D1000808

# The Reshaping of
# Plantation Society

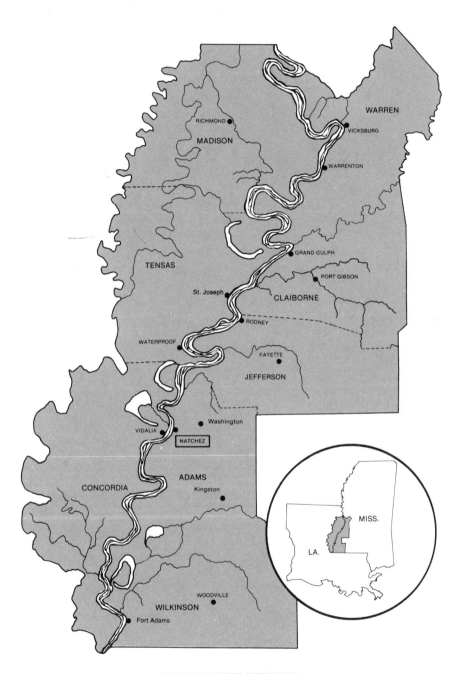

THE NATCHEZ DISTRICT

# THE RESHAPING OF
# PLANTATION SOCIETY

## The Natchez District, 1860–1880

MICHAEL WAYNE

Louisiana State University Press

Baton Rouge and London

Copyright © 1983 by Louisiana State University Press
All rights reserved
Manufactured in the United States of America

Designer: Albert Crochet
Typeface: Linotron Sabon
Typesetter: G & S Typesetters, Inc.
Printer: Thomson-Shore, Inc.
Binder: John Dekker & Sons, Inc.

LIBRARY OF CONGRESS CATALOGING IN PUBLICATION DATA

Wayne, Michael, 1947–
    The reshaping of plantation society.

    Bibliography: p.
    1. Plantations—Mississippi—Natchez (District)—History. 2. Natchez
        (Miss.: District)—Economic conditions. 3. Natchez (Miss.: District)—
        Social conditions. I. Title.
HD1471.U5W39 1983      307.7′2      82-7817
ISBN 0-8071-1050-7                  AACR2

*To my father and
to the memory of my mother*

# Contents

# Tables

# Acknowledgments

I have been generously assisted at every stage of my work. At the libraries and archives I visited I invariably received courteous treatment and patient guidance. Special thanks are due Michelle Hudson, Clinton Bagley, Caroline Killens, and the late Harriet Heidleberg at the Mississippi Department of Archives and History, which granted permission to quote from manuscript materials in its collections. Margaret Dalrymple, Merna Whitley, and Stone Miller, Jr., at the Department of Archives and Manuscripts, Louisiana State University were very helpful. I am indebted to them and to the staffs of the William R. Perkins Library, Duke University; the Southern Historical Collection, Library of the University of North Carolina at Chapel Hill; the library at Tulane University, New Orleans; the Louisiana State Library, Baton Rouge; and the Baker Library of the Harvard Business School. Funding for my research was provided by a fellowship from the Canada Council.

Various families in Natchez kindly allowed me to examine private papers in their possession. I am grateful to Ayres and Emily Haxton, Dr. and Mrs. William Godfrey, Mr. and Mrs. Boyd Sojourner, Mr. and Mrs. Hyde D. Jenkins, the late Waldo Lambdin and Mrs. Lambdin, Mr. and Mrs. Bazile Lanneau, and Mrs. Douglas MacNeil for this conspicuous display of southern hospitality. I am also grateful to Ron and Mimi Miller for putting me in touch with all these people and giving me a home in Natchez.

Many of my greatest intellectual debts were contracted during my years as a graduate student at Yale. My advisor was C. Vann Woodward. It happened that I was his last student—a dubious honor for him no doubt, but for me an obvious privilege. Professors William N. Parker and Stephen J. DeCanio helped me clarify my none too precise thinking regarding economic matters. A close friend, Paul Blanchard, currently of the Mathematics Department at Boston University, wrote computer programs that greatly facilitated my statistical investigation. Three other friends from my graduate school days, Larry Powell, Steven Hahn, and Ellen Moriarty, read the manuscript in its early stages and gave me the benefit of their thoughtful criticism. Their own subsequent accomplishments give an indication of how valuable that criticism was. All or part of drafts of this manuscript were also read by Don Doyle, Dewey Grantham, Eric Foner, Joel Williamson, David Brion Davis, and David Carlton. All these scholars have provided me with insight, and I only regret I have not in every instance been able to take into account their suggestions. Naturally, I alone bear responsibility for any errors.

Finally, my greatest debts are of a more personal nature. To my wife, not only for her advice on my work but for her material and emotional support throughout a period in which she had a manuscript of her own to complete and a new job to begin in a new country. And to my parents. This book is dedicated to them. We never talked much about history. But such insight as I have into the human experience, I believe, largely comes from them.

# The Reshaping of
# Plantation Society

# Introductory Remarks

The story is perhaps apocryphal but worth repeating. It concerns a prospector who sometime during the early 1830s—the exact date is not clear—stopped for the night at the home of a planter in southern Louisiana. At one point in the evening his host produced several ingots of metal, which he offered to the prospector for his examination. The metal, it appeared, was pure silver and the miner, his interest aroused, asked to know more. He was informed that the ingots had been left with the planter quite a few years earlier by a Spaniard who had supposedly uncovered, but not developed, a rich vein of ore in the cotton country along the Mississippi, somewhere south of Natchez.

The following day the prospector headed upriver in search of the rumored lode. Luck seems to have been with him because after only a few days he came across a deposit of silver that was, indeed, not only deep but as yet untapped. No doubt anticipating a substantial windfall, he approached the gentry of the neighborhood with a scheme for jointly building and working a mine. They, however, politely turned him down. It was not, they said, that they were skeptical of the value of the ore. But as one resident of the community noted, "What planter would exchange his cotton fields for a silver mine?"[1]

The Natchez district was the richest principality in the domain of King Cotton in the decades leading up to the Civil War. It is a moot point whether local planters did, as the story suggests, ignore precious metals in their midst. The fact is, nowhere in the antebellum South were the cotton economy and the slave plantation more dominant.

The following pages look at what happened to the plantation

1. [Joseph Holt Ingraham], *The South-West: By a Yankee* (2 vols.; New York: Harper, 1835), II, 140–41.

society of this region after Emancipation and into the 1880s. It is a history involving many participants. Freedmen played a major role as did storekeepers. Lesser parts went to Union and Confederate soldiers, Federal officials, Yankee lessees, New Orleans commission merchants, European immigrants, and Chinese laborers. Above all, however, it is the history of the gentry: of their successful efforts to preserve their material interests after the war, and of their failed efforts to preserve their world.

No claim is made that the experiences described here are typical of the experiences of the cotton South in general. On the contrary, the rationale for looking at the Natchez district has to do with the distinctive situation of the local planters. They were concentrated in greater numbers than were their counterparts elsewhere, and they were for the most part wealthier. In addition, due to the exceptional fertility of the soil along the banks of the Mississippi, years of exhaustive farming had not—as they had in other sections of the Black Belt—appreciably diminished the productivity of the land. This meant, presumably, that the gentry could expect their prosperity to continue well into the future. It meant also that many members of the planting elite belonged to families that had been in positions of prominence in the locality for decades, if not generations. As a result, they had developed a decided class consciousness and a belief in the superiority of their own lineage and way of life.

On the eve of the Civil War, then, the gentry of the Natchez district were uncommonly well placed to defend the existing social system and the interests of their class. They had psychological resources—the sense of authority, the sense of the justness of their rule—that accompanied a long planting tradition and were held in more pronounced form only by the aristocracy in declining communities to the east. And they had unparalleled economic resources. Nowhere would the challenge to the old order have more meaning.

PART I

# Before the War

CHAPTER ONE

# The Gentry and the Antebellum Plantation

I

Occupied by the French in the early eighteenth century, the land on the east bank of the Mississippi near the future town of Natchez was for years "little more than the theatre of Indian hostilities and warfare." Under the British, to whom the French ceded the territory in 1763, modest measures were taken toward the establishment of a settlement. But colonization advanced slowly, and in 1779, when the land fell into the hands of the Spanish, local inhabitants numbered barely five hundred, most of whom worked small plots and produced only enough for subsistence.[1] Spain attempted to turn the district into a buffer between its colonies on the Gulf and the aggressive new nation to the north. The government opened up trade along the Mississippi and offered prospective settlers a variety of benefits, including generous tracts of land and religious toleration. As a result of these policies, the population grew rapidly—more than tenfold in less than twenty years. But American expansionism was undeterred, and by 1795, Madrid had decided to relinquish the territory to the United States to avoid the possibility of war.

It was during the years of Spanish occupation that the groundwork was laid for a staple-based economy. In response to government incentives, local landowners took up the cultivation of tobacco in the 1780s and began to develop commercial ties with New Orleans. A change in official policy led to the abandonment

1. For discussion of the Natchez region under the French and British, see J. Dunbar Rowland, *History of Mississippi, the Heart of the South* (2 vols.; Chicago: S. J. Clarke, 1929), Vol. I, Chaps. 1 and 2; D. Clayton James, *Antebellum Natchez* (Baton Rouge: Louisiana State University Press, 1968), Chap. 1.

of that particular crop after several years. But the principle of production for the market had taken hold.

There followed a term of brief and largely unprofitable experimentation with indigo. Then, in 1795, the cotton gin arrived in the district. Within months, something of an agricultural revolution took place. Output of cotton rose from 36,351 pounds in 1794 to about 1.2 million pounds two years later. Stephen Minor alone shipped 2,500 bales to New Orleans in 1796, a consignment worth over $50,000 at prevailing prices. By the time the United States took control in 1798, cotton had become, in the words of one planter, the "universal crop" of the community.[2]

The region now entered a period of sustained and largely uninterrupted growth. Settlement began to press north through the bluffs of Mississippi and west into the bottomlands of Louisiana. The soil in both directions was remarkably productive. On the bluffs was a brown loam so fertile in its virgin state that Frederick Olmsted later pronounced it the richest he had ever seen. In Louisiana was an alluvial clay capable of producing two bales of cotton per acre. The upland loam was shallow and subject to rapid depletion by exhaustive farming. But the alluvial soil was deep, so deep in fact that geologists expressed little concern over the prospect of decades of unvaried cultivation. Indeed, certain sections of land along the Tensas River were said to be "almost inexhaustible."[3] Consequently, though particular long-settled corners of the region had begun to go into decline by the 1830s, in general the Natchez district continued to expand and flourish. By mid-century it emerged as a sprawling social and economic unit, roughly encom-

2. The years of Spanish occupation are covered in Rowland, *History of Mississippi*, Vol. I, Chap. 3; James, *Antebellum Natchez*, Chap. 2; Charles S. Sydnor, *A Gentleman of the Old Natchez Region: Benjamin L. C. Wailes* (Westport, Conn.: Negro Universities Press, 1970), 4–15. Spain agreed to surrender the land to the United States in Pinckney's Treaty of 1795 (ratified by the Senate in 1796), but delayed moving its troops out until 1798.

3. Frederick Law Olmsted, *The Cotton Kingdom*, ed. Arthur M. Schlesinger (New York: Knopf, 1953), 411; on the soil in these counties and parishes, see U.S. Bureau of the Census, *Tenth Census of the United States* (22 vols.; Washington, D.C.: Government Printing Office, 1884), V, 247–53, 323–27, 114–18; on movement into Louisiana, see James, *Antebellum Natchez*, 148; Thomas Affleck, "On the Hygiene of Cotton Plantations and the Management of Negro Slaves," *Southern Medical Reports*, II (1850), 431; Robert Dabney Calhoun, "A History of Concordia Parish, Louisiana," *Louisiana Historical Quarterly*, XV (1932), 44–67.

passing five counties in Mississippi—Wilkinson, Adams, Jefferson, Claiborne, and Warren—and three parishes in Louisiana—Concordia, Tensas, and Madison.[4]

And the 1850s ushered in "an era of unprecedented business and agricultural prosperity." In 1860 the region produced well over 400,000 bales of cotton, almost one-tenth the output of the entire South. Furthermore, over 30 percent of the production of Louisiana came from Tensas, Concordia, and Madison parishes, almost 20 percent from Tensas alone. While admittedly many parts of the South enjoyed good fortune in these days, it can justifiably be said that no place so clearly epitomized the enduring and triumphant nature of the reign of King Cotton.[5]

Nor did any place more obviously demonstrate the ascendancy of the plantation and of the planting "aristocracy." A Canadian journalist passing through the region several years before the Civil War noted that on each side of the Mississippi, "plantation succeeded plantation." In 1860 the number of district landowners holding fifty or more slaves was well over six hundred (see Table 1). And the elite controlled an enormous share of all acreage and wealth in real estate, more than 60 percent in Claiborne County, for instance, and almost 90 percent in Concordia Parish[6] (see

4. The term *Natchez district* actually derives from the name given by the French to the administrative district covering the triangular-shaped area extending from Fort Saint Peter near the mouth of the Yazoo River to a base line running eastward from the Mississippi about forty miles along the 31st parallel. Mississippians later came to refer to that area on the east bank of the Mississippi from Vicksburg south to the Louisiana border as simply "the Natchez." Harnett T. Kane, *Natchez on the Mississippi* (New York: Morrow, 1947), 9–10. There would have been little point in confining this study to the original political division. The social and economic boundaries of the region spread west across the Mississippi and did not reach so far east as the line established by the French. To the north lay the fertile, yet still largely unexploited, country of the Mississippi Delta, while to the east was pine land unsuited to the kind of plantation economy that emerged along the river. The southern and western boundaries used here are somewhat more arbitrary, since the society of Wilkinson County merged into the society of West Feliciana Parish to the south, and the alluvial land of Concordia Parish extended farther west into Catahoula Parish and south through Pointe Coupee Parish.

5. James, *Antebellum Natchez*, 166; U.S. Bureau of the Census, *Eighth Census of the United States* (4 vols.; Washington, D.C.: Government Printing Office, 1864), II, 66–67, 84–85, 184–185; Gavin Wright, *The Political Economy of the Cotton South: Households, Markets, and Wealth in the Nineteenth Century* (New York: Norton, 1978), 22.

6. William Kingsford, *Impressions of the West and South During a Six Weeks' Holiday* (Toronto: A. H. Armour, 1858), 47. The rationale for focusing on landholding rather than slaveholding in the concentration of wealth is that the former provides a basis for compari-

**Table 1.**   DISTRIBUTION OF SLAVEHOLDERS, 1860

|  | Size of Slaveholding | | | | | |
|---|---|---|---|---|---|---|
|  | 1–4 | 5–9 | 10–19 | 20–49 | 50+ | Total |
| *Mississippi* | | | | | | |
| Adams | 263 | 164 | 91 | 86 | 84 | 688 |
| Claiborne | 116 | 68 | 64 | 87 | 89 | 424 |
| Jefferson | 95 | 73 | 70 | 99 | 88 | 425 |
| Warren | 346 | 156 | 123 | 116 | 80 | 821 |
| Wilkinson | 144 | 98 | 91 | 84 | 82 | 499 |
| *Louisiana* | | | | | | |
| Concordia | 51 | 29 | 41 | 35 | 94 | 250 |
| Madison | 63 | 46 | 50 | 81 | 89 | 329 |
| Tensas | 51 | 36 | 34 | 98 | 111 | 330 |
| Total | 1,129 | 670 | 564 | 686 | 717* | 3,766 |

SOURCE: U.S. Bureau of the Census, *Eighth Census*, II, 230–32.
*Because some planters had multiple holdings spread over several counties and/or parishes, the total here does not indicate the exact number of large slaveholders in the district. From the manuscript census it appears that approximately 640 individuals belonged to this slaveholding elite.

**Table 2.**   DISTRIBUTION OF LANDHOLDERS, BY ACREAGE, CLAIBORNE COUNTY, 1857, AND CONCORDIA PARISH, 1860

|  | Total Number of Landowners | | | | |
|---|---|---|---|---|---|
|  | Acreage | | | | |
|  | 1–49 | 50–199 | 200–499 | 500–999 | 1000+ |
| Claiborne | 31 | 79 | 98 | 94 | 87 |
| Concordia | 10 | 29 | 34 | 22 | 88 |
|  | Percentage of Landowners | | | | |
|  | Acreage | | | | |
|  | 1–49 | 50–199 | 200–499 | 500–999 | 1000+ |
| Claiborne | 8% | 20% | 25% | 24% | 23% |
| Concordia | 5% | 16% | 19% | 12% | 48% |

SOURCES: U.S. Bureau of the Census, MS Agricultural Schedules for Concordia Parish, 1860; Claiborne County Land Rolls, 1857, in Mississippi Department of Archives and History, Jackson.

**Table 3.** CONCENTRATION OF ACREAGE, CLAIBORNE COUNTY, 1857, AND CONCORDIA PARISH, 1860

| | Percentage of Total Acreage Owned | | | | |
| | Acreage | | | | |
| | 1–49 | 50–199 | 200–499 | 500–999 | 1000+ |
|---|---|---|---|---|---|
| Claiborne | 0% | 4% | 11% | 25% | 60% |
| Concordia | 0% | 1% | 5% | 7% | 87% |

SOURCES: U.S. Bureau of the Census, MS Agricultural Schedules for Concordia Parish, 1860; Claiborne County Land Rolls, 1857.

**Table 4.** CONCENTRATION OF WEALTH, CLAIBORNE COUNTY, 1857, AND CONCORDIA PARISH, 1860

| | Percentage of Total Wealth Owned | | | | |
| | Acreage | | | | |
| | 1–49 | 50–199 | 200–499 | 500–999 | 1000+ |
|---|---|---|---|---|---|
| Claiborne | 1% | 3% | 10% | 22% | 64% |
| Concordia | 0% | 1% | 3% | 6% | 90% |

SOURCES: U.S. Bureau of the Census, MS Agricultural Schedules for Concordia Parish, 1860; Claiborne County Land Rolls, 1857.
NOTE: Wealth is defined as value of real estate holdings.

Tables 2, 3, and 4). Significantly, they particularly dominated the most fertile land—Concordia Parish was entirely alluvial.

Some of the wealthiest men in the South lived in the area, many in and around Natchez itself. Their landholdings extended far beyond the locality, and at least a few held considerable property and investments in the North. Some examples: in 1860 the Davis brothers—Samuel M., George, Alfred Vidal, and Frederick—together controlled 843 slaves and more than 14,000 acres in Louisiana; collectively their holdings were worth roughly $1.7 million. An acquaintance, Haller Nutt, owned 800 slaves and 42,947 acres

son with the postbellum period. At the same time, a landowner in the Natchez district with one thousand or more acres was roughly the equivalent of a slaveowner with fifty or more slaves, the usual designation for a large planter.

on twenty-one separate estates stretching from Adams County to the Louisiana Gulf Coast. During 1860 he reportedly earned over $225,000 from the sale of cotton and sugar. Then there was Dr. Stephen Duncan, at one time said to be the largest producer of cotton in the nation. His net worth in the early 1850s was conservatively estimated at almost $2 million, including $829,907 in slaves, $400,000 in lands, $479,500 in bonds and stocks, and $200,000 in outstanding personal notes.[7]

Planting was, of course, the "*ne plus ultra* of every man's ambition." It had been for a long time. "Young men who come to this country, 'to make money'," noted Joseph Holt Ingraham, a fascinated observer in the 1830s, "soon catch the mania, and nothing less than a broad plantation, waving with snow white cotton bolls, can fill their mental vision, as they anticipate by a few years in their dreams of the future, the result of their plans and labors."[8]

At one time such dreams had been attainable. Absalom Pettit moved to Mississippi from his native western Virginia in 1818. After two years in Jefferson County, he found employment as an overseer on the Warren County plantation of Judge Covington. Here he had the good fortune—or perhaps sense—to win the heart and hand of his employer's young daughter. Receiving an estate plus a full complement of slaves from the judge, he started planting on his own. By 1860 he had accumulated property worth well in excess of $150,000.[9]

Calvin Smith was born in Massachusetts in 1768. He emigrated to the Natchez district when still a young man and bought a small plot of land on which he erected a rude home. Hiring himself out as a carpenter in town by day while his wife cleared the earth, he

7. Joseph Karl Menn, *The Large Slaveholders of Louisiana, 1860* (New Orleans: Pelican Publishing Co., 1964), 105, 177–78, 202–203; James, *Antebellum Natchez*, 156, 150–51; Stephen Duncan and Stephen Duncan, Jr., Papers, VI, 291–93, Department of Archives and Manuscripts, Louisiana State University, Baton Rouge.

8. [Joseph Holt Ingraham], *The South-West: By a Yankee* (2 vols.; New York: Harper, 1835), II, 84.

9. *Goodspeed's Biographical and Historical Memoirs of Mississippi, Embracing an Authentic and Comprehensive Account of the Chief Events in the History of the State and a Record of the Lives of Many of the Most Worthy and Illustrious Families and Individuals* (2 vols.; Chicago: Goodspeed Publishing Co., 1891), Vol. I, Pt. 1, p. 317; U.S. Bureau of the Census, MS Population Schedules for Warren County, 1860, p. 173.

managed to put aside $100. With this small savings he purchased a slave and began farming. Hard work and judicious management enabled him to build up a substantial labor force over time and turn his few acres into a plantation. On the eve of the Civil War his heirs ranked among the elite of district society.[10]

Still, while such "rags to riches" stories were relatively common early in the century, their incidence declined noticeably in later years. Aspiring planters came to find that they needed substantial capital just to get started, much more capital, say, than Calvin Smith had needed in his day. With the passing of frontier conditions, real estate values had begun to rise. By 1860 they reached over $100 an acre for certain tracts in Louisiana. Meanwhile the price of slaves too had risen enormously, to as much as $2,000 for a prime field hand—and labor requirements were significantly greater in the district than elsewhere, because of the need to build and maintain levees in the bottomlands and because of the relative heaviness of the alluvial soil.[11]

The result of these developments was a serious decrease in social mobility. The local elite in the decade before the war was composed principally of second- and third-generation planters and large slaveholders recently emigrated from exhausted lands to the east. Their considerable wealth set these men apart, of course, but now so too did their distinctive style of life. Planters regularly took trips to the spas of Virginia and Tennessee, spent summers in the North, vacationed in Europe, and engaged in lavish display everywhere. Above all, they cultivated a learned and genteel manner, both in themselves and in their children. "I hope," wrote James Foster of Hermitage to his young son away at school in 1852, "that you are resolved that you will faithfully and indefatiguably [sic] labour to see what you can accomplish in the way of improvement of your mind, and in your temper and manners; for it is in the cultivation of the mind, and the subduing and controling [sic]

10. *Goodspeed's*, Vol. I, Pt. 1, pp. 371, 481; U.S. Bureau of the Census, MS Population Schedules for Adams County, 1860, pp. 122, 145; U.S. Bureau of the Census, MS Population Schedules for Claiborne County, 1860, p. 77.

11. Roger W. Shugg, *Origins of Class Struggle in Louisiana: A Social History of White Farmers and Laborers During Slavery and After, 1840–1875* (Baton Rouge: Louisiana State University Press, 1972), 5–6.

of the temper, and the grace and elegance of manner, that we find that which places men in a portion above the vulgar herd."[12] Most planters would have agreed with Foster on the central importance of education. They employed tutors on their estates, and sent their sons to local academies and, sometimes, to college in the North. Many also arranged for their daughters to receive private instruction in languages, music, and art.

As for their own intellectual endeavors, probably a majority of the gentry subscribed to at least a few of the more informed journals of the day, and some evidently had truly impressive libraries. Samuel S. Boyd of Arlington, for instance, owned some eight thousand volumes in a dozen different languages. In addition, large slaveholders were instrumental in the formation of several literary and philosophical societies and contributed generously to the various private schools and two colleges that were established in the district. David Hunt alone gave over $150,000 to the founding and development of Oakland College in Jefferson County.[13]

A handful of local planters even gained national recognition for their intellectual achievements. Benjamin L. C. Wailes produced a number of geological tracts that were highly regarded in academic circles in the North. Dr. Rush Nutt developed the widely used "Petit Gulf" strain of cotton and modified the cotton gin. Dr. John Carmichael Jenkins was a distinguished botanist and ornithologist who belonged to the Academy of Natural Sciences, the Pennsylvania Historical Society, and the American Pomological Society, among other organizations.[14]

Despite the visible accomplishments of the few, contemporaries differed over the general cultural level of the majority of local plan-

12. For examples of the gentry's trips and vacations, see [Ingraham], *The South-West*, II, 206; M. A. D. Conner to her sister, September 9, 1860, in Lemuel Parker Conner and Family Papers, Department of Archives and Manuscripts, Louisiana State University, Baton Rouge; Wm. H. Ker to his mother, March 31, 1858, in Mary Susan Ker Papers, Southern Historical Collection, University of North Carolina, Chapel Hill. James Foster to his son, January 10, 1852, in James Foster and Family Papers, Department of Archives and Manuscripts, Louisiana State University, Baton Rouge.

13. Kane, *Natchez*, 168; Sydnor, *Gentleman*, 125–26, 130, 144–48; *Goodspeed's*, Vol. I, Pt. 2, pp. 990–91.

14. James, *Antebellum Natchez*, 156; "Record of the Jenkins Family of Windsor Place" (MS in possession of Mr. and Mrs. Hyde D. Jenkins, Natchez). Sydnor, *Gentleman*, is a fine portrait of Wailes.

ters. Frederick Olmsted dismissed their way of life as "the farce of the vulgar rich." "Of course," he conceded, "there are men of refinement and cultivation among the rich planters of Mississippi, and many highly estimable and intelligent persons outside of the wealthy class, but the number of such is smaller in proportion to that of the immoral, vulgar, and ignorant newly-rich, than in any other part of the United States."[15]

By contrast, Robert Russell, a visitor from Britain, offered the opinion in 1857 that "there is as refined society to be found in Natchez as in any other part of the United States." Twenty years earlier Joseph Holt Ingraham had arrived at much the same conclusion. Praising the planters on their "*air distingué,*" he went on to compare them favorably to the landed gentry of England. The elite of the district could, he suggested, "successfully challenge any other community to produce a more intelligent, wealthy, and, I may say, *aristocratic* whole. But I do not like the term applied to Americans; though no word will express so clearly that refinement and elegance to which I allude and which everywhere indicate the opulence and high breeding of their possessors."[16]

In truth, most large slaveholders had less the substance of gentility than its veneer. But in any case, their particular bearing and style of life did identify them as the privileged segment of society. And they consciously cultivated their distinctiveness and drew attention to the social distance between themselves and their less fortunate neighbors. A district resident told Frederick Olmsted that the children of planters "do want so bad to look as if they weren't made of the same clay as the rest of God's creation." "Avoid as much as possible low company," a planter's wife admonished her son in 1859. "Associate with the refined for your manners soon tell what company you keep—Recollect dear son that you have a name to preserve."[17]

By the eve of the Civil War, then, indeed by some years before, the

15. Olmsted, *Cotton Kingdom*, 416–17.

16. Robert Russell, *North America, Its Agriculture and Climate: Containing Observations on the Agriculture and Climate of Canada, the United States, and the Island of Cuba* (Edinburgh: A. and C. Black, 1857), 258; [Ingraham], *The South-West*, II, 34, 50.

17. Olmsted, *Cotton Kingdom*, 416; R. A. Minor to James, October 21, 1859, in Minor Family Papers, Southern Historical Collection, University of North Carolina, Chapel Hill.

gentry had evolved into a stable, self-conscious elite, "slow to regard any as their equals," utterly convinced of their superior breeding. This development was perhaps best reflected in the changed pattern of marriage. Children of planters rarely wed outside their "station" now. And men of modest means—clerks, for example, and most overseers—could no longer hope to advance themselves through profitable unions. Note, in this regard, a casual remark by young Kate Stone of Brokenburn in 1861 and then recall, by way of comparison, the rise of the overseer Absalom Pettit more than a generation earlier. "Late this afternoon Mamma and I went down to see the wife of the new overseer. She seems entirely too nice a woman, and her fashion is evidently from the planter class. I wonder why she married him. She does not look like a contented woman."[18]

Intermarriage among the elite became so common that, in the words of one historian, "the proverbial Philadelphia lawyer would have been baffled by the complex family relations." One extended clan included the Surget, White, Bingaman, Lintot, Minor, Vousdan, and Chotard families, "each of which held title to vast cotton domains."[19]

The increasing exclusivity and public hauteur of the planters naturally bred a certain amount of local resentment. They were known as "Aristocrats" in a land where that term was frequently used in a pejorative sense. Less fortunate neighbors called them "Swell-heads" and accused them of "insufferable arrogance and ostentation." And yet, by virtue of their inordinate economic power and, perhaps, superior bearing, they were able to capture and retain the respect of many whites lower on the social ladder. They dominated the boards of local churches and schools, headed charitable institutions and recreational organizations, and generally took the lead in most social and economic affairs in the district. They were, in short, the leaders of the community. But then au-

18. H. S. Fulkerson, *Random Recollections of Early Days in Mississippi* (Vicksburg: Vicksburg Printing and Publishing Co., 1885), 15, 16, 144; John Q. Anderson (ed.), *Brokenburn: The Journal of Kate Stone, 1861–1868* (Baton Rouge: Louisiana State University Press, 1972), 15, 40.

19. James, *Antebellum Natchez*, 137. Still, wealth remained a paramount consideration in marriages. See, for example, Anderson (ed.), *Brokenburn*, 105.

thority came naturally to such men. They had learned its various dimensions on the plantation.[20]

II

Whatever its origins as a labor system, black servitude in the Natchez district, as elsewhere in the cotton South, emerged as more than just an economic institution. It took on social and political aspects that, on the plantation in particular, made it "less a business than a life." This manifold character of plantation slavery was a product of the dual legal system that evolved to deal with the contradictory role of the slave as property and person. Free men came together as equals before the law. The state set the rules and regulations that governed their lives and was the ultimate arbiter of differences between them. But slaves were property, and legislatures were reluctant to dictate how a man might use his possessions. Insofar as slaves could in fact commit very human crimes against free members of the polity, laws existed. And insofar as slaves might develop a very human class consciousness antithetical to an order that called for their subjugation, special restrictions on their behavior existed. But the state deemed it inappropriate to regulate the master-slave relationship itself, with the result that, as Robert Fogel and Stanley Engerman have observed, "for most slaves it was the law of the plantation, not of the state, that was relevant. Only a small proportion of the slaves ever had to deal with the law-enforcement mechanism of the state. Their daily lives were governed by plantation law. . . . Unlike the Northern manufacturer the authority of the planter extended not only to the conduct of business but to the regulation of the family lives of slaves, the control of their public behavior, the provision of their food and

20. Olmsted, *Cotton Kingdom*, 415; Sydnor, *Gentleman*, 269. For examples of planter dominance of social organizations, see "History of Methodist Churches" (Typescript in W.P.A. Records, RG 60, for Adams County, Folder: Churches, Methodist and Protestant Episcopal, Mississippi Department of Archives and History, Jackson), 35; "List of Members Belonging to the Pharsalia Association, 1860," in possession of Mrs. Douglas Mac-Neil, Natchez; Jefferson College Papers, Z 59, VI, 54, 60, 97, Mississippi Department of Archives and History, Jackson. James (*Antebellum Natchez*, esp. Chaps. 9 and 11) argues that in the town of Natchez itself, planters willingly surrendered social leadership to the middle class. Such was not the case in the district as a whole, however.

shelter, the care of their health, and the protection of their souls." Or as the young daughter of a prominent local slaveholder more simply put it, "Each plantation was a law unto itself."[21]

By and large such statutes as existed tended to buttress the rules of the plantation. But when the two came into conflict, more often than not it was the latter that took precedence. Mississippi and Louisiana routinely forbade large gatherings of slaves, for example, but district planters allowed their chattels to socialize with those from neighboring estates on special occasions and for religious services. More significant, almost all minor criminal offenses by slaves and even some major ones, up to and including murder, never reached the state courts. The gentry preferred to deal with legal transgressions at home and on their own terms. They sought a large degree of autonomy, and the state accorded it to them. Perhaps the essence of the regime was most aptly captured by Virginia Harris in speaking of her former owner, Nat Hoggatt of Madison Parish: "He knowed how to take care of his own business without calling for help."[22] Under the circumstances it is scarcely surprising that the black laborer came to assume that ultimate authority resided in his particular master and not in the government. The dual legal system fostered such a notion, and the slaveholders, for reasons of their own, encouraged it.

In theory this arrangement left the planter free to deal with his chattels in almost any manner he should choose. And, in fact, plantation law largely reflected the interests of the slaveholder. But slaves, while they lacked power as a class in society at large, did have a measure of leverage on their own plantations. They could control the productive process by, for instance, working slowly, feigning illness, breaking tools, or mishandling livestock. Further-

---

21. Ulrich Bonnell Phillips, *American Negro Slavery: A Survey of the Supply, Employment and Control of Negro Labor as Determined by the Plantation Regime* (Baton Rouge: Louisiana State University Press, 1966), 401. On the dual legal system, see Eugene D. Genovese, *Roll, Jordan, Roll: The World the Slaves Made* (New York: Pantheon Books, 1974), 25–49; Kenneth M. Stampp, *The Peculiar Institution: Slavery in the Ante-Bellum South* (New York: Vintage Books, 1956), Chap. 5. Robert William Fogel and Stanley L. Engerman, *Time on the Cross: The Economics of American Negro Slavery* (Boston: Little, Brown, 1974), 129; Anderson (ed.), *Brokenburn*, 6.

22. Sydnor, *Gentleman*, 107; George P. Rawick, Jan Hillegas, and Ken Lawrence (eds.), *The American Slave: A Composite Autobiography*, Supplement, Series 1 (12 vols.; Westport, Conn.: Greenwood Press, 1977), VIII, 941.

more, when sufficiently moved they proved willing to run away, kill the overseer, or actively "strike" in a bold attempt to ameliorate their condition. Often, of course, such actions represented personal rebellion against the condition of enslavement itself. But the vast majority of disruptions were directed toward improving the quality of life *within* slavery, toward getting, say, more leisure time on Saturday or regular access to a preacher.

Planters could respond to expressions of slave will with the whip, and often they did. But they also compromised, giving their chattels at least a few of the things they sought. Slaveholders generally chose to regard such benefits as privileges generously extended. But the slaves understood that privileges can be institutionalized over time, can, in short, become rights. As Eugene Genovese has expressed it, "If the law said they had no right to property, for example, but local custom accorded them garden plots, then woe to the master or overseer who summarily withdrew the 'privilege.' To these slaves the privilege had become a right and the withdrawal an act of aggression not to be borne."[23]

The slaves' notions of their rights developed and spread through the district side by side with the slaveholders' ideas about management and efficiency. In the end, the rules and regulations of one plantation came to resemble closely those of the next. Because this "plantation system" has been described at length by other historians, no attempt will be made to present it in detail here. What follows is merely a brief overview.

The division of labor was elaborate and, to a certain degree at least, efficient. Each hand fulfilled a specified role, be it that of servant, artisan, or, most often, field hand. The field hands worked in large gangs under the direction of an overseer or black driver, frequently both. Their hours were long—dawn to dusk on most places—and when it was too cold or wet to tend to the crop, or after all the cotton had been harvested, they were expected to perform various jobs pertaining to the general upkeep of the plantation, such as repairing fences and whitewashing the quarters.[24]

23. Genovese, *Roll, Jordan, Roll*, 30–31.
24. For examples of representative plantations, see the Aventine Plantation Diary (Z

Everywhere Sunday was a day of rest and on many places the slaves were also allowed time off on Saturday afternoon. In addition, they enjoyed a small number of holidays during the year. At Christmas, for instance, work would cease for anywhere from three days to a week. Usually the master would fete his hands with gifts and perhaps the makings of a dinner or dance. "Us'd be 'lowed to invite us sweethearts on other plantations," recollected one former bondsman. "Old Mis' would let us cook a gran' supper an' Marse would slip us some licquor. Dem suppers was de bes' I ever et. Sometimes us'd have wil' turkey, fried fish, hot corn pone, fresh pork ham, baked yams, chitlins, popcorn, apple pie, pound cake, raisins an' coffee."[25]

Of course, the principal return the slaves received for their labor was simply basic care and protection. They could expect food, clothing, and shelter, even during their unproductive years. Charles Sydnor, in his study of slavery in Mississippi, reported that he found "no instance of a master's failing to care for [the elderly and infirm] and they generally seem to have been treated as well as able-bodied field hands." While provisioning was, without question, more meager than Sydnor has suggested, his fundamental point remains valid: the system called for the basic support of even those who had outlived their usefulness to the slaveowner. Likewise it called for the support of those whose usefulness lay at some point in the future. Planters provided nurseries for the infants and young children of women who worked in the fields.[26]

The gentry also took responsibility for the medical care of their chattels. They set aside buildings in the quarters to serve as hospitals. And they demanded that overseers acquaint themselves with everyday diseases and conventional remedies. In cases of serious illness a physician would usually be called in, often the same physi-

175) and the Walter Wade Plantation Diaries (Z 270) (MSS in Mississippi Department of Archives and History, Jackson).

25. Benjamin Leonard Covington Wailes Letters and Papers, XXXII, 120, Manuscript Department, William R. Perkins Library, Duke University, Durham, N.C.; James S. Allen Plantation Book (Z 14) (Typescript in Mississippi Department of Archives and History, Jackson), 6; Charles S. Sydnor, *Slavery in Mississippi* (New York: D. Appleton-Century, 1933), 22; Rawick, Hillegas, and Lawrence (eds.), *The American Slave*, Supp., Ser. 1, Vol. X, pp. 2057–58.

26. Sydnor, *Slavery*, 66, 65; Russell, *North America*, 265.

cian who ministered to the slaveowner and his family. Cynics have justly derided the quality of treatment afforded blacks under these conditions. But it should be remembered that the health care available to whites was not all that much better. And in any case, there is no denying that for a mixture of humanitarian and selfish reasons the planters took seriously their obligation to provide for the ill among their hands. Note, for instance, the forthright instructions of Haller Nutt to his overseer on Araby in Madison Parish: "The first consideration is to feel the importance of attending to the sick. To *feel* that it is above all other duties of a plantation. . . . Now bear in mind that as soon as you place them on the sick list, they must be *strictly* & *regularly* attended to. You must feel its importance and take an interest in it—and in order to watch the changes of the disease & the effects of your medicine, you should visit them three times a day—*morning, noon,* & *night* and if much sicker oftener than that."[27]

Housing for the slaves consisted of rows of cabins near the Big House or the overseer's residence. Here they kept small gardens where they grew vegetables for their own consumption or, more rarely, for sale. Many also raised chickens and managed to accumulate a little cash through the marketing of eggs. Planters carefully monitored the financial dealings of their bondsmen; indeed, usually it was the slaveholder himself who purchased the limited produce of his laborers and sold them such goods as they desired and could afford, generally tobacco, sugar, molasses, and material for clothing. On occasion, however, the slave ventured into town and, at times openly, at times surreptitiously, traded with the small merchants there.[28]

The authority that the slaveowner exercised over his hands was extensive, going far beyond economic matters. He restricted their educational opportunities ("The only book learning we ever got was when we stole it," remembered one resentful former bondsman), closely watched their leisure activities, and intruded in their

27. Journal of Araby Plantation, 1843–50 (MS in Haller Nutt Papers, Manuscript Department, William R. Perkins Library, Duke University, Durham, N.C.).

28. Rawick, Hillegas, and Lawrence (eds.), *The American Slave*, Supp., Ser. 1, Vol. VII, p. 570, Vol. VIII, pp. 938, 1244; [Ingraham], *The South-West*, II, 54; Allen Plantation Book, 1–3.

marital and family arrangements.[29] Planter interference in slave religion is indicative. Most members of the gentry allowed or even encouraged their hands to practice Christianity. But they were careful to ensure that the word from the pulpit included sanctification of their own earthly interests. Recounted one freedman years after the Civil War, "De darkies went to de white fokes' church at Old Hopewell an' atter de white fokes preachin' den de preacher preached to us darkies. He would jes tell us not to steal our master's meat from de smoke house, or cotton or tatoes or 'lasses an' like that. An' do not kill each other." Less devout planters attempted to suppress religious observance altogether. "Once in a while, dey would have a little singing in the quarters," recalled Silas Spotfore, who lived on the Johnson estate near Fort Adams, Mississippi, "but you mustn't call on the law'd too much." Levi Ashley, who grew up on a plantation in the same neighborhood, saw his master whip two hands simply for attempting to organize a prayer meeting.[30]

Recent studies have established that blacks were able to develop a significant degree of autonomy within slavery—in their family life, in their relations with each other, and in their religious experiences.[31] These findings are an important corrective to earlier misconceptions. They make clear that, whatever the planter might have believed, his ability to mold the values and define the aspirations of most of his slaves was quite limited. All the same, his power to compel at least outward compliance with his will was real enough. It could scarcely have been otherwise in a society that placed few legal restrictions on its slaveowning class.

The principal means by which the master enforced his authority

29. Rawick, Hillegas, and Lawrence (eds.), *The American Slave*, Supp., Ser. 1, Vol. IX, p. 1664, Vol. VIII, p. 1345. For evidence of planter interference in the personal hygiene of the slaves, see E. McGehee to his son, July 20, 1860 (copy), in James Stewart McGehee Papers, Vol. I, Pt. 2, p. 430, Department of Archives and Manuscripts, Louisiana State University, Baton Rouge.
30. Rawick, Hillegas, and Lawrence (eds.), *The American Slave*, Supp., Ser. 1, Vol. X, pp. 2408–409; Silas Spotfore Slave Narrative (MS in W.P.A. Source Material, Folder: Slaves—Ex-slave Interviews, Louisiana State Library, Baton Rouge), 2; Rawick, Hillegas, and Lawrence (eds.), *The American Slave*, Supp., Ser. 1, Vol. VI, p. 76.
31. See, for example, Genovese, *Roll, Jordan, Roll*; John Blassingame, *The Slave Community: Plantation Life in the Antebellum South* (Rev. and enl. ed.; New York: Oxford University Press, 1979); Herbert G. Gutman, *The Black Family in Slavery and Freedom, 1790–1925* (New York: Pantheon Books, 1976).

was the lash. Recalled Virginia Harris of her youth on Nat Hoggatt's Madison Parish plantation: "Master didn't allow no beating
or knocking. They got whipped if they wouldn't do what they was
told to do, or if they runned off. They wasn't put in jail. Didn't
have none of them things. Just whipped and let go. That's all." The
lash was a cruel device, and the slaves understandably viewed it
with loathing. But what disturbed them the most, what indeed
touched them with fear, was not the whip itself, but the license the
planter had to act arbitrarily. The same slaveowner who might
reprimand a recalcitrant hand with a temperate strapping on one
occasion, might for any number of reasons give him a brutal beating on the next—or something far worse. James A. Stewart of
Wilkinson County had a particularly deplorable way of dealing
with the problem of petty theft, a grandson recalled.

> He was extremely skillful in the use of all sorts of traps and snares, and
> no man either white or black knew but what he would put his foot in a
> beartrap that would break a man's leg or on a board of spikes that
> would give him the lock-jaw, immediately upon crossing any boundary
> of the place. These spikes were nails filed to a needle-point and, being
> driven through a stout plank, the latter was placed underneath the soil,
> leaving the nails points up. Of course, at night they could not be seen
> at all, and even in the daylight in the grass or the watermelon vines
> were practically invisible. His hands were furnished as many comforts
> as the white people but thieving received no indulgence whatsoever.[32]

Planters could and did use moral suasion against neighbors who
they felt transgressed the bounds of decency.[33] But it was an ironic
consequence of the dual legal system that while it in principle secured the slave from disease, hunger, and the abuse of overseers, it
left him vulnerable before the one force that could cause him most
pain, his own master.

At its ideal, plantation law reflected the benevolent relationship
described by E. N. Elliott, president of the Planters' College in
Mississippi.

---

32. Rawick, Hillegas, and Lawrence (eds.), *The American Slave*, Supp., Ser. 1, Vol. VIII,
p. 940; J. S. McGehee Papers, III, 13.
33. Joseph Holt Ingraham (*The South-West*, II, 256) observed in the 1830s, "Those
planters who are known to be inhumanly rigorous to their slaves are scarcely countenanced
by the more intelligent and humane portion of the community."

> Slavery is the duty and obligation of the slave to labor for the mutual benefit of both master and slave, under a warrant to the slave of protection, and a comfortable subsistence, under all circumstances. . . . The master, as the head of the system, has a right to the obedience and labor of the slave, but the slave has also his mutual rights in the master; the right of protection, the right of counsel and guidance, the right of subsistence, the right of care and attention in sickness and old age. He has also a right in his master as the sole arbiter of all his wrongs and difficulties, and as a merciful judge and dispenser of law to award the penalty of his misdeeds.[34]

Of course, the plantation rarely, if ever, approached the benign reciprocity described by Elliott and other apologists of the regime. That would only have been possible in a world in which slaves accepted their own enslavement and masters willfully surrendered their own economic interests. The Natchez district was not that kind of world.

And yet, for all the inherent tension, what is striking is the extent to which the system functioned smoothly and efficiently. Slaves by and large went about their business, masters by and large fulfilled their tacit responsibilities. The rationale of the gentry will be touched on below. As for the slaves, clearly a functioning plantation law was preferable to no law at all. It ensured them, at least, a modicum of protection and some recognition of their essential humanity.

But there was a catch. To secure benefits within slavery the black laborer had to compromise his commitment to immediate emancipation. He had to show that he was willing to work conscientiously when his "rights" were respected and abide by the bulk of the regulations that his master might lay down. Above all, he had to forgo sustained, open resistance to the regime. Often this meant quietly accepting humiliating whippings, proffering insincere deference to those who would abuse him, and living with the painful potentiality, from time to time realized, of a disrupted family life. These degradations put in perspective for the slave, if not for the master, the kindnesses and rights that slavery allowed. Blacks were obedient, but out of pragmatism, not acquiescence or, as their

34. Quoted in Genovese, *Roll, Jordan, Roll,* 76.

owners liked to think, gratitude. The slave made at best a troubled peace with his condition.

### III

Historians have called the antebellum southern plantation "pater-nalistic." There are problems with this characterization. A man may act paternalistically toward his children, but scarcely toward his property. The slaves had aspects of both; and in a capitalist world, economic considerations all too often gave priority to the property aspect.

Still, if we confine our attention to plantation law, the father-child model does have a certain utility. For one, it can help us describe the particular kind of interaction that took place between master and slave. Think, for a moment, of a free labor economy. Here capital and labor face each other as theoretical equals in the marketplace, with the state setting the rules and regulations under which the system operates. The mutual obligations that the individual employer and his laborers undertake are largely confined to the economic sphere and depend principally on the ways in which their respective classes are affected by the forces of supply and demand. Under the circumstances, employers have little cause to take on responsibilities unenforceable in the marketplace and there is no reason for laborers to pledge themselves to enduring obedience. Normally a paternalistic kind of regime will not emerge.

In a slave society, on the other hand, conditions are quite different. Labor is dependent; its responsibilities, social as well as economic, are in the power of the slaveowning class. As Ulrich Phillips has pointed out, "Theoretically the master might be expected perhaps to expend the minimum possible to keep his slaves in strength, to discard the weaklings and the aged, to drive his gang early and late, to scourge the laggards hourly, to secure the whole with fetters by day and bolts by night, and to keep them in perpetual terror of his wrath."[35] As we have seen, however, such brutality was not characteristic of the Natchez district or, indeed,

35. Phillips, *American Negro Slavery*, 293.

of the cotton South in general. Here slaves acquired some rights and thereby gained a measure of protection. Although the master remained the guardian and arbiter of the law, his relationship to his chattels took on an appearance that can legitimately, if roughly, be described as paternalistic. The planter, fatherlike, provided care and supervision; the slave, childlike, returned obedience.

Every slave society carries within itself the potential to evolve along paternalistic lines. The slaveholder, to protect his investment, must provide at least rudimentary food and shelter. But this potential will not be realized in every instance, and, in fact, most slave societies of the Western Hemisphere did not take on a paternalistic aspect. Why the American South proved an exception is obviously a question of some importance, although one to which we do not yet have a definitive answer. No doubt the religious and intellectual heritage of the gentry played a role; perhaps so too did the particular demands of the cotton culture. It may well be, however, as Eugene Genovese has speculated, that the single most important factor was the residency pattern of the southern planter. Unlike slaveowners elsewhere, he lived on his estate or visited it regularly. Even in the Natchez district, where absentee rates were higher than normal, there was recurring personal contact between masters and slaves. Blacks used this contact to imprint their humanity on their owners. And for reasons that were presumably a mixture of conscience and expediency, the gentry responded by conceding their chattels a voice in the shaping of the rules and regulations governing the plantation.[36] Significantly, the American slave force reproduced itself, indeed expanded rapidly. This meant that estates came to be populated with blacks sensitive to the fragility of their position and educated in the nuances of plantation law. As the slaveholders used the law to secure obedience, so the bondsmen used it to gain protection. Further study of the specific origins of paternalistic interaction on the plantation is needed. But as the foregoing suggests, broadly speaking we can say that such interaction derived from the general nature of class relations in a

36. Eugene D. Genovese, *The World the Slaveholders Made: Two Essays in Interpretation* (New York: Pantheon Books, 1969), 96. Northern Brazil plantations also developed along vaguely paternalistic lines, despite the vastly different European heritage of that country. Significantly, as in the United States, slaveowners in northern Brazil by and large lived on their estates.

slave society and the particular environment in which those relations evolved in America.

There is a further reason for applying the father-child model to
the antebellum southern plantation, beyond that of describing a
pattern of behavior. In addition to acting in a roughly patriarchic
manner, the gentry thought of themselves as father figures to their
slaves. Paternalism, in short, entered into their ideology. In time it
became the principal weapon in the defense of slavery. Yet ironically, if significantly, at an ideological level paternalism was primarily racial. Most of the gentry accounted for the childlike status
of their chattels not by reference to a proper relationship of labor
to capital but to qualities allegedly inherent in all blacks: irre-
sponsibility and immaturity, the need for constant protection and
guidance. "Can't depend on niggers," a Natchez district planter
once informed Frederick Olmsted. And what, replied Olmsted, if
they should gain their freedom? "Get tired of that, I should think,"
answered the slaveowner. "A northerner looks upon a band of
negroes, as upon so many *men*," observed Joseph Holt Ingraham
from Natchez in the 1830s. "But the planter . . . views them in a
very different light." To the planter they were perpetual children,
placed in servitude by a merciful Providence. It was the duty and
burden of the slaveowner to give them guardianship and moral up-
lift. As William Newton Mercer wrote in his will, "One of my
greatest responsibilities has been to treat justly and kindly that
class of my fellow-beings who were made dependent on me by
Providence."[37]

To men and women who reasoned in this way, paternalism took
on a very narrow meaning. It stood for the special infirmity of
blackness, the particular control the Negro needed and the particular care. By the same token, characteristics associated with free
labor took on a racial construction of their own. If blacks were by
nature dependent, whites—even poor whites—could be expected
to look out for themselves. As one young planter put it shortly after
the war, "The motive power of the Teutonic is upward; that of the
Ethiopian is to sink to the brute level. The accumulative means

37. Olmsted, *Cotton Kingdom*, 413; [Ingraham], *The South-West*, II, 260; "Succession
of W. N. Mercer" (Typescript in William Newton Mercer Papers, Department of Archives
and Manuscripts, Louisiana State University, Baton Rouge).

which stimulate the former, act reversely upon the latter."[38] Apparently the same God who had placed the Negro in bondage intended the Caucasian for the egalitarian interaction of the marketplace.

Here the objection will perhaps be raised that racial paternalism was merely class paternalism undiscovered, that the planters were moving ideologically toward a full-scale critique of free labor, perhaps even of capitalism. This is the position taken by Eugene Genovese, for example, in *The World the Slaveholders Made*. He contends that the paternalistic attitudes of the planters were a natural outgrowth of the social organization of the antebellum plantation. Since the social organization of the plantation, whatever its racial dimension, derived fundamentally from the relationship between capital and labor in a slave society, the world view of the planters was bound to take on a class perspective.

This is a controversial argument but one to which developments in the Natchez district lend some support. As we have already seen, by the 1830s the gentry had begun to assume an increasingly elitist posture toward other members of white society. Furthermore, their response to abolitionist attacks on slavery often included derogatory remarks about the northern wage system.[39] Nevertheless, whatever direction planter ideology was likely to take in the future, at the rather unsophisticated level at which most large slaveowners were thinking in the days before the Civil War, paternalism was plainly a racial concept—the black was slave because he was childlike, not childlike because he was slave.

This raises an obvious and important question. Why, even if possibly only for the time being, did the gentry have a manifestly distorted vision of the world around them? More specifically, given that the paternalistic nature of the plantation derived from the social relations of slavery, why did the planter assume that it had something to do with the character of the Negro?

38. J. Floyd King to Lin [Caperton], September 8, 1866, in Thomas Butler King Papers, Southern Historical Collection, University of North Carolina, Chapel Hill.

39. See, for instance, George Daniel Farrar to his father, December 24, 1858, in Alexander K. Farrar Papers, Department of Archives and Manuscripts, Louisiana State University, Baton Rouge; S. R. Bertron to William Hughes, August 14, 1860, in William Hughes and Family Papers, Z 68, Folder 7, Mississippi Department of Archives and History, Jackson.

This is not easy to answer. To say simply that slaveowners were racists overlooks the fact that northern whites too considered blacks inferior but by and large did not come to regard them as children. No doubt the historical association of blackness with servitude in the South tended to blur the distinction between labor and race relations and to encourage planters to identify one with the other. But the presence of successful free Negroes in the South in general and in the lower Mississippi Valley in particular—"the barber of Natchez," William Johnson, being the most striking example—was proof enough that blacks could function in a capitalist world.[40]

To understand why the planters fixed their attention on race it is necessary to go beyond the plantation and look at the nature of the larger world that elevated them. In addition to their paternalistic relations with the slaves, the gentry had marketplace relations with various whites in the community. From time to time they hired white laborers to perform odd jobs around the plantation, and periodically they called upon the services of local artisans. They also had frequent dealings with district merchants and extensive commercial transactions with manufacturers and factors. Furthermore, the most successful slaveowners in the Natchez district, the richest and most "patrician"—Stephen Duncan and William Newton Mercer, Jacob Surget and Levin R. Marshall—invested heavily in the North, lived a portion of the year in New York or New England, and profited from the marketplace arrangement of free labor just as they did from the paternalism of the plantation. The gentry were complexly enmeshed in a dual society—comfortably enmeshed as well. They were among the principal beneficiaries of an America half-slave and half-free. As such they were scarcely in a position to frame an ideology antagonistic to the status quo. On the contrary, what they required was a justification of the very duality all around them, some sanction for the side-by-side exis-

40. See Eugene H. Berwanger, *The Frontier Against Slavery: Western Anti-Negro Prejudice and the Slavery Extension Controversy* (Urbana: University of Illinois Press, 1967); Leon F. Litwack, *North of Slavery: The Negro in the Free States, 1790–1860* (Chicago: University of Chicago Press, 1961); William R. Hogan and Edwin A. Davis (eds.), *William Johnson's Natchez: The Ante-Bellum Diary of a Free Negro* (Baton Rouge: Louisiana State University Press, 1951).

tence of two different kinds of social relations. Race answered that need. It allowed them to pose the egalitarianism of the market-place as the logical complement, rather than the antithesis, of the paternalism of the plantation. To be sure, not all planters were en-tirely at ease with the "Herrenvolk democracy" that, perhaps un-avoidably, accompanied such reasoning. But, then, political de-mocracy was arguably a small price to pay for social stability and peace of mind.[41]

Because the gentry had conspicuous aristocratic pretensions, some historians have dismissed their professions of white egalitari-anism as mere rhetoric designed to ensure the continued support of the nonslaveholders.[42] But if by *egalitarianism* we mean not full social equality but simply equality of opportunity in the mar-ketplace, the gentry were true believers. They had to be. Here was a world that served their interests, indeed served their interests very well. That the world was itself dualistic only convinced them that such dualism was perfectly natural and right. Again, all they required was a coherent explanation for this peculiar arrangement. And this explanation they found in race.

Of course, there remained the inherent flaw in their reasoning. Paternalism was rooted in the social relations of slavery, not the innate nature of the black laborer. Admittedly this discrepancy be-tween thought and reality did not matter much in the antebellum period, when class and race were closely intertwined. But it took on considerable importance in the years immediately following the war. For while Emancipation destroyed the social basis of pater-nalistic behavior, it did not alter assumptions about the character of the Negro. The birth of the New South plantation is really the story of how the paternalistic relations of slavery gave over to the marketplace relations of free labor in the face of an ideology that could neither condone the change nor explain the need for it.

41. On "Herrenvolk democracy," see Pierre L. van den Berghe, *Race and Racism: A Comparative Perspective* (New York: Wiley, 1967), Chap. 4; George M. Fredrickson, *The Black Image in the White Mind: The Debate on Afro-American Character and Destiny, 1817–1914* (New York: Harper & Row, 1971), 64–70.
42. See, for example, Fredrickson, *Black Image*, 63.

PART II

# Days of Transition

CHAPTER TWO

# Everything Seems Sadly Out of Time

I

The Federal invasion in the spring of 1863 brought widespread devastation to the lower Mississippi Valley. "I saw the first furnished house I ever saw forsaken & part of the furniture destroyed," wrote an obviously troubled Union surgeon in May, 1863. "I believe there [were] 40 or 50 mirrors from 4 to 15 ft high and sofas, marble toped [sic] tables & & c enough to commence a wholesale furniture store. There were over a doz bedsteads that cost $200.00 each. The building cost $200,000.00. Five miles from this was a building which cost $125,000.00. In this was a thousand dollar piano. Everything was being destroyed."[1]

As Whitelaw Reid observed shortly after the war, "Respect for the rights of absent property owners" was "nowhere . . . a very marked characteristic of the movements of Northern armies."[2] Or for the rights of resident property owners, one might add. Joshua James lived on Ion, a Tensas Parish plantation of about 1,300 acres along the Mississippi. When war broke out, three of his four sons went off to fight for the Confederacy. He, however, remained at home, electing to stay there even when Federal forces, beginning their flanking movement around Vicksburg, overran the area in April, 1863. Union officers gave him assurances that his property would be respected. But during the following weeks, troops proceeded to confiscate his cows, hogs, poultry, grain, and garden crops, and burn down his ginhouse, barn, stables, carriage, and slave quarters.

1. [Charles B. Tompkins] to Mollie [Tompkins], May 6, 1863, in Charles Brown Tompkins Papers, Manuscript Department, William R. Perkins Library, Duke University, Durham, N.C.
2. Whitelaw Reid, *After the War: A Southern Tour* (Cincinnati: Moore, Wilstach & Baldwin, 1866), 283.

Bitter but apparently undaunted, James continued to reside at Ion until the late summer of 1864. Then, on September 16, under instructions from Captain N. T. Willetts of the U.S. gunboat *Rattler*, he began to move his family and household belongings back from the river. Despite his genuine, if grudging, willingness to obey Federal orders, he was arrested on September 20 and jailed overnight. In his absence, Willetts burned the mansion at Ion to the ground.

Three days later, troops confiscated his steam engine, and three weeks after that, now residing at the home of a friend, he was arrested once more, robbed of $250 in gold and several hundred dollars in U.S. legal tender notes, his silver plate, gold watches, blankets, and clothing, and forced to accompany Federal soldiers on a pillaging raid through the neighborhood. Finally he was removed to Vicksburg, where he was imprisoned along with about seventy other wealthy fathers of rebel soldiers.[3]

As James's experiences illustrate, Federal depredations did not end with the successful taking of the lower Mississippi Valley in the spring and summer of 1863. Throughout the remainder of the war, Natchez served as a base for Union forays into southwest Mississippi and eastern Louisiana. The most famous such raid took place in early October, 1864, and culminated in the spectacular burning of the residence and cotton factory of Judge Edward McGehee of Wilkinson County. Troops helped themselves to his stores of goods and food and set fire to his ginhouse, 350 bales of cotton, and promissory notes due him worth about $80,000.[4]

Even the fall of the Confederacy did not bring an immediate end to the Yankee pillaging. Soldiers, and private citizens masquerad-

3. Joshua James to Major Genl. McClernand, April 27, 1863, [Joshua James] to Robert J. Walker, January 13, 1868 (unfinished copy), both in Joshua James Papers, Manuscript Department, William R. Perkins Library, Duke University, Durham, N.C.
4. John Stanford Coussons, "The Federal Occupation of Natchez, Mississippi, 1863–1865" (M.A. thesis, Louisiana State University, 1958), 21; sworn statement, November 19, 1869 (copy), in J. Burruss McGehee Papers, Department of Archives and Manuscripts, Louisiana State University, Baton Rouge; James Stewart McGehee Papers, Vol. I, Pt. 1, p. 75, Department of Archives and Manuscripts, Louisiana State University, Baton Rouge. From 1863 through the end of the war, the Union army controlled much of the district, including almost all the land along the river and most of the territory in Louisiana. Sections in Mississippi remained under Confederate control, however, especially in Wilkinson County.

ing as soldiers, continued to confiscate food and cotton through the summer and into the fall of 1865. In June, for instance, troops removed substantial quantities of corn from the Jefferson County plantation of Buckner Darden. Several months later, his brother Jesse reported that six hundred hogs and sixty loads of corn had been taken from a neighboring estate. Treasury Department agents roamed the countryside in search of cotton allegedly once held in the name of the Confederacy. The activities of these men were characterized by "much irregularity," as the secretary of the treasury later confessed. In July, James H. Maury of Claiborne County informed Governor William L. Sharkey, "There is a little lad here about 17 years of age who is said to be a treasury agent. He or the provost both undertake to decide whose property is confiscable, and seize & carry off cotton—leaving the owner to pursue it through the maze of military judicial proceedings. Like the popish plot, the charge of having been a rebel is all sufficient to cover any case." Things finally became so desperate that planters placed armed guards over their cotton and forcibly began to resist seizure.[5]

But Federal soldiers were not the only agents of destruction in the region. In 1863 the Confederate government ordered that all cotton along the Mississippi be burned, lest it fall into northern hands. Although many slaveholders ignored the directive, tens of thousands of bales went up in flames. Later, during the two years of occupation, southern troops carried out sporadic raids against the plantations of Union sympathizers and Yankee lessees. Levin R. Marshall and Ayres P. Merrill reaped numerous benefits from their favorable relations with Federal officials in Natchez; but, as a consequence, Confederate guerrillas razed Marshall's Poplar Grove and Merrill's The Hedges. The frequency and violence of rebel activities in the vicinity of Vicksburg forced lessees to abandon over one-third of the land originally rented there.[6]

5. Susan Sillers Darden Diary (MS in Darden Family Papers, Z 82, Mississippi Department of Archives and History, Jackson), II, June 16, October 8, 1865; *Senate Executive Documents*, 43rd Cong., 2nd Sess., No. 23, p. 2; Jas. H. Maury to W. L. Sharkey, July 3, 1865, in Governors' Correspondence, Box 61, Mississippi Department of Archives and History, Jackson; statement by James H. Maury to Colonel Lilly, [1865?], in James H. Maury Papers, Z 733, Mississippi Department of Archives and History, Jackson.

6. F[rank] S[urget] to Dr. [Stephen Duncan], July 31, 1865, in Stephen Duncan Corre-

Actually, most planters experienced some losses at the hands of both sides. Haller Nutt was an avowed Unionist, but "stragglers" from the invading army burned down his cotton gins and ransacked his two Tensas Parish plantations. "*Every living thing,*" he lamented, "was either destroyed or carried away." Dempsey P. Jackson willingly advanced over $5,000 to the cause of secession. But Confederate authorities impressed a like value of his livestock and set fire to his cotton. Then there was the rather typical plight of Charles Whitmore of Adams County. He wrote to a cousin in England in late 1863, "Our principal diff'y is the position which we occupy outside the picket lines which prevents us from getting the necessary supplies & yet close enough to be in hearing & in sight of the Federals & what is worse in danger of inroads from the Confederates."[7] Allegiances, under the circumstances, were cautious and fleeting.

Finally, it is well to remember that there was a third party active in the "appropriation" of planter property. "Negroes in town come to the places where they formily resided," complained James A. Gillespie of Adams County at the end of the war, "& steel horses & other stock & run them to Natchez & even across the river for use or sale: Being familiar with the localities & oftain aided by the hired labor."[8] No doubt most freedmen thought that they were just taking what was rightfully theirs. To the planter it was theft. In any case, the results were the same.

In sum, the vast majority of former slaveowners in the district suffered some form of severe property damage or loss as a result of

spondence, Department of Archives and Manuscripts, Louisiana State University, Baton Rouge; "Under the Stars and Bars" (Typescript, in W.P.A. Records, RG 60, for Adams County, Folder: Civil War, Mississippi Department of Archives and History, Jackson); H. C. Minor to his mother, December 13, 1863, in William J. Minor and Family Papers, Department of Archives and Manuscripts, Louisiana State University, Baton Rouge; B. I. Wiley, "Vicissitudes of Early Reconstruction Farming in the Lower Mississippi Valley," *Journal of Southern History*, III (1937), 446.

7. [Haller Nutt] to Reverdy Johnson, October [?], 1863 (microfilm copy from Huntington Library), in Haller Nutt Papers, Manuscript Department, William R. Perkins Library, Duke University, Durham, N.C.; "List of money and equivalent given to the Confederate cause," in possession of Mr. and Mrs. Boyd Sojourner, Natchez; Chas. Whitmore to Mary Anne Welsh, November 23, 1863 (copy), in Charles Whitmore Diary (MS in Southern Historical Collection, University of North Carolina, Chapel Hill).

8. Jas. A. Gillespie to [?], May 29, 1865, in James A. Gillespie and Family Papers, Department of Archives and Manuscripts, Louisiana State University, Baton Rouge.

the conflict. James L. Sellers has concluded that southern wealth, exclusive of slaveholdings, declined 43 percent over the war years. Natchez area landowners fared worse than most. Individual planters placed their losses in the tens of thousands of dollars—hundreds of thousands if the value of emancipated slaves and unrealized cotton profits is included. Charles Whitmore, for instance, reckoned that the war cost him $100,000. Dempsey P. Jackson placed his own losses at $600,000. The destruction of his plantation and factory and the emancipation of his slaves reportedly cost Judge Edward McGehee about $1,150,000, exclusive of any decline in the value of his land.[9]

Enormous rebuilding expenses represented only part of the financial problem confronting the gentry in 1865. Many planters also faced substantial debts, a significant portion of which had been contracted prior to 1865. In a letter to Governor Benjamin G. Humphreys in March, 1866, George Torrey of Jefferson County bemoaned "the indebtedness of the Country." "Unless we can devise some measure of relief," he warned, "the Speculators, that were amongst us during the war, and the moneyed men of the North, will, in a few years, own all the property of the South— and the rising generation go without an education." Alexander K. Farrar of Adams County owed his friend and neighbor Stephen Duncan more than $61,600; other planters owed Farrar $25,000. Catherine Eustis confessed at the end of 1865 that even the suggested sale of her 1,280-acre river plantation at $55 an acre would not enable her to avoid bankruptcy.[10]

There was an irony here. Few of those burdened with outstand-

9. James L. Sellers, "The Economic Incidence of the Civil War in the South," *Mississippi Valley Historical Review*, XIV (1927–1928), 183; Chas. Whitmore to Mary Anne Welsh, November 25, 1863 (copy), in Whitmore Diary; scrap of paper, undated, in possession of Mr. and Mrs. Boyd Sojourner, Natchez; J. S. McGehee Papers, Vol. I, Pt. 1, p. 75.

10. Geo. Torrey to B. G. Humphreys, March 29, 1866, in Governors' Correspondence, Box 65; Stephen Duncan and Stephen Duncan, Jr., Papers, V, 212, Department of Archives and Manuscripts, Louisiana State University, Baton Rouge; "List of debts due A. K. Farrar in Wilkinson County," in Alexander K. Farrar Papers, Box 6, Folder 38, Department of Archives and Manuscripts, Louisiana State University, Baton Rouge; C. C. Eustis to Uncle William, December 4, 1865, in W. J. Minor Papers. Although the currency in which many debts had been contracted was repudiated, private debts made prior to and during the war were considered valid at its close and efforts to secure their abrogation by law proved unsuccessful. John K. Bettersworth, *Confederate Mississippi: The People and Policies of a Cotton State in Wartime* (Baton Rouge: Louisiana State University Press, 1943), 129.

ing antebellum debts in 1865 had actually been in financial difficulty before the war. The 1850s had been boom times, with ambitious planters borrowing freely to expand their estates and slaveholdings; only after the war did their indebtedness become oppressive. Joseph D. Shields provides a case in point. In 1860, Oscar Kibbe sold him a half interest in Pecano, a large Tensas Parish plantation, for $84,000—$14,000 in advance and the remainder in installments of $10,000 per year for seven years with 8 percent interest. At the time it seemed a sound investment, ensuring Shields a secure future. Then the war intervened. Six years later, he stood "pecuniarily ruined." Pressed by Kibbe for $7,500 of the outstanding balance, he replied, "It would be a useless gratuity on my part to give you my note for I have no more chance of redeeming it than skating to heaven on a moonbeam."[11]

Obviously creditors too suffered under these circumstances, and quite a few planters were creditors. One, Stephen Duncan, personally held almost fifty notes worth over $250,000 in 1863. To be sure, a man like Duncan, with vast and varied northern interests, could afford to be patient. Most creditors had far less to fall back on, however, and were desperate. Chesley S. Coffey of Jefferson County, for instance, wrote to Charles D. Hamilton in June, 1865, for help in collecting on an outstanding note. A mutual friend, "very much Distroid" by the war, had fled to Europe owing Coffey $3,000. "I want to get the money secured or Get Cotton for it," explained Coffey. "I have been a very heavy Sufferer for *my* means in the war." Henry L. Conner also approached Hamilton for assistance, although his request was of a somewhat more delicate nature: "I find myself at the end of this unfortunate war entirely without money or the ability to raise any. Having understood that you have been very fortunate in cotton speculations, I therefore take this occasion to enquire of you whether you can not settle your note either in full or part. I loathe to ask you for the payment of money at a time like this, & would not now were I not reduced

11. Jo. D. Shields to Buckner & Newman, July 19, 1866, Jo. D. Shields to Buckner & Co., October 20, November 23, 1866, Jo. D. Shields to Oscar Kibbe, October 31, 1866, January 31, 1867, Jo. D. Shields to J. R. Jones, December 15, 1866, all in Joseph D. Shields Papers, Department of Archives and Manuscripts, Louisiana State University, Baton Rouge.

to the last extremity so that I hope you will excuse this apparently unreasonable request."[12]

Encumbered with debts, their slaves emancipated, their property destroyed, most planters were precariously situated in 1865. But there were exceptions. As the wife of a Federal officer pointedly observed, "Some of the far-seeing men of means, while giving the semblance of their allegiance to the Confederacy, hedged against its failure by transferring their bank accounts from New Orleans to Liverpool and Paris." Charles D. Hamilton kept funds in England during the war, as did Charles Whitmore of Adams County. Clarissa Young, wife of a wealthy Claiborne County planter, had almost £1000 on deposit with the Liverpool firm of Rankin, Gilmour & Co. in January, 1865.[13]

These individuals were adequately fixed to withstand at least some of the adverse economic consequences of the war. But only those planters with large-scale northern or European investments were entirely secure. There were relatively few such men—perhaps no more than a score in the district—but they ranked among the most prominent members of the local aristocracy.

In 1864, Stephen Duncan owned stocks and securities worth over $170,000. Among his investments were shares in the New York Central Railroad, the Michigan Central Railroad, the Erie Railroad, the Bank of New York, and the Bank of Louisville. He also held $18,000 in United States bonds. William Newton Mercer too owned U.S. bonds and, in addition, held vast tracts of land in Illinois and shares in the New York Central Railroad, the Reading Railroad, the Pittsburgh and Fort Wayne Railroad, the Old Colony and Newport Railroad, the Newport and New York Steam Ship Company, and the California Quicksilver Company. Nor did the war curtail his financial activities. During July, 1864, for example,

12. Duncan Papers, VI, 19–20; C. S. Coffey to C. D. Hamilton, June 16, 1865, Henry L. Conner to C. D. Hamilton, September 26, 1865, both in Charles D. Hamilton and Family Papers, Z 98, Mississippi Department of Archives and History, Jackson.

13. Matilda Gresham, *Life of Walter Quintin Gresham, 1832–1895* (2 vols.; Chicago: Rand, McNally, 1919), I, 258–59; James Belknap to Lizzie Hamilton, April 26, 1869, in C. D. Hamilton Papers; C[harles] W[hitmore] to Joseph Lyon, August 13, 1863 (copy), Whitmore to Welsh, November 25, 1863 (copy), both in Whitmore Diary; account statement, January 1, 1865, in William Hughes and Family Papers, Z 68, Folder 7, Mississippi Department of Archives and History, Jackson.

he purchased 250 shares of New York Central Railroad stock for $37,392; during September he bought 50 shares of preferred Erie Railroad stock, 43 shares of Hudson River Railroad stock, and 86 shares of Philadelphia and Reading Railroad stock for a total of $15,000. Both he and Duncan continued to have extensive dealings with Liverpool brokers throughout the conflict. Audley C. Britton transacted business affairs through his brother in New York during the war as did other wealthy Natchez planters.[14]

These southern men with northern interests were the first to come to terms with Federal authorities during the occupation. It was in their homes that Yankees found shelter and society, and it was they to whom officials turned for advice in restoring stability to the region. Predictably, their behavior and professed Unionism won them favored treatment. They were allowed to lease their plantations at great profit and were given access to markets for their cotton. In the end their financial position was scarcely diminished by the conflict, which explains why a northern officer could claim that he "had never seen in New York or elsewhere anything approaching the style of living [in Natchez]."[15]

For the vast majority of planters, however, the war brought only distress. "There is great suffering here now," wrote a Union soldier from Natchez in April, 1865, "and it is not [to] be much better for some time to come. Families that were in the most affluent circumstances before the war, are now in want of bread to eat, and don't know where it is to come from." A year later, a young Georgian reported, "As about Savannah, poverty is the order of the day with the people of this section, where there was once great wealth."[16]

The former slaveowners themselves spoke most passionately of

14. Duncan Papers, VI, 66–67, III, *passim*; list of stocks, in Diary for January–August, 1865 (MS in William Newton Mercer Papers, Department of Archives and Manuscripts, Louisiana State University, Baton Rouge); tax receipts for March 26, April 1, 1867, account notices for January 20, 1865, June 25, 1863, all in Mercer Papers; W. A. Britton to his brother, April 15, 21, 1864, Brown Brothers & Co. to Audley C. Britton, March 20, 1865, all in Audley Clark Britton and Family Papers, Department of Archives and Manuscripts, Louisiana State University, Baton Rouge.

15. Quoted in Coussons, "The Federal Occupation of Natchez," 100.

16. Glyde [Swain] to his sister, April 15, 1865 (microfilm copy from Wisconsin Historical Society), in Samuel Glyde Swain Papers, Mississippi Department of Archives and History, Jackson; J. Floyd King to Virginia [King], March 28, 1866, in Thomas Butler King Papers, Southern Historical Collection, University of North Carolina, Chapel Hill.

their losses: "[The South] was once the finest, fairest, happiest country on the face of the earth! But all is changed: and the people once rich, hospitable, *powerful* are now poor, and like 'Samson of old' shorn of their pride and strength." And poignantly: "How still and lifeless everything seems. . . . The bare echoing rooms, the neglect and defacement of all. . . . Everything seems sadly out of time."[17]

## II

Economic difficulties were compounded by uncertainty about the future. Ingrained attitudes made the gentry fearful. It was widely assumed that blacks would never respond to marketplace incentives; only force, it was said, would keep them at their tasks. J. T. Trowbridge, in his travels through the district, received repeated assurances that the former slaves would not work except under "despotic compulsion." Carl Schurz heard the same argument and later complained that "every irregularity that occurred was directly charged against the system of free labor." It may well be, as James W. Garner has suggested, that not one planter in ten believed that free black labor could be made profitable.[18]

Nor, for that matter, would the former slaveowners admit that the freedman was competent to care for himself and his family. After all, inherent black improvidence had been the ideological cornerstone of the defense of slavery. The gentry were scarcely in a position now to deny the correctness of their traditional assumptions. On the contrary, most professed to see a bleak future for the Negro. "That slavery is an evil, I have never doubted," wrote William Newton Mercer during the closing days of the war, "and for more than twenty years have been convinced it could not be pre-

17. A. C. Britton to his sister, June 19, 1866, in Britton Papers; John Q. Anderson (ed.), *Brokenburn: The Journal of Kate Stone, 1861–1868* (Baton Rouge: Louisiana State University Press, 1972), 364–65.
18. J. T. Trowbridge, *The South: A Tour of Its Battlefields and Ruined Cities* (New York: Arno Press, 1969), 349; *Senate Executive Documents*, 39th Cong., 1st Sess., No. 2, pp. 16–17; James Wilford Garner, *Reconstruction in Mississippi* (New York: Macmillan, 1901), 133; Leon F. Litwack, *Been in the Storm So Long: The Aftermath of Slavery* (New York: Knopf, 1979), 158.

served, in opposition to the spirit of the age, the dictates of humanity and the teaching of experience. In regard to any personal interests, I would have been perfectly willing to have manumitted my own slaves. But I did not believe that an immediate, and so great a change would have been to their advantage. On the contrary, I felt convinced that they are now exposed to a dreadful ordeal."[19]

Should we pay attention to such transparently self-serving statements? Probably. Admittedly, the gentry engaged in more than their share of rhetoric. But remember, for years they had both publicly and privately justified their own economic elevation by treating slavery as a relationship in which the laborer received at least as much, probably more, than he gave. For their self-esteem they *had* to predict misery ahead for the freedman. Anyone who doubts the depth of their sincerity should consider the following remarkable passage from a letter written by Joseph D. Shields of Adams County to a friend in September, 1865: "Let me describe a scene that has just passed before my door. Mary is sitting backwards in Dades wagon. Cy & Daniel & Caius & Hinds are the mule Team while Walter is the driver—Huntz stands in the house and dictates the track—They are enjoying themselves just as much as though they were not Free."[20]

And yet, for all their doubts about the capacity of the freedman to act responsibly, most former slaveowners had by no means abandoned hope for the future. Slavery itself as a legal institution was gone, of that there was little doubt. But if the old paternalistic relations could be imposed on a slaveless world, much might be salvaged. As a Tensas Parish planter remarked to J. T. Trowbridge, "I think God intended the niggers to be slaves. . . . Now since man has deranged God's plans, I think the best we can do is keep 'em as near a state of bondage as possible. . . . My theory is feed 'em well, clothe 'em well, and then, if they don't work . . . whip 'em well!"[21] Not many former slaveowners were so candid with outsiders, but most would have subscribed to the underlying message: success

19. Litwack, *Been in the Storm So Long*, 359–61; Mercer Papers, XXX, April 10, 1865.
20. [Joseph D. Shields] to Mary J. Conway, September 23, 1865, in Shields Papers.
21. Trowbridge, *The South*, 392.

under a system of free black labor was dependent on preservation of antebellum plantation law.

Historians have largely overlooked the ironic quality of this reasoning. Emancipation had seemingly relieved the gentry of not only the rights of slaveholding but its responsibilities as well. As the *Southern Cultivator* noted in July, 1865, "The Law which freed the negro at the same time freed the master. At the same moment and for both parties, all obligations springing out of the relations of master and slave, except those of kindness, cease mutually to exist." Yet here was the planter proposing to provide rations and care, shelter and moral direction, as in the past. Kindness, of course, had little to do with it. His antebellum ideology simply allowed for no alternative. "The niger we Know him the mass of them are stupid and indolent," explained one former slaveowner from Tensas Parish. They "ever will require guardians."[22]

If preservation of traditional relations was necessary, it was also attainable—or so the gentry imagined at the end of the war. Planters believed that by binding the blacks to contracts—a practice introduced to the region by Federal authorities during the occupation—and choosing the wording carefully, they could reinstitute the rules and regulations of the antebellum plantation while, outwardly at least, complying with the legal forms of free labor. In practice, contracts varied little during the spring and summer of 1865. Typically the landowner would sign all his laborers to a single, brief agreement. In it he would promise to provide nominal wages plus rations, shelter, clothing, and moral oversight; the freedmen would pledge obedience. The former slaves on J. F. Sessions' plantation east of Natchez, for instance, committed themselves to "good and faithful service during the remainder of the year 1865, in whatever capacity the said J. F. Sessions may direct." Joseph Shields contracted to give the freedmen on Pecano in Louisiana "just treatment wholesome food comfortable clothing & quarters fuel and necessary medical attention."[23] Note that questions of

---

22. Quoted in Edgar T. Thompson, "The Natural History of Agricultural Labor in the South," in *American Studies in Honor of W. K. Boyd* (Durham, N.C.: Duke University Press, 1940), 170; undated note, [postbellum], in possession of Mr. and Mrs. Boyd Sojourner, Natchez.

23. Memorandum of an agreement, August, 1865, in J. F. Sessions Papers, Z 608, Folder

quantity and quality were left to his discretion as, presumably, was the interpretation of what constituted "just treatment."

Clearly the gentry were hopeful—perhaps they even expected—that the contracts of 1865 represented a final settlement of the labor question. It seemed evident from the perspective of the former slaveowner that the fundamental character of the Negro both demanded and made possible a return to a paternalistic form of social organization. Because of their innate carelessness and promiscuity, blacks would ever need a guardian and master; because of their spiritual torpor and intellectual weakness, they would inevitably look to responsible whites for direction.

But here the gentry miscalculated, betrayed by their delusive reading of the past. The paternalistic nature of the plantation had derived not from the personality of the slave but from the internal logic of the slave labor system. With slavery gone, there was no reason to suppose that antebellum plantation law would or should be perpetuated. On the contrary, tendencies inherent in free labor demanded their own forms of accommodation between planter and freedman. As would soon become apparent, Emancipation had opened the way for the marketplace to have a significant influence in the shaping of relations on the plantation. If the gentry hoped to retain control over the former slaves, they would have to develop effective devices for regulating or circumventing the process of supply and demand. The contracts of 1865 had been written with other considerations in mind and, despite their blatantly coercive aspect, were inadequate to protect the interests of the planters. They represented an epilogue to the old order, not a preface to the new.

That as late as the spring of 1865 the former slaveowners of the Natchez district were still visibly wedded to the past has to do in large measure with the policies of the Federal forces during the two years of wartime occupation. Several different plans for implementing free labor were tried in this period, and several men exercised some authority in the region, but all proposals were guided

---

4, Mississippi Department of Archives and History, Jackson; agreement with freedmen, May 26, 1865, in Shields Papers.

and all officials governed by the assumption that the continuingly unstable military situation demanded that the freedman remain on his home plantation, receiving care and a regulated wage in return for his labor. This would enable the military to minimize its expenses, encourage northern leasing of abandoned plantations, and possibly win the loyalty of slaveowners who had elected to remain on their estates. What it obviously would not do was introduce the marketplace into the planter-laborer relationship. As Colonel John Eaton, general superintendent for freedmen's affairs in the Mississippi Valley, later recalled, "The problem before us at first . . . was to afford not the best wages to the individual which free competition in an open market might assure him, but a livelihood for the entire population under a condition of military and industrial disorder which temporarily necessitated some form of definite regulation and precluded unrestricted competition."[24]

The end result of such thinking was a program in which planters and freedmen were required to act as if they had certain fundamental reponsibilities to each other that existed outside the laws of supply and demand. The gentry were not merely advised to continue acting like patriarchs, they were ordered to do so. Indeed, to a conspicuous extent the regulations imposed by the Yankees served to affirm the organization of the antebellum plantation. Consider the instructions given to the provost marshals who temporarily had authority at the end of the war. These read in part: "Freedmen must be encouraged to remain where they are now. . . . They must be made to understand that when they hire themselves to any one, they are under his control, and must be obedient to his orders. . . . Contracts must secure support, maintenance, clothing and medical attention to the laborer." In addition, freedmen were prohibited from showing "insubordination" or creating disorder, while employers were directed to provide "just treatment, whole-

---

24. See, for instance, James W. Garner's discussion of the Federal program in *Reconstruction in Mississippi*, 249–53; James E. Yeatman, *Report to the Western Sanitary Commission, in Regard to Leasing Abandoned Plantations, with Rules and Regulations Governing the Same* (St. Louis: Western Sanitary Commission Rooms, 1864); John Eaton, *Grant, Lincoln and the Freedmen: Reminiscences of the Civil War with Special Reference to the Work for the Contrabands and Freedmen of the Mississippi Valley* (New York: Longmans, Green, 1907), 129, 219–20.

some rations, comfortable clothing, quarters, fuel, and medical attendance, and the opportunity for instruction of children." Gardens were to be made available to the hands. Only the introduction of education represented a departure from traditional practices, and the authorities, by according oversight to the planter, ensured that even this innovation would be limited.[25]

Here, then, we have the old pattern of reciprocal responsibilities formalized, set down in detail, and given the stamp of Federal approval. And increasingly subject, incidentally, to enforcement by officials convinced that the surest and most sensible way to return stability to the region was to further the interests of the local elite. The government appointed provost marshals sympathetic to the gentry or, as in the case of the Warrenton district of Warren County, simply conferred the office on a resident planter.[26]

In view of the nature of their introduction to free black labor, it is scarcely surprising that many members of the gentry believed that traditional relations could be preserved under cover of the contract. Seemingly the occupation forces had destroyed slavery only to sanction the very duties and obligations that slavery itself had created. The freedmen, however, had ideas of their own. They turned the briefness of the agreements to personal advantage. In April, 1866, Amelia Montgomery of Belmont complained to her husband, "I wish our contract had been more specific with regard to Baling. These negroes don't like to bale for us, say it was not in the contract." Later in the year, she cautioned him to spell out every duty clearly in the future:

In your contract you ought to have a lean [sic] on the crop, & a time specified for the payment of it, & the cotton or a part of it to be shiped [sic] to you (delivered at Rodney) as early as it is baled, some by the first Nove'r to help us live, pay house rent & c. &c. & that no wood was to be sold off the place only by your special permission, what stock was left to be taken care of, & they to have the use of the cows, & to divide the butter with us if they had it to spare instead of selling it. Allowing them a proportion of the few hogs that might be raised for taking care of them if we should leave any, there are many other little

25. Regulations of Provost Marshals of Freedmen, in James S. Allen and Family Papers, Z 1239, Box 3, Folder 27, Mississippi Department of Archives and History, Jackson.
26. Appointment, June 14, 1865, in Allen Papers.

things ought to be included about cutting too much timber on this side of the road, & *distinctly* understood about our individual privileges here about house room & c.[27]

Apparently the freedmen were determined to pursue interests of their own. Even more unsettling for the planters, evidence was accumulating that the former slaves were willing to move around if necessary to secure their objectives. George D. Reynolds, acting assistant commissioner of the Freedmen's Bureau in southern Mississippi, observed during the summer of 1865, "They will remain this year on their old places for a support, and such remuneration as the crop raised can give them, but say next year they will leave and make other arrangements. They say that they have tried their old masters, know what they require, and how they will be treated, and that, as they are now free, they will try some other place and some other way of working. They take this view not because they are tired of working, or because they want to be idle, but because they are now free."[28]

By taking to the road, the freedmen let it be known that they would not be satisfied with a social order structured along antebellum lines. In the process, they introduced the marketplace into the labor settlement. As James Lucas succinctly noted many years later, "One ob de rights ob bein free wuz dat we could move around en change bosses."[29] It was a right the former slaves evidently meant to exercise.

To be sure, not all movement in the early days was linked to the forces of supply and demand. During the occupation and in the months following, many former slaves left home simply to experience freedom, to test the character and extent of their newfound liberty. Some set out to join family members on neighboring plantations or in other communities. Three of the best hands on Wil-

27. A. F. Montgomery to her husband, April 12, October 25, 1866, both in Joseph A. Montgomery and Family Papers, Department of Archives and Manuscripts, Louisiana State University, Baton Rouge.

28. *Senate Executive Documents*, 39th Cong., 1st Sess., No. 2, p. 101; Litwack, *Been in the Storm So Long*, 331.

29. George P. Rawick, Jan Hillegas, and Ken Lawrence (eds.), *The American Slave: A Composite Autobiography*, Supplement, Series 1 (12 vols.; Westport, Conn.: Greenwood Press, 1977), VIII, 1348.

liam Newton Mercer's Buckhurst, for example, decided to return to their old homes in Maryland and Virginia at the end of 1866.[30] But even in 1865 most movement was local and inspired by the belief that somewhere down the road there might be a better life.

This is the context in which to understand the Black Codes of late 1865 and early 1866. Passed by the state legislatures established under the presidential plan of Reconstruction, these laws represented the first formal response by the former slaveowner to the introduction of the marketplace into the labor settlement. As such, they were highly involved and impractical in the extreme. Guided by their preconceptions of the character of the Negro, the gentry were not content merely to regulate competition. They sought, as well, to legislate the freedman back into the kind of paternalistic arrangement that had existed before the war. Inevitably the laws reflected this confusion of intentions—now restricting the opportunities of the former slave, now confirming his antebellum rights and responsibilities. As Leon Litwack notes, "The Black Codes were . . . very much a product of post-war southern thinking, both a legal expression of the lingering paternalism (to protect the ex-slave from himself) and a legislative response to immediate and pressing economic problems."[31]

Both Mississippi and Louisiana passed vagrancy laws designed to drive freedmen out of the towns and back to the plantations; and both states enacted statutes apprenticing orphans to landowners. More significant, Mississippi prohibited blacks from leasing or purchasing real estate, while Louisiana authorized a plantation system closely modeled on antebellum forms:

> When in health the laborer shall work ten hours during the day in summer and nine hours during the day in winter unless otherwise stipulated in the labor contract; he shall obey all proper orders of his employer or agent. . . . Failing to obey reasonable orders, neglect of duty, or leaving home without permission will be deemed disobedience; im-

30. Wilmer [Shields] to Doctor [William N. Mercer], November 18, 1866, in Mercer Papers.

31. Litwack, *Been in the Storm So Long*, 366; see also Daniel A. Novak, *The Wheel of Servitude: Black Forced Labor After Slavery* (Lexington: University of Kentucky Press, 1978), 1; Theodore Brantner Wilson, *The Black Codes of the South* (University, Ala.: University of Alabama Press, 1965).

pudence, arguing, or indecent language to, or in the presence of, the employer, his family, or agent, or quarreling and fighting with one another shall be deemed disobedience. . . . Laborers will not be required to labor on the Sabbath, except to take necessary care of stock and other property on the plantation. . . . No livestock shall be allowed to laborers without the permission of the employer. Laborers shall not receive visitors during work hours. All difficulties arising between the employer and laborers, under this section, shall be settled, and all fines imposed by the former.[32]

In addition to the laws regulating black labor, there were various statutes dealing with the position of the former slave in southern society. A few of these measures extended protection to the freedman, but most were designed to curtail his civil liberties—limiting his rights in the courts, for instance, or denying him permission to bear arms. The clear intention of such legislation was to place the former slave in a caste status closely akin to that of the free Negro before the war. Indeed, many of the laws were drawn directly from antebellum statutes.[33]

In sum, the Black Codes were an elaborate and extensive attempt to control labor, reimpose the paternalistic arrangement of the plantation, and reaffirm the inferior position of the black in southern society. Planters were active in formulating this legislation, and undoubtedly a majority of former slaveowners from the district regarded the laws as at least somewhat beneficial, especially those provisions pertaining to labor relations. But doubts were soon raised. In early 1866, George Torrey, a prominent Jefferson County landowner, wrote to his friend and fellow planter, Benjamin G. Humphreys, now governor of Mississippi,

I think our Legislators Legislated too much—Insted of that long act in relation to their giving evidence in court, I think there should not have

32. William C. Harris, *Presidential Reconstruction in Mississippi* (Baton Rouge: Louisiana State University Press, 1967), Chaps. 6 and 7; indentures of various freedmen with G. W. Humphreys, 1865, in George Wilson Humphreys and Family Papers, Z 29, Folder 10, Mississippi Department of Archives and History, Jackson; *Laws of the State of Mississippi Passed at a Regular Session of the Mississippi Legislature, Held in the City of Jackson, October, November, and December, 1865* (Jackson, 1866), 82–93; *Senate Executive Documents*, 39th Cong., 2nd Sess., No. 6, p. 182.
33. Harris, *Presidential Reconstruction*, 152; Ira Berlin, *Slaves Without Masters: The Free Negro in the Antebellum South* (New York: Pantheon Books, 1974), 382.

been more than one section—Allowing all freedmen, free negroes, and mulatoes, to give evidence in all courts of the State, subject to the rules of evidence in courts—I think they should have been allowed to rent, or lease lands, as they will not be able for years to come, to do much in the way of farming. I think the laws preventing any person from giving or selling spiritsous [*sic*] liquors, good laws if they could be enforced— If they are realy free, which we all concede, can they be deprived of their rights.[34]

Such reservations were rarely humanitarian. Natchez district planters were discovering that overly stringent legislation threatened their own economic recovery. Freedmen from the interior of Mississippi and Louisiana were relocating on the rich and fertile land along the river. They were unlikely to continue doing so if the terms of labor and their economic opportunities were the same everywhere. Already there were suggestions that blacks in poorer states to the east were abandoning thoughts of immigration because of the severity of the Mississippi and Louisiana codes.[35]

The prospect of reduced black immigration would not have disturbed the planters had there been a labor surplus. But by 1865, death, conscription, and flight to the towns had seriously depleted the number of former slaves available to work on the plantations. Before the war, over four hundred hands had lived on William Newton Mercer's four Adams County places; in the fall of 1865, fewer than three hundred remained. Even planters situated on the most productive land were deeply concerned. Zinas Preston wrote dejectedly to Stephen Duncan from Burn Place in Tensas Parish at the end of the year, "The labor is not in the county [*sic*] to fill up entirely *all the front* plantations on the River, & leave back of them (or in the places back) two hands where there was 10 before the war. It is fortunate for me that I am as near the River as I am & as near the vilage or I would despair of doing anything at all."[36]

The gentry could scarcely work up enthusiasm for legislation

34. Torrey to Humphreys, March 29, 1866, in Governors' Correspondence, Box 65. See also Vernon Lane Wharton, *The Negro in Mississippi, 1865–1890* (New York: Harper & Row, 1965), 90.

35. Clement Eaton, *The Waning of the Old South Civilization, 1860–1880's* (Athens: University of Georgia Press, 1968), 128; Litwack, *Been in the Storm So Long*, 437.

36. Mercer Papers, XXX, September 26, 1865; Z. Preston to Dr. S. Duncan, December 28, 1865, in Duncan Correspondence.

that would settle relations on the plantation only at the cost of creating an enduring labor shortage. Historians who attribute the failure of the Black Codes to pressure from the North must ask whether the statutes represented a viable solution to the long-range economic needs of the planting elite. It should tell us a great deal that landowners along the river generally applauded the enactment of the laws—then ignored them in practice when it served their interests to do so, raised few objections to their repeal, and into the 1880s resisted state efforts to introduce new regulatory measures.[37]

The dilemma posed by the Black Codes reflected the paradoxical situation of the planters in late 1865. They still believed that the character of the Negro demanded a particular kind of plantation order. And yet, for practical reasons, they had to bid for the services of former slaves determined to change that order. Region was not merely set against region; neighbor faced neighbor as potential competitors. "Gloster has not left my place as yet, nor been rebellious," wrote Clarissa Young to Charles D. Hamilton in June, 1865. "Therefore I think hard that you would employ him without first consulting me about him. I am sure I would not employ your servant man John without your approbation."[38]

Old bonds wavered under the strain. When Cicero Stampley approached Susan Sillers Darden in January, 1866, for permission to hire one of her former slaves, she turned him down. In deference to her wishes, and out of respect for their long-standing friendship, he promised not to pursue the matter further. Two days later, however, apparently thinking better of his pledge, he contracted secretly with the hand in question. The Dardens were not above retaliation in such instances. When another neighbor lured away a laborer the following year, Jesse Darden ventured into the culprit's quarters and endeavored to hire his cook. Even family ties weakened in the frantic bidding for freedmen. Amelia Montgomery of Belmont wrote bitterly to her husband in the summer of 1866, "Would you believe it, James [their son] sent for & hired Beverly when I expressly told him, I had a contract with his mother for

37. Wharton, *The Negro in Mississippi*, 95.
38. C. Young to C. D. Hamilton, June 12, 1865, in Hughes Papers, Folder 7.

him, & would not consent to give him up, & now he sets me at defiance, & because you are away I have to submit to it. I feel quite provoked."[39]

The competition among planters opened the way for the freedman to exercise considerable influence in the shaping of labor arrangements. Commenting on the situation at the end of 1865, Whitelaw Reid noted, "In November nothing could exceed the hatred which seemed everywhere felt to the freedmen. Now this feeling was curiously and almost ludicrously mingled with an effort to conciliate them. Cotton was no longer king, but the cotton-maker was. Men approached the negro with an effort at kind manners, described to him the comforts of their plantations, and insinuatingly inquired if he wouldn't like to enter into contract for a year."[40]

Both planters and Federal officials publicly derogated the demands of the freedman. His reasons for moving from one place to the next, they argued, were neither rational or consistent. "The negroes as a class have not yet learned the fact that their labor is their capital," complained General Philip H. Sheridan of the Louisiana Freedmen's Bureau in 1866, "and therefore are too ready to quit their work for the most trivial reasons."[41] But what stands out in retrospect is the extent to which the former slaves acted purposefully to effect changes in their condition. For all those who moved impetuously, there were many more who were deliberate and had clearly defined goals. Sheridan to the contrary, these individuals did treat their labor as their capital; they understood full well that it was the only real asset that they had.

All this is not to suggest that the freedmen were, as a group, well organized or even that they invariably sought changes favorable to their long-term interests. It is simply, but emphatically, to point out that they had ideas of their own about how to reform the plantation regime and that they moved around to achieve their objec-

39. Darden Diary, II, January 2, 3, 4, 1866. Ben Montgomery reported from Warren County that Louisiana planters were scouring Mississippi for laborers. Ben [Montgomery] to Jos. E. Davis, May 6, 1867, in Joseph E. Davis and Family Papers, Z 1028, Mississippi Department of Archives and History, Jackson. A. F. Montgomery to her husband, August 16, 1866, in Montgomery Papers.
40. Reid, *After the War*, 446. Compare Novak, *Wheel of Servitude*, 19.
41. *Senate Executive Documents*, 39th Cong., 2nd Sess., No. 6, p. 70.

tives. They learned to exchange information, negotiate with would-be employers, and evaluate the comparative advantages of each opportunity. The planter who would retain his laborers from one year to the next found that he had at least to match the benefits being offered by other landowners in the vicinity. Typical was the situation facing William Newton Mercer of Adams County at the end of 1866. "Our immediate neighbors are the cause of all this doubting," noted his manager bitterly. "Metcalfe I hear is making efforts to get a very large force, offering every inducement, with plenty of whiskey and every latitude & liberty to do as they please, so they work for him. And Hutchins tampers with our negroes and those who left us, particularly old Daniel at E., offering to furnish mules utensils and all plantation gears & tools for half the cotton made." The hands on John Williams' place in Jefferson County demanded that he give them, word for word, the same contract used by his neighbor, Jesse Darden. Rather than risk their departure, he agreed.[42]

Should his current employer prove unaccommodating, the former slave was quite prepared actively to seek employment with a planter known for his liberality. William Ker of Elba in Concordia Parish reported to his sister in early 1867, "When I came out last Monday, I found that some hands from the Alexander place wanted to come to me, and I have been busy all week moving them down and getting them settled." Those like Ker who treated their laborers well and were willing to accede to some of their demands enjoyed comparative success securing and holding on to laborers after 1865. Because the labor shortage persisted, however, those who acted otherwise experienced recurring difficulties. In any locality, there were likely to be certain former slaveholders who were far less troubled by labor turnover than were their neighbors. Susan Sillers Darden noted in January, 1866, that in her corner of Jefferson County all of Doctor Wade's hands had chosen to remain with him, while all of Captain Montgomery's had left as had all but two of Gabe Fowler's.[43]

42. Wilmer [Shields] to Doctor [William N. Mercer], December 1, 1866, in Mercer Papers; Darden Diary, II, January 13, 1869.
43. Wm. H. Ker to his sister, February 1, 1867, in Mary Susan Ker Papers, Southern Historical Collection, University of North Carolina, Chapel Hill; Darden Diary, II, January 8, 1866.

Still, competition pleased almost no one—which explains why, as early as the summer of 1865, most landowners began to involve themselves in efforts to organize locally. Throughout the district, groups of planters met to exchange ideas on the labor crisis and try to find some mutually acceptable way of standardizing hiring and provisioning practices. In late 1866, for example, landowners in Jefferson County passed a series of resolutions in favor of uniformity in labor agreements and appointed a body to recommend practicable and enforceable steps to that end. The immediate results of this particular action are unknown, but later a committee in the county circulated pamphlets that set down rules "for governing contracts, regulating labor, ensuring order, and affording protection to the property of all classes and colors." In Jefferson County as almost everywhere else, however, attempts at organization foundered on the unwillingness of some members of the community to sacrifice personal advantage to larger class interest. James Gillespie touched on the crucial issue in describing the collapse of a meeting in the Kingston area of Adams County: "Each one wished to be untrammelled & free to act as judgment might direct."[44]

For the moment, then, the marketplace was triumphant. What direction negotiations would take in the future, how the organization of the plantation would change and with what consequences, remained to be seen. But if it was not yet clear what the rights and responsibilities of planters and laborers would be under the new regime, it was at least apparent that the process for determining rights and responsibilities had itself been radically altered.

44. Wharton, *The Negro in Mississippi*, 94; Litwack, *Been in the Storm So Long*, 323; Jas. A. Gillespie to A. K. Farrar, April 26, 1876, in Gillespie Papers. See also Theodore Saloutos, "Southern Agriculture and the Problems of Readjustment, 1865–1877," *Agricultural History*, XXX (1956), 67; Robert Higgs, *Competition and Coercion: Blacks in the American Economy, 1865–1914* (New York: Cambridge University Press, 1977), 47–49, 129–31.

# CHAPTER THREE

# Considered Alternatives

I

The realization that the postbellum settlement would be significantly determined by marketplace competition came as an aftershock of Emancipation to most planters. Convinced that blacks were inherently subservient, they could hardly be expected to negotiate willingly with the former slave as an equal. Understandably, emigration emerged as one well-considered alternative.

It no doubt tells us something that those former slaveholders with investments outside the South were among the first to abandon the district after the war, generally going north or to Europe. "Many of our friends wish to leave this part of the country," observed Rebecca Minor from Natchez in October, 1865, "and those who can, and if their purses will admit, go to France." Members of the Tullis clan explored the possibilities of settling near Tours. Eustace Surget returned to his ancestral Bordeaux and took up residence in a four-hundred-year-old mansion.[1]

Among those who headed north was Robert Carter of Concordia Parish. He disposed of a portion of his extensive holdings in Louisiana and moved to Newport, Rhode Island. During the next fifteen years he lived there and in Philadelphia and traveled widely on the Continent. Several prominent Natchez district planters settled in New York, including two of the wealthiest and most influential members of the old elite, Stephen Duncan and Levin R. Marshall.[2]

1. R. A. Minor to her uncle, October 20, 1865, in Stephen Duncan Correspondence, Department of Archives and Manuscripts, Louisiana State University, Baton Rouge; [Joseph D. Shields] to Mary J. Conway, September 23, 1865, in Joseph D. Shields Papers, Department of Archives and Manuscripts, Louisiana State University, Baton Rouge; I. S. Boyd to Miss Mary [Ker], December 16, 1867, in Mary Susan Ker Papers, Southern Historical Collection, University of North Carolina, Chapel Hill.
2. Various mortgages, October 15, 1866, in Concordia Parish General Mortgages,

In general, however, there was antipathy toward the North and resentment of those who fled there. Most interest in emigration focused on Latin America. Through 1865, former Confederate officers toured the lower Mississippi Valley, expounding on the various bounties of Brazil, Mexico, and British Honduras. They received a respectful and at times enthusiastic hearing, especially from the gentry. "Gen Liddell is still here making up an emigrant company to move to Brazil," reported Frank Surget from Natchez in June, 1865. "He has some 75 or 80 names, amongst them I hear are some of the *Metcalf* [*sic*], Dave Williams, his mother and others. . . . When it was first started, those people thought . . . that they could take their slaves along with them."[3]

Wishful delusion, as in the above instance, may explain some of the early interest in Latin America. Still, slavery did exist in Brazil and for some of the gentry that was inducement enough. The Whitaker family of Warren County, to cite one example, moved to the vicinity of São Paulo and purchased some laborers. Eventually they took up farming near a colony of Englishmen.[4]

Although slavery per se was not legal in Mexico, Emperor Maximilian, eager to attract Americans, offered prospective settlers not only cheap land and generous tax advantages but a labor code that left room for familiar southern arrangements.[5] Regulations stated that blacks, though free,

---

Vol. O, pp. 81–97, Concordia Parish Courthouse, Vidalia; *Goodspeed's Biographical and Historical Memoirs of Mississippi, Embracing an Authentic and Comprehensive Account of the Chief Events in the History of the State and a Record of the Lives of Many of the Most Worthy and Illustrious Families and Individuals* (2 vols.; Chicago: Goodspeed Publishing Co., 1891), Vol. I, Pt. 1, pp. 625, 676; R. G. Dun & Co. Collection, Louisiana VII, 12, Baker Library, Harvard Graduate School of Business Administration, Boston.

3. See, for example, Wm. H. Ker to his sister, January 3, 1869, in Ker Papers. F. Surget to Dr. [Stephen Duncan], June 14, 1865, in Duncan Correspondence. See also James L. Roark, *Masters Without Slaves: Southern Planters in the Civil War and Reconstruction* (New York: Norton, 1977), 125–31. Regarding British Honduras, see J. P. Harrison to A. K. Farrar, November 13, 25, 1867, both in Alexander K. Farrar Papers, Department of Archives and Manuscripts, Louisiana State University, Baton Rouge; A. F. Montgomery to her husband, January 2, 1868, in Joseph A. Montgomery and Family Papers, Department of Archives and Manuscripts, Lousiana State University, Baton Rouge; "Southern Emigration—Brazil and British Honduras," *De Bow's Review*, After the War Series, IV (November, 1867), 541–45.

4. Vicksburgesque, I, 13, Old Court House, Vicksburg; interview with V. Blaine Russell, January 16, 1975, Vicksburg.

5. Henry W. Allen to Judge [John Perkins], October 22, 1865, in John Perkins Papers, Southern Historical Collection, University of North Carolina, Chapel Hill; Clement Eaton,

may make contracts with the employer who has engaged or may engage them, by which such employer shall bind himself to feed, clothe, and lodge them, and give them medical attendance and also pay them a sum of money according to whatever agreements they may enter into with him. . . . The laborer shall, on his part, obligate himself to his employer to perform the labor for which he is employed, for a term of not less than five nor more than ten years. The employer shall bind himself to support the children of his laborers. In the event of the father's death, the employer will be regarded as the guardian of the children and they will remain in his service until they become of age, on the same terms as those agreed to by their fathers.

John Perkins, Jr., the respected Madison Parish planter and politician, emigrated to Vera Cruz shortly after the war and subsequently became the imperial colonization agent at Córdoba. Later he purchased a part interest in a coffee hacienda in Venta Parada.[6]

Although those former slaveowners who settled in the North and those who went to Latin America were scarcely of like mind, they operated from the same premise. Black free labor was unworkable. Better to remove to a more congenial and more practicable society. One group chose a region where labor was free but not black, the other a region where labor was black but not free.

Clearly most planters shared the doubts of the emigrants regarding the freedman. But in the end few decided to leave the South. Only a total of four thousand to six thousand southerners settled in Brazil.[7] And no more than a handful of former slaveowners from the Natchez area, albeit some of the wealthiest, permanently relocated in the North or in Europe. As for Mexico, the prevailing sentiment was well expressed by Joseph D. Shields in a letter to his wife: "George wants to know my opinion of Mexico. It is this, here we are in Purgatory there we would be in a little hotter place. We are about ninety years old & have had but one civil war. They are about forty years & have had about twenty civil wars." John

*The Waning of the Old South Civilization, 1860–1880's* (Athens: University of Georgia Press, 1968), 116. Some southerners brought slaves to Mexico in the guise of servants. Roark, *Masters Without Slaves*, 125.

6. Office of Colonization, Mexico, *Decrees for the Encouragement of Immigration and Colonization* (Mexico, November, 1865), 10, in Perkins Papers; Sterling Price, Isham G. Harris, and John Perkins to M. F. Maury, November 24, 1865, Richard L. Maury to John Perkins, April 29, 20, 1866, agreement, October 26, 1866, all in Perkins Papers.

7. C. Eaton, *Waning of the Old South*, 116.

Perkins, Jr., is the only member of the district gentry known to have gone to Mexico, and he remained there but a short time.[8]

Indeed, the vast majority of planters not only rejected emigration, they declined to part with their real estate even though demand drove prices as high as $40 to $50 an acre for bottomland at the end of 1865. Significantly, many of those who left the region, and particularly those who went north or to Europe, held on to their local property. Perkins, for one, kept his Louisiana interests. And Eustace Surget, though he never returned from France, retained a plantation in Concordia Parish that he leased out from year to year.[9]

Given the widespread destruction of the countryside and the general suspicion of free black labor, it is logical to ask why so few former slaveowners elected to leave the district. Part of the reason has to do with the well-publicized difficulties of the earliest emigrants. Southerners who moved to Brazil found much of the available land unsuitable for cotton and at a distance from existing markets; meanwhile, Mexico was going through a period of political upheaval. Many of those who went to Latin America eventually came back, bitter and disappointed. In 1874, Edward King journeyed upriver from New Orleans with one such disillusioned gentleman. "There is ez good a country ez the sun shines on," remarked the returning planter as they approached the familiar bluffs at Natchez, "and if all them cussed fools as went to the Brazils was hyar now, they would say so too. Give me old Mississippi in mine."[10]

8. Jo. D. Shields to Mrs. Jo. D. Shields, April 23, 1866, in Shields Papers; Maury to Perkins, April 20, 1866, in Perkins Papers. No other planters from the district were registered in a list of ninety-four recent American emigrants to Mexico published in the *Mexican Times*, September 16, 1865. For a discussion of the largest colony of Americans in Mexico, see Carl Coke Rister, "Carlota: A Confederate Colony in Mexico," *Journal of Southern History*, XI (1945), 33–50.

9. Whitelaw Reid, *After the War: A Southern Tour* (Cincinnati: Moore, Wilstach & Baldwin, 1866), 480, 564–65; Roger W. Shugg, *Origins of Class Struggle in Louisiana: A Social History of White Farmers and Laborers During Slavery and After, 1840–1875* (Baton Rouge: Louisiana State University Press, 1972), 261; C. C. Eustis to Uncle William, December 4, 1865, in William J. Minor and Family Papers, Department of Archives and Manuscripts, Louisiana State University, Baton Rouge; memorandum of agreement, March 1, 1870, in Perkins Papers; lease, January 5, 1871, in Concordia Parish General Mortgages, Vol. P, p. 91.

10. Susan Sillers Darden Diary (MS in Darden Family Papers, Z 82, Mississippi Department of Archives and History, Jackson), II, October 5, 1867; "Southern Emigration—Brazil

Still, even had the earliest emigrants fared well in Latin America, it is doubtful that many of their countrymen would have followed. Constraints of duty and feeling, as well as economic considerations, militated against any large-scale exodus.

Men who might under other circumstances have been inclined to seek their fortunes elsewhere remained to attempt an honorable settlement of their debts. "At first I felt overwhelmed at the array of figures," remarked one beleaguered planter, "but then I thought it was worth the struggle," adding, "I am more than anxious to be punctual." "I am beginning to think," confessed another, "that I will never see the end of debts which are pouring in upon me and of the existence of which I had never had the least idea. God knows that I had almost rather be dead than to be compelled to bear a burden that galls me more than I can express, and if I were not *desperate*, as far as business is concerned, I would give up everything and leave the country."[11]

Then, too, it was difficult for men of compassion to leave a land they cared for deeply and their homes and friends. "While many . . . citizens are entertaining and discussing ideas of emigration," wrote Alexander K. Farrar of Adams County in the summer of 1865, "I am directing my thoughts to the possibility of things being reorganized upon living terms, such as will admit of my remaining here, so that my bones too, shall rest with those I have loved."[12]

There was sentiment involved here, but also a sense of responsibility, for neighbors and for region. Proud men, the planters did not regard their commitments lightly. "You were born upon the soil—raised here and . . . have a deeper interest in the soil than the Yankee and a common interest in the unfortunate people left here," wrote E. D. Farrar of Madison Parish to his friend John Perkins,

---

and British Honduras," 540; Rister, "Carlota," 48. Most newspapers were opposed to emigration and publicized information detrimental to the movement. William C. Harris, *Presidential Reconstruction in Mississippi* (Baton Rouge: Louisiana State University Press, 1967), 28. Edward King, *The Great South* (New York: Arno Press, 1969), 776.

11. Jo. D. Shields to Buckner & Newman, July 19, 1866, in Shields Papers; Wm. H. Ker to his sister, December 17, 1866, in Ker Papers. Those who left were severely maligned for not settling their debts. See, for example, E. D. Farrar to John Perkins, Jr., September 18, 1866, in Perkins Papers.

12. A. K. Farrar to William L. Sharkey, June 27, 1865, in Governors' Correspondence, Box 60, Mississippi Department of Archives and History, Jackson.

Jr., now in Mexico. "Return to your country and take your place among your own people." "The time is not distant," prophesied another Perkins acquaintance, "when the West and South, politically united, will control this government for many a year to come. We must wait quietly for that time, and endeavor by steady industry to build up our broken fortunes in the meanwhile."[13]

Nevertheless, pride and responsibility would presumably have counted for little, without accompanying prospects for economic recovery. Certainly many more planters would have emigrated had they thought it impossible to repair "broken fortunes" in the South. In fact, however, most of the gentry were at least guardedly hopeful in 1865; some were downright confident. No less a person than Jefferson Davis imagined that he could do quite well by a return to planting. "Should I regain my liberty before 'our people' have become vagrants," he told his wife, "there are many of them whose labor I could direct so as to make it not wholly unprofitable." Dempsey P. Jackson estimated that if he rebuilt and restocked his Tensas Parish plantation and worked it with wage laborers, he would turn a profit of no less than $36,000, and likely more than $42,000, in just one year.[14]

Obviously such optimism ran directly counter to the prevailing opinion of free black labor. Confidence did exist, but it derived from the product, not the producer. To all appearances King Cotton had reclaimed his throne. And it seemed that his bounty would more than compensate for any losses occasioned by the emancipation of the slaves. William J. Minor got to the heart of the issue in a letter to his old friend Stephen Duncan in August, 1865: "I think we could arrange matters so as to obtain at least one half as much labor as we did before the great secession blunder was made. The expenses in time will not be greater, & if we can get a proportionate increase of price, we may do, in a pecuniary sense, as well as ever."[15]

13. E. D. Farrar to Perkins, September 18, 1866, F. H. Farrar to Jno. Perkins, September 21, 1866, both in Perkins Papers.

14. Mrs. Jefferson Davis to Joseph E. Davis, September 5, 1865 (copy), in Mary Stamps Papers, Southern Historical Collection, University of North Carolina, Chapel Hill; "Calculations About Planting with Free Nigers [sic]" (MS in possession of Mr. and Mrs. Boyd Sojourner, Natchez).

15. W. J. Minor to Dr. S. Duncan, August 6, 1865, in Duncan Correspondence.

The critical "proportionate increase of price" was a glorious reality in 1865. Cotton was bringing three times what it had in the years immediately preceding the war. Through 1865, the staple did not fall below thirty cents a pound at New Orleans; generally it exceeded forty cents. In England, the failure of Indian cotton to meet prevailing quality standards increased demand for the American variety. Southern "middling uplands" averaged nearly twenty pence on the Liverpool market during 1865.[16]

The Natchez district was alive with commercial activity. An agent of a New Orleans factorage firm reported to the home office in early July, "There is very little cotton in this section (say Adams, Jefferson, Wilkinson & Adams [sic]) & nearly the whole of which is in the hands of speculators who are, & have been, offering fabulous prices. As high as 20 [cents] per lb in gold, delivered on the plantation has been paid in this vicinity for Cotton of an indifferent quality & in bad order. The country is full of buyers crazy to invest at these high rates."[17]

Planters who had not yet taken the amnesty oath hastened to do so now to regain control of their property. Past allegiances were quickly forgotten. "Shields, Boyd, Metcalfs [sic] & nearly all the other fireeaters have taken [the oath]," sniped the Unionist Frank Surget in June. "In fact as is always the case the most rabid come forward first." The story of Andrew Johnson's conciliatory policy toward the old elite is well known. As early as July, Surget informed Stephen Duncan that "almost all who app[l]y for pardon, receive it." Those landowners whose plantations had not been leased out by the government began to lay crops even before they had been granted amnesty. Jesse Darden, for instance, signed a contract with his hands on August 22, 1865; he did not even contemplate petitioning for a pardon until two days later.[18]

16. James E. Boyle, *Cotton and the New Orleans Cotton Exchange: A Century of Commercial Evolution* (New York: Country Life Press, 1934), 155; M. B. Hammond, *The Cotton Industry: An Essay in American Economic History* (New York: Johnson Reprint Corp., 1966), 121.

17. Campbell Marsh to James Garner, July 5, 1865, in Bower, Garner and Harrison Papers, Department of Archives and Manuscripts, Louisiana State University, Baton Rouge.

18. F. Surget to Dr. [Stephen Duncan], June 14, July 17, 1865, in Duncan Correspondence; *House Executive Documents*, 39th Cong., 1st Sess., No. 11, pp. 3–5; William S. McFeeley, *Yankee Stepfather: General O. O. Howard and the Freedmen* (New Haven: Yale University Press, 1968), 103–105; Claude F. Oubre, *Forty Acres and a Mule: The Freed-*

Of course, credit had to be obtained. But this was available on relatively easy terms from Yankee investors or, more often, from rejuvenated New Orleans commission houses, themselves backed by northern money.

Yet despite the high price of cotton, there remained at least one major obstacle to the full-scale resumption of planting. The gentry, as we have seen, had little faith in the reliability of the freedman. Some alternative to operating with black labor would have to be found. In the immediate postbellum period, two options seemed to present themselves. In the short term, it was proposed to lease out estates to wealthy northerners until conditions became more settled; in the long run, it was proposed to bring in immigrant workers, either whites, who presumably would respond dependably to marketplace incentives, or Orientals, who might, it was hoped, prove more amenable than the former slave to some variation of traditional plantation law.

II

The countryside must have taken on a curious appearance with the arrival of the various immigrant groups. The Conners of Adams County experimented with Irish laborers, while a neighbor, Dr. James Metcalfe, hired fifty Dutchmen to work on his York and Bourbon places. Others introduced Germans, Swiss, and Danes to the district.[19] It was the Chinese, however, who attracted the greatest attention and apparently fostered the highest hopes. Charles G. McGehee of Wilkinson County wrote to his brother Micajah in California in the summer of 1869 for information on the employment of Chinese laborers, "as with great probability . . . they will

men's Bureau and Black Land Ownership (Baton Rouge: Louisiana State University Press, 1978), 35–43; Darden Diary, II, August 22, 24, 1865.

19. Fanny E. Conner to her husband, August 21, 1865, in Lemuel Parker Conner and Family Papers, Department of Archives and Manuscripts, Louisiana State University, Baton Rouge; Wilmer [Shields] to Doctor [William N. Mercer], December 19, 1865, in William Newton Mercer Papers, Department of Archives and Manuscripts, Louisiana State University, Baton Rouge; J. Floyd King to [Lin Caperton], December 29, 1865, J. Floyd King to Mallery [King], January 18, 1866, both in Thomas Butler King Papers, Southern Historical Collection, University of North Carolina, Chapel Hill.

be introduced in large numbers ere long." At about the same time, *De Bow's Review* published a communication from the prominent Adams County landowner, Ayres P. Merrill, arguing the merits of the Oriental laborer over the European. Not only, Merrill contended, could the former be induced to work in gangs, but "having no attachment for other countries than his own, he is not likely to covet ownership of the soil, and being content with any government which protects him in the fruits of his labor, he is not likely to become a politician."[20]

As for the leasing of plantations to northerners, it began under the aegis of Federal authorities in 1863. Most of the estates rented during the occupation had been abandoned by their owners and were under the jurisdiction of the Treasury Department. However, a few Unionist planters—Levin R. Marshall and Stephen Duncan, for example—asked for and received permission to lease their lands privately. The profits they realized served as an example to others, and with the end of hostilities and the subsequent restoration of property to returning members of the gentry, leasing increased dramatically.[21]

Enterprising Yankees flocked to the district, anxious to try their hand at planting under the new conditions. They found the former slaveowners more than willing "to let others try the experiment." The northerners were attracted by the current high price of cotton, but unlike their Southern counterparts they had little doubt about the comparative efficiency of free black labor or about their own abilities to control it. "A northern man knows from actual experience what free labor is," explained Carl Schurz shortly after the war, "and understands its management, which the late slaveholder,

20. C. G. McGehee to Micajah McGehee, August 28, 1869 (copy), in James Stewart McGehee Papers, Vol. II, Pt. 2, p. 279, Department of Archives and Manuscripts, Louisiana State University, Baton Rouge; A. P. Merrill, "Southern Labor," *De Bow's Review*, After the War Series, VI (July, 1869), 586–92; Leon F. Litwack, *Been in the Storm So Long: The Aftermath of Slavery* (New York: Knopf, 1979), 352.

21. For a good general overview of leasing during the occupation, see Bell Irvin Wiley, *Southern Negroes, 1861–1865* (New Haven: Yale University Press, 1965), Chaps. 12 and 13. Lawrence N. Powell, *New Masters: Northern Planters During the Civil War and Reconstruction* (New Haven: Yale University Press, 1980), is the definitive study of the men who came to the South. See also Louis S. Gerteis, *From Contraband to Freedman: Federal Policy Toward Southern Blacks, 1861–1865* (Westport, Conn.: Greenwood Press, 1973).

still clinging to the traditions of the old system, does not." "It is supposed," wrote an Illinois relative to Alexander K. Farrar, "that a Northern man will get more work out of Negroes in the present disturbed state of affairs, which is without doubt true."[22]

Naturally, some of the Yankees who came to the district did so with the intention of purchasing land of their own. Although, for reasons already discussed, only a limited number of estates were up for sale, it was not uncommon for a former slaveowner to offer a part interest in his plantation to a wealthy outsider. W. D. Anderson of Tensas Parish took on an associate, as did at least one of his neighbors. Such partnerships took a wide variety of forms, with in some cases the northerner, in some the southerner taking responsibility for management.[23]

Still, the majority of former slaveholders and Yankees regarded renting as the most desirable arrangement. Few northerners wished to remain in the region permanently; most assumed that the profits from one, or at the most two, crops would allow them to return home wealthy men. A lessee on Lake Providence told Whitelaw Reid that he anticipated making $65,000 in one year, working a single 1,500-acre plantation. His expectations were not out of line with those of his fellow countrymen.[24]

By 1866, most of the great cotton estates bordering the Mississippi, and not a few of those inland, were in the hands of lessees. J. T. Trowbridge, traveling through the district, found "men from the Middle States and the great West . . . everywhere." Of sixteen large plantations on Lake Concordia, only six were cultivated by their owners. Here and there a planter agreed to let his property out in small plots to aspiring white farmers, but the general preference was for a financially secure individual or a firm of known standing. Alfred Vidal Davis leased his Pittsfield estate to Gen-

22. A. F. Montgomery to her husband, September 5, 1865, in Montgomery Papers; *Senate Executive Documents*, 39th Cong., 1st Sess., No. 2, p. 28; Ben Swayze to A. K. Farar [*sic*], October 9, 1865, in Farrar Papers. See also James Wilford Garner, *Reconstruction in Mississippi* (New York: Macmillan, 1901), 136; Powell, *New Masters*, 125.

23. See "Southern Estates in the Market," *De Bow's Review*, After the War Series, II (December, 1866), 667–68, for a list of local plantations advertised for sale. R. G. Dun & Co. Collection, Louisiana XXII, 9, 15, 16.

24. Reid, *After the War*, 415; J. T. Trowbridge, *The South: A Tour of Its Battlefields and Ruined Cities* (New York: Arno Press, 1969), 380.

eral Lorenzo Thomas. Levin R. Marshall rented Cabin Teele to Frank P. Blair, Jr., another Union officer with connections in the government.[25]

Agreements differed from place to place. Some former slave-holders rented for shares. Columbia E. Dobyns of Jefferson County, for example, leased Buena Vista to Nelson Newman for half the crop. Antonio Yznaga del Valle rented Ravenswood and Consuelo, his two Louisiana plantations, to James D. Waters and George G. Klapp on similar terms. Most transactions were for cash, however, with half the rent coming in the form of a down payment and the remainder at the end of the year.[26]

Competition among would-be lessees pushed the price of rentals up "enormously" through 1865. The very best land around Natchez was going for as much as thirty dollars an acre at the end of the year. Along the river as far north as Lake Providence, rates ranged from eight to twenty-two dollars an acre. Whitelaw Reid noted that "fifteen thousand dollars seemed a common rent for a thousand acres of good land, with the use of agricultural implements, gin, and saw and grist-mills."[27]

It would have been quite remarkable had the crop of 1866 actually reached the elevated expectations of the lessees. Yet, in all fairness, no one could have rightly foreseen the terrible problems that lay ahead. High water poured over and through the makeshift Louisiana levee system, flooding numerous estates. In late summer, armyworms descended on the emerging cotton. "In a few days the fields were blackened like fire had swept over them," remembered one horrified witness. Labor difficulties only aggravated the cruelties of nature; implementation of the new system had proven much

25. Trowbridge, *The South*, 380; Reid, *After the War*, 579; "Concordia Parish, La." (Typescript in W.P.A. Source Material, Louisiana State Library, Baton Rouge), 28; John Taylor Moore to Wm. L. Sharkey, July 25, 1865, in Governors' Correspondence, Box 61; Powell, *New Masters*, 123.

26. Lease, October 31, 1865, in Jefferson County Deed Records, Vol. L, p. 169, Mississippi Department of Archives and History, Jackson; articles of copartnership, November 18, 1865, in Concordia Parish Conveyance Records, Vol. O, p. 5, Concordia Parish Courthouse, Vidalia; Powell, *New Masters*, 113.

27. Reid, *After the War*, 414, 451, 454, 480; Richard W. Griffin, "Problems of the Southern Cotton Planters After the Civil War," *Georgia Historical Quarterly*, XXXIX (1955), 107.

more difficult than the Yankees had imagined. As for those planters who had the good fortune to produce a few bales, they faced
heavy state and Federal taxes on cotton.[28]

The end of the harvest brought a grim final reckoning. "Most
persons that attempted to plant last year were ruined," reported
Joseph E. Davis to his brother Jefferson in March, 1867, "usually
northern men." J. Floyd King, who managed plantations in Louisiana for the New York concern of Hoyt, Sprague & Co., confided
to a friend, "As all the Lessees, they have lost heavily. The freedmen and unprecedented bad seasons have cost that class of enter-
prisers many 'hundreds of thousands' in the Valley." Many of the
Yankees whose leases expired at the end of 1866 elected to return
to the North. Their conspicuous failure precluded a major influx
of newcomers.[29]

And yet the picture was not entirely bleak. Cotton prices remained inordinately high. Through 1866, the staple stayed above
thirty cents a pound at New Orleans. Under the circumstances, a
significant element of lessees was ready, indeed determined, to believe that the problems of the previous year had been extraordinary and that another crop would more than make up for initial
losses. Many plantations were again rented in 1867, and observers
noted "feverish excitement" at the onset of the planting season.[30]

Understandably, rents were substantially below what they had
been in 1866. But they were still sufficient to provide the former

28. John Q. Anderson (ed.), *Brokenburn: The Journal of Kate Stone, 1861–1868*
(Baton Rouge: Louisiana State University Press, 1972), 369; Jo. D. Shields to J. R. Jones,
August 21, 1866, in Shields Papers. The Federal cotton tax enacted in 1862 reached as high
as five cents a pound in 1865; in the summer of 1866 it stood at three cents. Congress did
not repeal the tax until 1868. Milton M. McPherson, "The Federal Cotton Tax in the
South, 1862–8" (M.A. thesis, University of Alabama, 1959). In November, 1865, the legis-
lature of Mississippi enacted a special tax of two dollars per bale on cotton. "Report of
Special State Tax Collected in Adams Co., Dec. 29, 1865" (MS in Records of the Auditor of
Public Accounts, Folder: Reports of Special Taxes, January 8, 1865–December 29, 1865,
Mississippi Department of Archives and History, Jackson).

29. Joseph E. Davis to Jefferson Davis, March [?], 1867, in Hudson Strode (ed.), *Jeffer-
son Davis: Private Letters, 1823–1889* (New York: Harcourt, Brace & World, 1966), 263;
J. Floyd King to Lin [Caperton], December 23, November 7, 1866, both in King Papers;
Alvan C. Gillem to [J. S.] Fowler, March 23, 1867, in Joseph S. Fowler Papers, Southern
Historical Collection, University of North Carolina, Chapel Hill.

30. Boyle, *Cotton and the New Orleans Cotton Exchange*, 180; U.S. Department of Agriculture, *Report of the Commissioner of Agriculture, 1867* (Washington, D.C.: Government Printing Office, 1868), 416.

slaveowner with at least an adequate income. Robert Carter, for instance, leased Vidalia, his plantation in Concordia Parish, to Benjamin Teel for $7,000; the previous year he had rented it to the same man for $12,500. Eliza Sanderson let out Overton, fifteen miles southeast of Natchez, for $1,500. Thomas R. Shields received $1,000 for Hermitage, his estate straddling the boundary line between Adams and Jefferson counties.[31]

Unfortunately for planter and lessee alike, most of the problems recurred the following year, with a few new ones unkindly thrown into the bargain. An early spell of dry weather hindered cultivation, and then, during picking season, the armyworms returned. Flooding remained a concern in Louisiana. General Alvan C. Gillem, head of the Freedmen's Bureau in Mississippi, reported that cotton production did not exceed "half of what was regarded as an average crop." At the end of the year the Natchez *Democrat* observed,

> The efforts of the South to cultivate cotton with profit to the planters, since the war, have proven to be utter failures. Last year, a planter was facetiously pitied in proportion to the number of acres of cotton he had under cultivation, for upon that depended how much he would be in debt at the end of the year. Made desperate by the disasters of that year . . . the planters redoubled their efforts in the vain hope that a good crop this year would partially retrieve their losses and place them again on the high road to prosperity. They were doomed to still greater disappointment.[32]

This time, demand for the staple offered no saving grace. By December, 1867, cotton was under fifteen cents a pound at New Orleans, less than half what it had been a year earlier.[33] In seasons of

31. Leases, December 12, 1865, December 29, 1866, in Concordia Parish General Mortgages, Vol. O, pp. 73, 153; leases, November 14, December 1, 1866, in Adams County Deed Records, Vol. OO, pp. 287, 493, Adams County Courthouse, Natchez.

32. Anderson (ed.), *Brokenburn*, 372; "Department of Commerce," *De Bow's Review*, After the War Series, IV (July, August, 1867), 105–106; Alvan C. Gillem to Major General E. C. C. Ord, December 10, 1867 (typescript), in W.P.A. Records, RG 60, for Warren County, Folder: Reconstruction, Mississippi Department of Archives and History, Jackson; Natchez *Democrat*, October 3, 1867, quoted in Ross H. Moore, "Social and Economic Conditions in Mississippi During Reconstruction" (Ph.D. dissertation, Duke University, 1937), 74.

33. Boyle, *Cotton and the New Orleans Cotton Exchange*, 180; U.S. Department of Agriculture, *Report of the Commissioner of Agriculture, 1867*, 416; Gillem to Ord, December 10, 1867, (typescript), in W.P.A. Records for Warren County, Folder: Reconstruction.

normal production this price would have been more than sufficient to ensure the landowner a considerable profit. Now it was hopelessly inadequate. Planting had become a nightmare.

III

Members of the old elite suffered terribly. "Nobody has any [money] to spare to lend," complained Amelia Montgomery of Claiborne County in March, 1868. "Nobody will try to pay debts now if they can possibly avoid." Her sons put off trips to town lest they be dunned for outstanding bills. One distraught former slaveowner wrote to the governor of Mississippi for aid in securing the position of consul to the seaport towns of Cuba: "My object is to visit the Island as soon as I can for the purpose of finding out what my experience as a Planter may be worth to me, as that is my capital & worth nothing here."[34]

Creditors hastened to call in outstanding old notes; and many slaveholders who had taken out loans in the 1850s now paid a heavy price for their lack of clairvoyance. Prior to the war, John Kingsbury Elgee had borrowed over $600,000 from David D. Withers, a New York financier. As security for the loan he had given Withers a mortgage on his three Wilkinson County plantations, several tracts of land in Adams County, and 515 slaves. In April, 1867, almost $300,000 remained due, and Withers, despairing now of ever receiving payment, foreclosed on Elgee's heirs. Sale of the property netted a mere $10,250.[35]

Some prominent names disappeared from the ranks of the elite in these difficult times. William Cannon had been adjudged "one of our stanchest & most acute bus[iness] men" before the war by

34. A. F. Montgomery to her husband, March 5, 16, 1868, both in Montgomery Papers; Cortez Chambliss to B. G. Humphreys, March 12, 1867, in Governors' Correspondence, Box 68.

35. *David D. Withers* v. *Heirs of John Kingsbury Elgee*, final decree, November 21, 1867, in Adams County Chancery Court Minute Book, Vol. 1856–70, p. 312, Adams County Courthouse, Natchez. For other instances of former slaveholders closed out during these years, see deed, June 3, 1867, in Claiborne County Deed Records, Vol. GG, p. 5, Mississippi Department of Archives and History, Jackson; *Henry D. Patterson* v. *A. E. Wall, W. D. Wall et al.*, in Wilkinson County Chancery Court Final Records and Index, I, 477, Mississippi Department of Archives and History, Jackson.

the local representative of the R. G. Dun Mercantile Agency. Although "wrecked by war," he still owned $30,000 in real estate at
the beginning of 1866 and was widely regarded as "honorable."
Two years later he was dead, his estate insolvent. The unfortunate
story of John N. Helm is told in the Tensas Parish credit ledgers of
the Dun Agency:

| | |
|---|---|
| May, 1860 | excellent char and bus habits, good . . . plantation & 75 or 85 Negroes . . . other property in Adams Co. Miss., prompt, not speculative, perfectly safe |
| July, 1866 | Owns fine large plantation about 7 miles from Water-proof, making crop on place this season, in debt, but solvent, excellent general and fair bus habits |
| April, 1867 | Involved |
| March, 1868 | Heavily involved, still planting |
| July, 1868 | Has left the Point, not very solvent[36] |

And yet, these examples are not really representative. As bad as
things were, they might well have been worse for the majority of
former slaveowners. Some—principally those who had borrowed
heavily to resume planting in 1866 and 1867—did indeed lose
their land: John S. Minor, Lemuel P. Conner, Zebulon York, and
E. J. Hoover are cases in point. But most did not. Creditors found,
as did David D. Withers, that there was little to be gained from
forced sales. Poor crops had discouraged potential buyers, driving
down real estate values. One planter reported in January, 1867,
"Lands are now far less valuable, generally sold at two thirds less
than formerly; and still depreciating."[37] After a time, the spate of
foreclosures abated.

Still, it was not only a shortage of prospective purchasers that
allowed the gentry to hold on to their estates. By leasing, many
former slaveowners had escaped the worst effects of two crop fail-

36. R. G. Dun & Co. Collection, Mississippi II, 51, Louisiana XXII, 11; mortgage,
April 29, 1867, in Jefferson County Deed Records, Vol. L, p. 507. Evidently the Dun agent
seriously underestimated Helm's holdings before the war. The manuscript census shows
him with 189 slaves on his Tensas Parish place in 1860.
37. See various mortgages, in Concordia Parish General Mortgages, Vol. O, pp. 14, 21,
25, 28, 58, 62, 75, 130. J. Floyd King to Lin [Caperton], November 7, 1866, in King Papers. See also Shugg, *Origins of Class Struggle*, 192, 261. The depreciation of land values
was even greater if measured in terms of greenbacks. Harris, *Presidential Reconstruction*,
165.

ures. Those who had insisted on cash and some kind of down payment—and most had—had something to show for their foresight; those who had taken shares or were never paid by defaulting Yankees had at least saved themselves the expense of running their plantations. All told, the result was much as Jefferson Davis had predicted it would be, though perhaps not arrived at in quite the way he had imagined: "The land will not pass to any great extent from its former proprietors. They will lease it for a few years to men with capital, and then resume working it themselves, or sell portions of it with the same object, not materially decreasing their own possessions."[38]

By the time 1868 arrived, few Yankee lessees were left in the district. Of necessity, almost all former slaveowners were operating their own plantations or renting to freedmen. In light of the experiences of the previous two seasons, there was widespread pessimism. And then—as if Providence had summoned the armyworms solely to drive the outlanders from the region—things took a turn for the better. Cotton prices rose again and, more important, yields increased dramatically. By October, Will D. Gale was able to write from Satartia in the Delta, "The condition of the country is vastly improved since last winter." The firm of Fleming & Baldwin reportedly made $70,000 in 1868 running a single plantation below Natchez.[39] If not everyone did quite so spectacularly, at least now there was room for hope. For the planters, the nightmare was over.

IV

Meanwhile, the immigration movement was falling far short of expectations. By 1870, the gentry would largely abandon attempts at switching to white or Chinese labor. The reasons were diverse. For one thing, it was proving much more difficult to attract Europeans

38. Quoted in Powell, New Masters, 43–44.
39. Boyle, Cotton and the New Orleans Cotton Exchange, 180; James L. Watkins, King Cotton: A Historical and Statistical Review, 1790–1908 (New York: Negro Universities Press, 1969), 176–78, 200–202; Griffin, "Problems of the Southern Cotton Planters," 111; Will [D. Gale] to his wife, October 19, 1868, in Leonidas Polk Papers, Southern Historical Collection, University of North Carolina, Chapel Hill; Darden Diary, II, November 27, 1868.

than had been imagined. Edward King observed a decade after the war that would-be immigrants were insulted by "the wages offered them by the old school of planters—namely, a trivial sum yearly, and the rations of meal, pork, and molasses, with which the negro is easily contented." Those who did come to the Natchez district were quick to abandon the plantations for superior opportunities in the towns. J. Floyd King wrote from Tanglewood, in Concordia Parish, in March, 1866, "Daily I grow less hopeful of the Emigrants [*sic*]—the country is so destitute of 'help,' and the demand in the cities, and thro' out the plantations, so high for any 'white being' to replace the blacks employed, that imported laborers, having no law to retain them, leave and seek work in more agreeable situations than they occupy as field hands." Even many of the Chinese deserted the plantations, although their objective was usually self-employment as fishermen and truck farmers.[40]

Too, the financial demands of the immigrants distressed the gentry. Amelia Montgomery complained in 1866 that white hands were too expensive; she would have to keep her old servants. George W. Montgomery of Montrose in Madison Parish hired a Chinese cook for fifteen dollars a month in early 1875 but soon replaced her with a black cook who was willing to work for five dollars a month less.[41]

Furthermore, many planters had rather naïvely supposed that the foreigners would be of loyal, obedient, sturdy peasant stock. Instead, a significant number came from poor, urban environments and were entirely unprepared for the considerable demands of plantation life. James S. McGehee recalled that a band of white laborers, newly arrived on his father's estate, quickly succumbed to the tortures of a Louisiana summer: "They would begin the day with a breakfast of bread and coffee. Between ten and eleven o'clock

40. Hammond, *The Cotton Industry*, 123; Oscar Zeichner, "The Transition from Slave to Free Agricultural Labor in the Southern States," *Agricultural History*, XIII (1939), 25–26; Rowland T. Berthoff, "Southern Attitudes Towards Immigration, 1865–1914," *Journal of Southern History*, XVII (1951), 328–60; King, *The Great South*, 792; J. Floyd King to Lin [Caperton], March 4, 1866, in King Papers; Shugg, *Origins of Class Struggle*, 254–55. Planters complained, additionally, that many whites were only interested in securing land of their own. Reid, *After the War*, 563.

41. A. F. Montgomery to her husband, November 22, 1866, in Montgomery Papers; George W. Montgomery Account Books (MSS in Department of Archives and Manuscripts, Louisiana State University, Baton Rouge), VI, 101.

they would eat a substantial meal of beans and pork. This they would repeat between two and three and wind up at eventide with another heated meal. . . . Summer was not fairly begun before they were depleted with fever and digestive troubles."[42]

However, probably the main argument against immigrant labor, and no doubt for the former slaveowner the most surprising, was the accumulating evidence that the freedmen were generally performing better than their highly sought replacements. J. Floyd King of Concordia Parish wrote with some irony to his brother Mallery at the beginning of 1866, "We have here Dutch, German, Dain and Swiss Emigrants. Many of the two first have deserted; the latter seem more quiet and more honest—but they all eat at least one third to one half more than the negro, and do not accomplish more than two thirds as much work. When, however, there are two or three at work among the negroes, which they do not at all object to here, they work once as well again."[43]

With increasing frequency and invariably with expressions of amazement, the planters began to bear witness to the viability of free black labor. In March, 1867, J. H. Bowman reported in *De Bow's Review* that freedmen in his area of the district, near Vicksburg, had worked better in 1866 than anticipated. Several months later, a correspondent for the Louisville *Journal* traveled through the lower Mississippi Valley and observed that the former slaves were working well, "much better than last year."[44] Will D. Gale wrote to his wife in March, 1867, from the Delta north of Vicksburg, "We are exceedingly fortunate in having such good negroes. I have never at any time seen negroes more respectful, obedient, and industrious. And the amount of work accomplished has been more than even I anticipated." Five years later, Samuel Postlethwaite of Westmoreland happily informed an uncle, "The planta-

42. John Richard Dennett, *The South as It Is: 1865–1866*, ed. Henry M. Christman (New York: Viking Press, 1965), 366; J. S. McGehee Papers, III, 26.

43. J. Floyd King to Mallery [King], January 18, 1866, in King Papers.

44. "Department of Agriculture," *De Bow's Review*, After the War Series, III (March, 1867), 306; "Department of Commerce," 106. Vernon Lane Wharton (*The Negro in Mississippi, 1865–1890* [New York: Harper & Row, 1965], 120) contends that the gentry reconciled themselves to the new order after 1867. Ross H. Moore ("Social and Economic Conditions," 67) puts the date at about 1870.

tion is going on now very smoothly & negroes are working better & giving less trouble than for years past. You probably won't believe me when I tell you that I have had to issue stringent orders, to prevent their taking the mules to the field to plow before daylight."[45]

Travelers to the district in the 1870s were struck by how changed the atmosphere was from the first months after the war. The former slaveowner seemed at ease with the new order now, and reconciled to the future. Charles Nordhoff, who visited the region at mid-decade, commented, "Everywhere planters have been ready to demonstrate to me the profitableness of free labor, and to acknowledge that all their fears of disorganization had proved groundless."[46]

It would be easy to exaggerate the rapidity and completeness of the gentry's accommodation to free black labor. Complaints may have dwindled after the crop failures of 1866 and 1867, but there were always landowners anxious to blame their troubles on the former slave. What was unmistakably new was the ideological capitulation of the planter to the notion that it was possible, even practicable, to deal with the freedman in the marketplace. Emancipation may have altered the nature of relations on the plantation; the labor force itself would remain predominantly black.

45. Will [D. Gale] to his wife, March 30, 1867, in Polk Papers; Sam Postlethwaite to Uncle [James] Gillespie, March 4, 1872, in James A. Gillespie and Family Papers, Department of Archives and Manuscripts, Louisiana State University, Baton Rouge.

46. Charles Nordhoff, *The Cotton States in the Spring and Summer of 1875* (New York: D. Appleton, 1876), 56. See also Roger L. Ransom and Richard Sutch, *One Kind of Freedom: The Economic Consequences of Emancipation* (New York: Cambridge University Press, 1977), 21–22.

PART III

# Emergence of the New South Plantation

# CHAPTER FOUR

# Survival of the Old Elite

I

The crop of 1868 resurrected hopes of a full return to prosperity. And in the years ahead, there were those among the old elite who succeeded in recovering their former affluence. The journalist Edward King reported finding "many wealthy families in Natchez" in 1874, "independent of the war and its abasements." Hampton Elliott, when he died in 1872, left a plantation on Pine Ridge and a personal estate worth roughly $70,000. A year earlier, the local representative of the Dun Agency remarked of Alfred Vidal Davis, "He passes most of his time in New Orleans. He owns in his own right at least one dozen valuable plantations & personal property in proportion most of which is in Concordia Parish, La. He owes oo$ at this time for which he could not give his check. . . . If Mr. Davis is not worth 500m$ he is not wor[th] one cent." J. M. Gillespie was reported to be the "wealthiest man in North Louisiana" in 1878, "wo[rth] 200m$, has no debts & good for all he buys."[1]

Indeed, some former slaveowners were able to extend their landholdings significantly during Reconstruction. P. H. McGraw of Natchez owned $60,000 in real estate on the eve of the war; by 1873, he had more than tripled his holdings. A. D. Rawlings held one plantation in the district in 1860. At his death in 1887, he had seven, not to mention an estate in Catahoula Parish, five town lots in and around Natchez, and various stock in local commercial and industrial enterprises.[2]

---

1. Edward King, *The Great South* (New York: Arno Press, 1969), 293; estate of Hampton Elliott, in Adams County Chancery Court Records, Box 91, Adams County Courthouse, Natchez; R. G. Dun & Co. Collection, Mississippi II, 76, Louisiana XXII, 47, Baker Library, Harvard Graduate School of Business Administration, Boston.

2. R. G. Dun & Co. Collection, Mississippi II, 4; valuation of property, September 19, 1887, receipt, December 2, 1882, memorandum, May 17, 1879, receipt, April 10, 1889, all

The fact is, however, few former slaveowners were in a position to contemplate expansion in the years prior to 1880. On the contrary, most faced serious and enduring financial problems. Although cotton prices remained, by antebellum standards at least, normal or above normal, yields were down—the freedmen, notwithstanding their willingness to work hard, were disinclined to put in as long hours as in the past. With the credit structure of the region still in something of disarray as a result of the war, and with additional pressures created by Reconstruction, many former slaveowners found it a struggle merely to maintain solvency.[3]

Especially during the depression from 1873 to 1879, planting was precarious. "You will probably expect me to say something of what we are doing or more properly what we intend doing this year," wrote H. K. Hutton of Oakland to a friend in early 1876, "but as this is not a very agreeable subject the less said the better— Everything looks so very discouraging & the prospects ahead are so very gloomy that perhaps the less one does the better." Another planter observed from Concordia Parish two years earlier, "We are so depressed about the hard times, and we find it a very serious matter to live even in a plain way."[4]

Not all such testimony can be taken at face value. James A. Gillespie complained throughout Reconstruction of personal misfortune; but in his will he left two plantations, several tracts of land in Arkansas, and something over $200,000. Nevertheless, most planters did indeed have serious financial problems of one sort or another. Charles Nordhoff remarked in 1875, "There is no

---

in T. Otis Baker Papers, Z 72, Box 3, Folder 30, Mississippi Department of Archives and History, Jackson.

3. M. B. Hammond, *The Cotton Industry: An Essay in American Economic History* (New York: Johnson Reprint Corp., 1966), 327–28, App. 1; James E. Boyle, *Cotton and the New Orleans Cotton Exchange: A Century of Commercial Evolution* (New York: Country Life Press, 1934), 155; Roger L. Ransom and Richard Sutch, *One Kind of Freedom: The Economic Consequences of Emancipation* (New York: Cambridge University Press, 1977), Chap. 3. For a recent discussion of the cotton economy after the war, see Gavin Wright, *The Political Economy of the Cotton South: Households, Markets, and Wealth in the Nineteenth Century* (New York: Norton, 1978), Chap. 6.

4. [H. K. Hutton] to Albert [N. Cummings], February 21, 1876, in Cummings-Black Family Papers, Tulane University Library, New Orleans; Vic to his sister Sala, March 24, 1874, in Douglas Papers, Southern Historical Collection, University of North Carolina, Chapel Hill.

doubt that there has been much suffering in the South since the war among a class of people who formerly scarcely knew what even prudent economy meant." One district planter recounted, at about the same time, "Nine years ago we came from N.O. having been there to purchase supplies for Home and Bayou macon, expecting to realize profitable returns for the investment, but the wheel of our fortunes, had somehow got to turning the wrong way & has been doing so ever since. We were then tolerably well supplied with money & could afford to be comfortable. But now the money is in a great measure gone, & our wants more numerous."[5]

Debt was at the heart of the problem in most cases. Formerly a convenience of business, it now became a necessity of life. "As a general rule, the cotton-planters are more in debt now than during the first year after the war," read the *Report of the Commissioner of Agriculture for the Year 1874.* "Their condition is outwardly improved, but inwardly debt is silently gnawing at their vitals." Meanwhile, credit had become increasingly difficult to obtain. The Jefferson County representative of the R. G. Dun Mercantile Agency observed of one partnership in 1874, "I could not rec them to unlim cr. In fact I would advise great caution in dealing with any Planters in this country as labor is scarce & nearly every one plants all cotton & during the past yr but very few made their expenses."[6]

Understandably, the terms of credit had changed from those before the war, to the extreme disadvantage of the borrower. "I am sorry to hear my dear Uncle that you are so hard up," wrote Samuel Postlethwaite to James A. Gillespie in April, 1871. "If I find any one with more money than they want I will send them to you but with a sorrowful heart, as I dont like to see you mortgage yr property, that I suppose never k[n]ew a mortgage before." This last was a reasonable assumption. Only rarely had plantations

5. Will of James A. Gillespie, October 1, 1873, in James A. Gillespie and Family Papers, Department of Archives and Manuscripts, Louisiana State University, Baton Rouge; Charles Nordhoff, *The Cotton States in the Spring and Summer of 1875* (New York: D. Appleton, 1876), 24; Jones-Smith Plantation Journal (Z 890) (MS in Mississippi Department of Archives and History, Jackson), February 28, 1875.

6. C. W. Howard, "Condition of Agriculture in the Cotton States," in U.S. Department of Agriculture, *Report of the Commissioner of Agriculture for the Year 1874* (Washington, D.C.: Government Printing Office, 1875), 226, 236; R. G. Dun & Co. Collection, Mississippi XI, 334.

been mortgaged to secure loans before the war.[7] Now such transactions were increasingly common, even for relatively small advances. Washington Ford secured a loan of $7,800 in 1885 with a
deed of trust on his 2,894-acre Adams County plantation.[8] In
April, 1873, James C. Brandon of the same county mortgaged his
section of the Hoggatt estate to A. D. Rawlings, a fellow planter,
to secure a note for only $1,284. If the complaints of landowners
can be believed, the value of property mortgaged was generally
three to four times the amount of the loan, and never less than
double that amount.[9]

Whether or not the new system of credit was just, it unquestionably put a severe strain on the resources of the old elite. An
observation made in 1877 about W. T. Magruder by the Claiborne
County representative of the Dun Agency might well have been applied to other former slaveowners in the district: "Considbly involved, his ppty is all covered up for more than its value. Continues
to run his plantn & is dg the best he can, nothing can be made out of
him his crop being covered for advances and supplies."[10]

Debt was not the only serious financial problem facing the gentry
during Reconstruction. Taxes had risen dramatically, with landowners bearing the brunt of the burden. In Mississippi the state
levy in 1869 was three times higher than that of 1861. And rates
continued to climb into the 1870s (see Table 5). Even after Redemption, state taxes remained well above antebellum levels.[11]

7. Sam P[ostlethwaite] to Uncle [James A.] G[illespie], April 28, 1871, in Gillespie Papers; Hammond, *The Cotton Industry*, 111. See John S. Lobdell to J. Alex Ventress, May
29, 1857, in Trask-Ventress Family Papers, Z 607, Folder 259, Mississippi Department of
Archives and History, Jackson, for references to instances in which antebellum mortgages
were demanded.
8. Deed of trust, May 16, 1885, in Baker Papers, Box 2, Folder 21. A deed of trust is
identical to a mortgage, with the exception that the property in question is deeded to a third
party for a nominal sum rather than to the lender. Should the debt not be paid, the third
party is empowered to sell the property at public auction and give proceeds from the sale to
the lender.
9. Deed of trust, April 29, 1873, in Baker Papers, Box 3, Folder 30; address by Put
Darden (MS in possession of Mrs. Waldo Lambdin, Natchez); Jefferson College Papers,
Z 59, VI, 196, Mississippi Department of Archives and History, Jackson.
10. R. G. Dun & Co. Collection, Mississippi VI, 161.
11. Nordhoff, *The Cotton States*, 57; James Wilford Garner, *Reconstruction in Mississippi* (New York: Macmillan, 1901), 323. During Redemption there was, however, a significant cut in taxation, particularly on real estate. Robert L. Brandfon, *Cotton Kingdom of*

Table 5.   STATE TAXES, MISSISSIPPI

| Year | Rate (in mills) |
| --- | --- |
| 1869 | 1 |
| 1870 | 5 |
| 1871 | 4 |
| 1872 | 8.5 |
| 1873 | 12.5 |
| 1874 | 14 |
| 1875 | 9.25 |
| 1876 | 6.5 |
| 1877 | 5 |
| 1878 | 3.5 |

SOURCE: Garner, *Reconstruction in Mississippi*, 323.

County levies too were high, generally exceeding the state assessment (see Table 6). In Jefferson County in 1870, for example, landowners paid a poor tax set at 35 percent of the state levy, a "special" tax for the same amount, two separate bridge taxes totaling 150 percent of the state tax, a general county tax for 120 percent of the state levy, and a tax of four cents per acre for redemption of outstanding county warrants. Small wonder that Edward King adjudged taxation in the district "very oppressive" in 1874 or that at least one planter concluded that the policy of the Mississippi Republicans was "to ruin by taxation."[12]

Realistically, the hardships of the gentry cannot be attributed to changes in the tax structure, or at least not principally so. Had similarly high levies been in effect before the war, most large slaveholders would have had little difficulty in meeting their obligations. As one visitor to the region remarked in 1875, taxation seemed

*the New South: A History of the Yazoo Mississippi Delta from Reconstruction to the Twentieth Century* (Cambridge: Harvard University Press, 1967), 170.

12. Garner, *Reconstruction in Mississippi*, 313; Order of Board of Police of Jefferson County, January 3, 1870, in Records of the Auditor of Public Accounts, Mississippi Department of Archives and History, Jackson; King, *The Great South*, 295; James A. Gillespie to Jesse Cage, August 10, 1871, in Gillespie Papers.

**Table 6.**   MISSISSIPPI STATE AND COUNTY TAXES, 1874

| County | State Tax | County Tax | Total |
| --- | --- | --- | --- |
| Adams | 14 | 17.7 | 31.7 |
| Claiborne | 14 | 10.5 | 24.5 |
| Jefferson | 14 | 17.5 | 31.5 |
| Warren | 14 | 14 | 28 |
| Wilkinson | 14 | 19 | 33 |

SOURCE: Garner, *Reconstruction in Mississippi*, 313.
NOTE: Tax figures are in mills.

burdensome "mainly because of the straitened circumstances of the people." Still, the increased levies clearly aggravated an already severe situation. "I shall have to go in debt myself to pay my own taxes which in Adams co. are $1000.63, in Wilkinson on Tarbert alone they are $1406.00," wrote John Flavel Jenkins to a friend in 1871. "How is that for very agonizing."[13]

Their new financial vulnerability forced planters to make drastic adjustments in their way of life. Lavish expenditure gave way to a close counting of pennies. William H. Ker wrote to his sister Mary in 1869:

> Owing to my arrears to my hands and to my desire to buy a vehicle and a horse to drive with my mare, I have been compelled to draw on Mr. Hare for nearly $900.00 *before* I could hear from him and be absolutely certain that he would advance to me, and *not* protest my drafts. This is a thing that I *should* not do under any other circumstances than those I am placed in, and just after the mortification I felt in having had to write to Mr. Hare to that affect [*sic*], I think it is rather hard to know that you have had to have more money and have gone to Mr. Hare for it. If you knew how harrassed [*sic*] I am about our prospects, and how galling it is to me to think that I am *always* to have debts dragging me down, you would feel sorry for me, and I think you would not spend money simply because you have it—for I cannot

13. King, *The Great South*, 315. Furthermore, there is some evidence that during Reconstruction many acres were assessed at nominal figures. See newspaper fragment from the Woodville *Sentinel*, August 2, 1873, in Benajah R. Inman and Family Papers, Department of Archives and Manuscripts, Louisiana State University, Baton Rouge. John [Jenkins] to Julia [Dunbar], February 3, 1871, in John C. Jenkins and Family Papers, Department of Archives and Manuscripts, Louisiana State University, Baton Rouge.

imagine what occasion you have for spending much. I feel like giving up entirely, for the more I struggle and just when I think I have cause to feel a little relief, something occurs to bring everything before me. I had rather have a man shoot at me than ask me for money that I owe him and cant pay him, and I never go on the streets, that I don't feel like dodging men, lest they should dun me. If I live a thousand years, I don't think I should ever get over this feeling.

In a like vein, Ker's wife, Josie, complained of the "extravagant" habits of her in-laws: "Butter is one thing—if they would use it sparingly they could sell enough to keep them in sugar & coffee."[14]

Planters with training in law or medicine now returned to practice, intending to supplement their income from cotton. Wives and daughters of the elite secured employment as teachers in local schools or offered private instruction in music and languages. A few even earned a little cash selling services to former slaves. Nellie Ker did some sewing for the hands on the estate Chevy Chase. Jane Gillespie earned $76 in 1870 making clothes for the freedmen on Hollywood.[15]

Each family sought its own way to save money. George Marshall began raising livestock at his residence near Natchez. Mrs. F. W. Boyd sold some of her furniture. Amelia Montgomery considered taking in boarders. Jesse Darden terminated his life insurance policy. For those driven to more desperate straits, there remained the recourse of selling a portion of their land. In 1876, for instance, Prosper K. Montgomery deeded 1,400 acres of his 2,400-acre Jefferson County plantation to Meyer Eiseman, a local merchant, to liquidate a debt. J. M. Coffey sold 100 acres to the same man for $720.[16]

14. Wm. H. Ker to his sister, January 26, 1869, Josie C. Ker to her sister[-in-law], December 20, 1874, both in Mary Susan Ker Papers, Southern Historical Collection, University of North Carolina, Chapel Hill.

15. See, for example, Susan Sillers Darden Diary (MS in Darden Family Papers, Z 82, Mississippi Department of Archives and History, Jackson), II, February 8, 1867; notice, September 22, 1866, in Good Hope Plantation Papers, Department of Archives and Manuscripts, Louisiana State University, Baton Rouge; Kate D. Foster Diary (MS in Manuscript Department, William R. Perkins Library, Duke University, Durham, N.C.), February 5, 1872; Laura to Bec, July 25, 1870, in Drake-Satterfield Papers, Z 96, Box 2, Folder 22, Mississippi Department of Archives and History, Jackson. Nellie Ker to her aunt, April 15, 1879, in Ker Papers; Gillespie Papers, XV.

16. Harnett T. Kane, *Natchez on the Mississippi* (New York: Morrow, 1947), 185; C. C. Boyd to Mary [Ker], October 2, 1874, in Ker Papers; A. F. Montgomery to her hus-

Unfortunately for most planters, such expedients often proved only temporary. The travails of Lemuel P. Conner provide a case in point. A wealthy slaveholder before the war, with estates in Concordia Parish and Adams County, Conner sustained "great pecuniary losses" planting in 1866 and 1867. He struggled to remain solvent by curtailing expenditures, opening a distillery, and borrowing from relatives. But indebtedness soon overwhelmed him and in 1868 he was forced into bankruptcy.[17]

The following year he entered into a partnership with a friend and fellow planter, Antonio Yznaga del Valle, for cultivation of Innisfail in Concordia Parish. Del Valle was to provide the working capital, with Conner contributing some equipment and livestock and taking responsibility for management. This arrangement, though promising, proved short-lived, and Conner next took out a bank loan and purchased a sugar plantation some miles to the south, in Iberville Parish. Here he remained for six years, planting with at best indifferent success and falling deeply into debt again. As before, pressure from creditors eventually forced his hand. He sold the property and took employment as manager of Hard Times, an aptly named, if decrepit, sugar plantation in West Baton Rouge Parish owned by the Mechanics' and Traders' Bank of New Orleans.[18]

From Hard Times he spent the next few years trying to secure any of several public offices in Concordia Parish: sheriff, tax collector, member of the levee board. Each effort met with failure.

band, November 21, 1867, in Joseph A. Montgomery and Family Papers, Department of Archives and Manuscripts, Louisiana State University, Baton Rouge; Darden Diary, II, March 29, 1877, August 27, 1876; deed, October 14, 1880, in Jefferson County Deed Records, Vol. II, p. 212, Mississippi Department of Archives and History, Jackson.

17. Indenture, December 25, 1867, J. Brickell to Lem [Conner], September 21, 1866, Lemuel P. Conner to Fanny [Conner], May 10, 1867, authorization, July 31, 1867, M. L. McMurran to her sister, June 26, 1868, E. E. Norton to Farrar B. Conner, November 20, 1868, bankruptcy judgment, December 4, 1869, all in Lemuel Parker Conner and Family Papers, Department of Archives and Manuscripts, Louisiana State University, Baton Rouge.

18. Agreement, January 1, 1869, in Concordia Parish Conveyance Records, Vol. O, p. 400, Concordia Parish Courthouse, Vidalia; J. G. Conner to her mother, January 20, 1869, Fanny E. Conner to her husband, February 13, 1869, A. Yznaga del Valle to Mr. Conner, December 27, 1872, A. E. to Lemuel [Conner], January 8, 1873, Fanny E. Conner to her husband, January 15, 1875, A. Hardenbrook to Major L. P. Conner, March 6, 1875, Lemuel Conner to Fanny [Conner], March 5, 1875, B. Pope to Maj. L. P. Conner, April 4, 1875, Fanny E. Conner to her husband, April 26, May 3, 1875, all in Conner Papers.

The depth of his resulting exasperation and despair can be measured in an appeal he made in 1877 to an influential acquaintance in New Orleans: "I am told there are several districts in this state presided over by U.S. Commissioners of Internal Revenue—U.S. offices—If not too troublesome can you find out the lands on these districts and some approximation of the income. . . . Of course such positions in the City would be taken by very prominent politicians—I might possibly get a scrap bone in the country." This plea, too, was ignored, however.[19]

Happily for Conner, things improved during the 1880s. His son, Lemuel, Jr., opened a law office in Vidalia and took in his father as a partner. Together they built up a clientele extending throughout northeastern Louisiana. For the Conner family, hard times ended here.[20]

Not all struggling former slaveowners eventually enjoyed a return to prosperity. In 1867, John O. Hutchins of Adams County secured an advance from his New Orleans factor, Given, Watts & Co., with a mortgage on Glen Aubin, his 870-acre estate near the town of Kingston. When the firm went out of business several years later, he transferred the mortgage to the Natchez banking concern of Britton & Koontz for a loan of $1,500. In November, 1872, he gave James Carradine, a local merchant, a second mortgage on the property as security for a debt of $1,000. The following year, he paid off both notes with money borrowed from a neighbor, Wilmer Shields, to whom he yet again mortgaged Glen Aubin. By now, it seemed, he was beginning to lose the means, or perhaps the will, to carry on. A few months later, he sold out to Shields for $4,500.[21]

19. Lemuel P. Conner to Gov. Francis T. Nicholls, January 8, 1876, R. E. Conner to his brother, January 29, 1877, Lemuel P. Conner to James W. Brickell, February 6, 1877, all in Conner Papers.

20. Lemuel P. Conner, Jr., to his mother, January 9, 1878, [Lemuel P. Conner, Jr.] to his mother, [?], 188[?], both in Conner Papers; Lemuel P. Conner to Capt. T. Otis Baker, September 23, 1887, in Baker Papers, Box 3, Folder 30.

21. Mortgage, January 14, 1867, in Adams County Deed Records, Vol. OO, p. 355, Adams County Courthouse, Natchez; mortgage, March 24, 1870, in Adams County Deed Records, Vol. QQ, p. 63; mortgage, November 21, 1872, deed of trust, April 23, 1873, in Adams County Deed Records, Vol. SS, pp. 18, 413; deed, December 31, 1874, in Adams County Deed Records, Vol. UU, p. 272.

**Table 7.**   ANTEBELLUM PLANTERS WHO FORFEITED LAND FOR
NONPAYMENT OF TAXES

| Year | Adams County | Concordia Parish |
|------|:---:|:---:|
| 1851 | 0 | — |
| 1866 | 6 | 18 |
| 1867 | 5 | 18 |
| 1868 | 0 | 16 |
| 1869 | 3 | 15 |
| 1870 | 8 | 15 |
| 1871 | 3 | 16 |
| 1872 |   | 12 |
| 1873 |   | 23 |
| 1874 | 27 | 22 |
| 1875 | 14 | 18 |

SOURCES: "List of Lands in Adams County Delinquent for Non-Payment of Taxes Thereon for the Fiscal
Year 1851," in Records of the Auditor of Public Accounts, Box 30–31; Record of Lands Sold for
Taxes, in Adams County Courthouse, Natchez; Concordia Parish General Mortgages, Vol. P,
pp. 362–435, Vol. Q, pp. 320–55, Vol. R, pp. 2–48, 174–222, Vol. S, pp. 135–76, Vol. T,
pp. 3–23, in Concordia Parish Courthouse, Vidalia.
NOTES: The antebellum planters include the large slaveholders, their spouses and children.
The figure for Adams County for 1874 is cumulative for 1872, 1873, and 1874.

A significant portion of the old elite were forced to forfeit their
land for nonpayment of taxes during these years. Table 7 provides
figures for Adams County and Concordia Parish. In Wilkinson
County in 1851 there were a total of only 23 delinquent taxpayers,
none of whom was a planter. Sixteen years later, 649 separate
tracts were forfeited to the state, with at least 28 members of the
old gentry losing their land. In Jefferson County, only 9 landowners failed to pay their taxes in 1851 and of these, none owed
more than $6.07. In 1874, 15 of the surviving gentry forfeited all
or part of their holdings; their debts to the state totaled over
$30,000.[22]

22. "List of Lands and Town Lots in Wilkinson County Delinquent for Non-Payment of
Taxes Thereon for the Year 1851," "Wilkinson County—Land Sold to and Held by the
State for Taxes, July 13, 1877," "A List of Lands and Town Lots in Jefferson County Delin-
quent for the Non Payment of Taxes for the Fiscal Year A.D. 1851," "List of Lands Sold to

A few former slaveowners ended their lives in near or real poverty. Dr. Philomel Chew was a onetime member of the Louisiana Senate who owned over 60 slaves and a large plantation in Tensas Parish before secession. He "lost nearly everything" in the war and was forced to return to practicing medicine. "As a Physn he is A1," reported the Dun agent for the parish in 1872. But five years later, he was doing poorly. "Has not a $ of Property in the World, has no property beyond his professional experience as a Physician and in our Judt is not a responsible man as far as property is concerned, is honest but being a poor collector, generally is without funds." When Dr. Tom West died in April, 1872, he was buried by the Masons. "His family are left destitute," commented a neighbor, "he had to give up his comfortable home this year & build a log house on a part of his place." Joseph Davenport had to sell sheep to raise money for his wife's coffin.[23]

For some planters, this fall from grace was too much to bear. The ledgers of the Dun Agency tell the tragic story of Nathanial Jefferies, Jr., scion of one of the leading families of antebellum Claiborne County:

May, 1870   Is single, 22 yrs of age, good char, habits & capac, dg sm bus in Lumber, dg tolerably well as a planter, his father owns the place, stands well & is regarded reliable.

Oct. 1870   In his bus 3 yrs. R. E. 25m$. His father transferred to him the R. E., there are Mortgs against the ppy & various judgts. They are not running the Saw Mill. They are compromising at 25% & are expected to succeed in clearing matters up

May, 1871   heavily mortgaged

Sept., 1872   all his R. E. [mortgaged] recently to Joseph Brady, prosps tolerable

Feb., 1873   Sold out to Joseph Brady

July, 1873   Drinking, dissipated young man wor nothing dont keep his engagements & unsafe to trust[24]

the State of Mississippi on the 10th Day of May A.D. 1875—for the Taxes of 1874," all in Records of the Auditor of Public Accounts. Land in Mississippi was purchased by the state, whereas land in Louisiana merely reverted to the state.

23. R. G. Dun & Co. Collection, Louisiana XXII, 13; Darden Diary, II, April 12, 1872, May 12, 1869.

24. R. G. Dun & Co. Collection, Mississippi VI, 144B.

II

In view of the foregoing, it should come as something of a surprise that, despite the existence of widespread indebtedness, despite the forfeiture of property for nonpayment of taxes, most former slave-owners were able to hold on to their land. Indeed, to a striking extent the gentry managed to maintain their dominant place in the local economic hierarchy. The evidence for this conclusion comes from the extant tax rolls for Mississippi and Louisiana (see Appendix I). Though admittedly incomplete and flawed, these records constitute a reasonably reliable—in fact, the only reasonably reliable—overview of property holding after the war. What they reveal is that military defeat, Emancipation, crop failures, and, in the 1870s, depression did not seriously diminish the relative economic position of the old elite.

Tables 8 to 13 summarize the necessary information. For purposes of analysis, five categories have been chosen, roughly dividing landowners by acreage into small farmers (1−49 acres), middle-sized farmers (50−199 acres), large farmers (200−499 acres), small planters (500−999 acres), and large planters (1,000 or more acres). (See Appendix I.) As Tables 8 and 9 indicate, in Claiborne County to a substantial extent and to a lesser degree in Concordia Parish, there was an expansion of the farmer class in general after the war. In Claiborne County this development was undoubtedly related to a decline in the size of the landholding elite. In Concordia Parish considerable new land was brought into cultivation, and all groups grew in magnitude. It is suggestive, however, that in Louisiana, where land was by and large more productive than it was across the river, the relative advance of the small planter was as marked as that of the farmer. It is worth noting, too, that the number of planters with 1,000 acres or more actually increased somewhat in Concordia Parish over the course of the depression that lasted from 1873 to 1879.

Although the size of a class is scarcely in and of itself an adequate yardstick of economic power, the substantial increase in smallholders after the war does imply that they were taking on a new significance, potential or otherwise. An examination of the

**Table 8.**   DISTRIBUTION OF LANDHOLDERS, BY ACREAGE

| | Total Number of Landowners | | | | |
|---|---|---|---|---|---|
| | Acreage | | | | |
| | 1–49 | 50–199 | 200–499 | 500–999 | 1,000+ |
| Concordia Parish | | | | | |
| 1860 | 10 | 29 | 34 | 22 | 88 |
| 1873 | 11 | 42 | 58 | 50 | 91 |
| 1880 | 29 | 55 | 65 | 50 | 96 |
| Claiborne County | | | | | |
| 1857 | 31 | 79 | 98 | 94 | 87 |
| 1866 | 28 | 73 | 101 | 91 | 101 |
| 1879 | 72 | 170 | 157 | 96 | 76 |

SOURCES: U.S. Bureau of the Census, MS Agricultural Schedules for Concordia Parish, 1860; Concordia Parish Assessment Rolls, 1873, 1880, in Louisiana State Capitol, Baton Rouge; Claiborne County Land Rolls, 1857, 1866, 1879, in Mississippi Department of Archives and History, Jackson.

**Table 9.**   DISTRIBUTION OF LANDHOLDERS, BY ACREAGE

| | Percentage of Landowners | | | | |
|---|---|---|---|---|---|
| | Acreage | | | | |
| | 1–49 | 50–199 | 200–499 | 500–999 | 1,000+ |
| Concordia Parish | | | | | |
| 1860 | 5% | 16% | 19% | 12% | 48% |
| 1873 | 4% | 17% | 23% | 20% | 36% |
| 1880 | 10% | 18% | 22% | 17% | 33% |
| Claiborne County | | | | | |
| 1857 | 8% | 20% | 25% | 24% | 23% |
| 1866 | 7% | 20% | 26% | 23% | 26% |
| 1879 | 13% | 30% | 27% | 17% | 13% |

SOURCES: U.S. Bureau of the Census, MS Agricultural Schedules for Concordia Parish, 1860; Concordia Parish Assessment Rolls, 1873, 1880; Claiborne County Land Rolls, 1857, 1866, 1879.

concentration of wealth and acreage, however, serves to put this development into perspective (see Tables 10 and 11).

In Claiborne County the gentry did experience some diminution of their relative economic strength. Whereas before the war large planters had owned 60 percent of the acreage in the county, in 1879 they owned only 51 percent; whereas before the war they had held 64 percent of all wealth in real estate, in 1879 they held but 51 percent. And yet, in the end, the point of overriding interest is that the elite still controlled a disproportionate share of the land.

The case of Concordia Parish is even more indicative in this regard. Large planters owned 79 percent of all acreage in 1880 and 84 percent of all wealth. Although, again, these figures were down from antebellum days, the decline hardly seems important. Those with 1,000 acres or more remained the dominant element in the community. Indeed, for both Claiborne County and Concordia Parish, if we take into account the relative decline in the size of the planting elite, wealth was arguably even more concentrated in 1880 than it had been before the war (see Table 12).[25]

If, then, the large planter class remained economically preeminent through Reconstruction, there remains the question of to what extent that class derived from the antebellum aristocracy. Table 13 provides the answer (see Appendix I). The old gentry were clearly the foundation for the new. To be sure, as the figures for Adams County reveal, the war and its immediate aftermath took a heavy toll on the former slaveholders. In 1866, 84 percent of the large planters in the county had identifiable roots in the prewar gentry; by 1870, the proportion had dropped to 65 percent. In addition, at least in Concordia Parish the depression of the 1870s served further to reduce the stature of the old elite. But, by the

25. Jonathan M. Wiener (*Social Origins of the New South: Alabama, 1860–1885* [Baton Rouge: Louisiana State University Press, 1978], Chap. 1), using a somewhat different statistical approach, divided the landholders into deciles and found that the top decile increased its share of landed wealth after the war. Kenneth S. Greenberg ("The Civil War and the Redistribution of Land: Adams County, Mississippi, 1860–1870," *Agricultural History,* LII [1978], 292–307) used a similar approach and reached a similar conclusion about Adams County. The problem with such a methodology is that it fails to take into account changes in the distribution of landownership that may have affected the size of the local elite. Still, the findings of Wiener and Greenberg are suggestive and entirely consistent with the conclusions reached about the Natchez district.

**Table 10.**   CONCENTRATION OF ACREAGE

| | Percentage of Total Acreage Owned | | | | |
| | Acreage | | | | |
| | 1–49 | 50–199 | 200–499 | 500–999 | 1,000+ |
|---|---|---|---|---|---|
| Concordia Parish | | | | | |
| 1860 | 0% | 1% | 5% | 7% | 87% |
| 1873 | 0% | 2% | 5% | 11% | 82% |
| 1880 | 0% | 2% | 7% | 12% | 79% |
| Claiborne County | | | | | |
| 1857 | 0% | 4% | 11% | 25% | 60% |
| 1866 | 0% | 3% | 11% | 22% | 64% |
| 1879 | 1% | 7% | 17% | 24% | 51% |

SOURCES: U.S. Bureau of the Census, MS Agricultural Schedules for Concordia Parish, 1860; Concordia Parish Assessment Rolls, 1873, 1880; Claiborne County Land Rolls, 1857, 1866, 1879.

**Table 11.**   CONCENTRATION OF WEALTH

| | Percentage of Total Wealth Owned | | | | |
| | Acreage | | | | |
| | 1–49 | 50–199 | 200–499 | 500–999 | 1,000+ |
|---|---|---|---|---|---|
| Concordia Parish | | | | | |
| 1860 | 0% | 1% | 3% | 6% | 90% |
| 1873 | 1% | 1% | 4% | 7% | 87% |
| 1880 | 1% | 2% | 5% | 8% | 84% |
| Claiborne County | | | | | |
| 1857 | 1% | 3% | 10% | 22% | 64% |
| 1866 | 1% | 5% | 9% | 20% | 65% |
| 1879 | 2% | 7% | 17% | 23% | 51% |

SOURCES: U.S. Bureau of the Census, MS Agricultural Schedules for Concordia Parish, 1860; Concordia Parish Assessment Rolls, 1873, 1880; Claiborne County Land Rolls, 1857, 1866, 1879.
NOTE: Wealth is defined as value of real estate holdings.

**Table 12.** RELATIONSHIP BETWEEN THE SIZE OF THE LARGE
PLANTING CLASS AND ITS SHARE OF ACREAGE AND WEALTH

| | Landowners Who Own 1,000 or More Acres | | |
| --- | --- | --- | --- |
| | Percentage of All Landowners | Share of Acreage | Share of Wealth |
| Concordia Parish | | | |
| 1860 | 48% | 87% | 90% |
| 1873 | 36% | 82% | 87% |
| 1880 | 33% | 79% | 84% |
| Claiborne County | | | |
| 1857 | 23% | 60% | 64% |
| 1866 | 26% | 64% | 65% |
| 1879 | 13% | 51% | 51% |

SOURCES: U.S. Bureau of the Census, MS Agricultural Schedules for Concordia Parish, 1860; Concordia Parish Assessment Rolls, 1873, 1880; Claiborne County Land Rolls, 1857, 1866, 1879.
NOTE: Wealth is defined as the value of real estate holdings.

**Table 13.**   PERSISTENCE OF THE SLAVEHOLDING ELITE

Percentage of Those with 1,000 Acres or More
Who Had Belonged to the Class of
Large Slaveholders Before the War

Adams County

| 1866 | 1870 | 1879 |
| --- | --- | --- |
| 84% | 65% | 59% |

| Concordia Parish | | Claiborne County | |
| --- | --- | --- | --- |
| 1873 | 1880 | 1866 | 1879 |
| 61% | 51% | 76% | 59% |

SOURCES: U.S. Bureau of the Census, MS Population and Slave Schedules for Adams County, Claiborne County, Concordia Parish, 1860; Adams County Land Rolls, 1861, 1866, 1870, in Mississippi Department of Archives and History, Jackson; Adams County Land Rolls, 1879, in Adams County Courthouse, Natchez; Claiborne County Land Rolls, 1857, 1866, 1879; Concordia Parish Assessment Rolls, 1873, 1880.

same token, over half of the large planters in the district in 1880 can be directly traced to the antebellum aristocracy. And this proportion understates the true figure. Due to the limitations of the sources, it has not been possible to identify those women who were daughters of slaveholders but came to hold land under their married names. Nor has it been possible to determine those large planters who, though new to the district, had actually belonged to the slaveholding elite elsewhere in the South before the war. All in all, it seems reasonable to conclude that fully 60 percent, perhaps more, of those with one thousand or more acres in 1880 were actually descended from the aristocracy of bygone days. As subsequent chapters will show, substantial changes took place in the district as a result of war and Emancipation; a revolution in land titles was not one of them, however.[26]

### III

A logical question arises. Given that the old elite were burdened with debts and unprecedented high taxes, given that there is substantial evidence of bankruptcy and forfeiture of land, how is it that most families were able to retain their plantations and their dominant position in the local economic hierarchy?

There are a number of explanations. For one thing, struggling planters were occasionally able to secure assistance from more fortunate friends and relatives. Neighbors regularly approached Jesse Darden of Jefferson County for loans during the 1870s; although burdened with financial difficulties of his own, he rarely turned down a plea for aid. Jefferson College, whose board of directors

26. Until recently, most historians tended to assume that the old elite was largely displaced after the war. See, for example, Fred A. Shannon, *The Farmer's Last Frontier: Agriculture, 1860–1897* (New York: Farrar & Rinehart, 1945), 80; Clement Eaton, *The Waning of the Old South Civilization, 1860–1880's* (Athens: University of Georgia Press, 1968), 153. Jonathan M. Wiener's investigation of Alabama (*Social Origins*, 8–16) and Kenneth S. Greenberg's examination of Adams County ("The Civil War and the Redistribution of Land") cast considerable doubt on this conclusion as does the present study. Indeed, in the Natchez district, as in Alabama, the persistence rate of the elite was not noticeably affected by the conflict and its aftermath. In Adams County, for instance, 63 percent of those with one thousand acres or more in 1861 had belonged to the slaveholding elite in 1850. By comparison, the persistence rate from 1860 to 1870 was 65 percent.

was composed predominantly of members of the old elite, made numerous advances to planters in need.[27]

For those who sought a more permanent solution to their problems, there remained the possibility of an advantageous marriage. William Dunbar Jenkins wed a daughter of the prominent Natchez banker George W. Koontz and received a "handsome marriage portion." Scott McGehee also effected a profitable union. "The dowry of $100,000 is quite a nice sum in these hard times," remarked an envious acquaintance. "He must have looked out the money before he thought of marrying." William H. Ker wrote to his sister from Natchez in 1869, "Every body here has run crazy on the subject of weddings, parties, & c and I am disgusted with the way people talk and act. Steve Duncan could marry any girl here, I believe, at the drop of a hat, but the very people who are such worshippers of riches would be horrified if you told them so, and ridicule the idea of anyone's marrying for money."[28]

Still, there were few enough eligible heirs and heiresses around during Reconstruction. And in view of the difficult times, debt-ridden former slaveowners could hardly count on the financial assistance of friends. It happened, then, that many members of the gentry took steps of frankly dubious legality to secure their plantations. Or as the wife of one planter bluntly noted, "it does seem as if every body is trying to swindle each other."[29]

In one relatively widely used ploy the indebted planter would deliberately fail to meet mortgage payments, thereby inducing foreclosure. With the price of land in the district declining, it was often possible to have a friend purchase the encumbered plantation at public auction for a sum considerably below the value of the mortgage. Later the original owner, now free of his creditors, would buy the property back from his accomplice. Charles D. Hamilton saved his Louisiana plantation Allendale in this way. B. H. Buck-

27. Darden Diary, II, December 20, 1870, May 25, 1874; Jefferson College Papers, VI, *passim.*

28. R. G. Dun & Co. Collection, Mississippi II, 184; W. P. S. Ventress to Charlotte D. Ventress, May 18, 1872, in Trask-Ventress Family Papers, Folder 237; Wm. H. Ker to his sister, January 28, 1869, in Ker Papers.

29. A. F. Montgomery to her husband, January 23, 1868, in Montgomery Papers.

ner of Madison Parish took similar steps to clear himself of obligations amounting to over $120,000.[30]

Without question, though, the most popular and effective means for an insolvent planter to hold on to his property was to sign it over to a relative, generally his wife. The Dun Agency credit ledgers cite literally scores of instances of former slaveowners attempting to get around their problems in this way. Martin N. Hulbert owned over 1,600 acres in Claiborne County before the war. But the Dun representative found him "Badly in debt" in 1866. "Insolvent & tricky. Has considerable estate in his wifes name??" Six years later, the verdict was much the same: "Prospects are so mixed up and impared [sic] divided between his wife & children that you could not tell to who it belonged. Look out for him he has a vy honest face." Nor were such tactics employed only by those of doubtful reputation. Samuel J. Bridgers was known throughout Claiborne County as a man "in every way reliable & responsible." But he too transferred his holdings to his wife to dodge creditors. So did a neighbor, John Taylor Moore, widely regarded as a "gentleman, a scholar & a soldier."[31] Often the planter, having dispossessed himself of his property, would wait an appropriate period of time and then declare bankruptcy, thus freeing himself of outstanding debts.

In strict terms, such practices were illegal. The Mississippi Supreme Court repeatedly ruled that transfers of property to defeat creditors were null and void. But fraud was evidently difficult to prove, and, in any case, litigation was expensive. "Injunction after injunction can be gotten out," reported one observer.[32] In the end, most planters who attempted to turn their plantations over to their wives were able to do so. Table 14 suggests the pervasiveness of

30. B. S. Stevens to C. D. Hamilton, April 28, 1867, in Charles D. Hamilton and Family Papers, Z 98, Mississippi Department of Archives and History, Jackson; R. G. Dun & Co. Collection, Louisiana VII, 14. This practice is described in detail in J. T. Belknap to Lizzie Hamilton, November 30, 1869, and E. D. Farrar to Lizzie Hamilton, May 6, 1869, both in C. D. Hamilton Papers.

31. R. G. Dun & Co. Collection, Mississippi VI, 154, 160H, 166, 159.

32. See, for example, *James K. Wilson* v. *C. F. Kohlheim*, in State Supreme Court of Mississippi, *Mississippi Reports*, XLVI (Chicago: Callahan, 1872), 346–74; J. Brickell to [Mrs. Lemuel P. Conner], May 4, 1875, in Conner Papers. A. H. Polk to Meck, January 18, 1866, in Leonidas Polk Papers, Southern Historical Collection, University of North Carolina, Chapel Hill.

**Table 14.** WOMEN AMONG THE PERSISTING ELITE

Landowners Who Own 1,000 or More Acres

Claiborne County

| | Total | Women | Percentage Women |
|---|---|---|---|
| 1857 | 87 | 2 | 2% |
| 1866 | 77 | 12 | 16% |
| 1879 | 44 | 18 | 41% |

Concordia Parish

| | Total | Women | Percentage Women |
|---|---|---|---|
| 1860 | 88 | 5 | 6% |
| 1873 | 56 | 9 | 16% |
| 1880 | 44 | 13 | 30% |

Adams County

| | Total | Women | Percentage Women |
|---|---|---|---|
| 1860 | 97 | 18 | 19% |
| 1866 | 73 | 14 | 19% |
| 1870 | 49 | 16 | 33% |
| 1879 | 40 | 9 | 23% |

SOURCES: U.S. Bureau of the Census, MS Population and Slave Schedules for Adams County, Claiborne County, Concordia Parish, 1860; Adams County Land Rolls, 1861, 1866, 1870, 1879; Claiborne County Land Rolls, 1857, 1866, 1879; Concordia Parish Assessment Rolls, 1873, 1880.
NOTE: The landowners with 1,000+ acres include only those who had belonged to the class of large slaveholders (including their spouses and children) before the war.

this course of action. In Claiborne County in 1857, only two of eighty-seven large planters were women. Nine years later, seventy-seven landowners with 1,000 acres or more came from families belonging to the antebellum elite, and of these seventy-seven, twelve were women. In 1879 the number of surviving gentry had fallen to forty-four, but now fully eighteen were women, or over 40 percent. The figures for Concordia Parish show the same trend as, to a lesser extent, do those for Adams County (see Appendix I).

Some former slaveowners transferred property to their children or parents. W. S. Lum of Warren County turned his holdings over to his offspring to defeat a claim of the Mississippi Valley Bank for

$1,500 and several other obligations. J. T. Watson of Tensas Parish deeded his lands to his mother in 1871 and "left his creditors in [the] cold to [the] tune of $25,000."[33]

Taxation was another matter. As was indicated earlier, each year planters turned over considerable acreage to the state for nonpayment of taxes. But property that had been forfeited was subject to redemption, within two years in Mississippi, within six months in Louisiana.[34] As Table 15 demonstrates, apparently most former slaveowners were able to take advantage of this provision of the law. Of twenty-seven parties in Adams County who forfeited all or part of their acreage in the years 1872 to 1874, at least twenty-two succeeded in recovering their land. Furthermore, although in cases of forfeiture, title formally passed into the hands of the state, within the period allowed for redemption the defaulting landowner was permitted to remain in possession of the property in question.

Of course, those seeking to redeem their holdings had to come up with the wherewithal to pay outstanding levies and any penalty charges. But from time to time the state waived penalty charges and occasionally even arrearages.[35] In any case, most planters seem to have been able to raise limited amounts of capital whenever necessary. Indeed, the regularity with which some plantations were forfeited and recovered, forfeited and recovered, suggests that certain former slaveowners regarded default as a necessary part of a program of rational financial management.

Theoretically, land not redeemed within the period specified by law would be sold at public auction. But through the 1870s and especially during the years of depression, planters found that they could largely ignore deadlines for redemption. The reason was simple enough. As Charles Nordhoff observed in 1875, land was

33. R. G. Dun & Co. Collection, Mississippi XXI, 42D, Louisiana XXII, 11.

34. Darden Diary, II, August 7, 1871; deed, [?], 1873, in Concordia Parish General Mortgages, Vol. P, p. 287; *The Revised Code of the Statute Laws of Mississippi* (Jackson: Alcorn & Fisher, 1871), 344–68; *Acts Passed by the General Assembly of the State of Louisiana at the First Session of the Third Legislature Begun and Held in New Orleans, January 6, 1873* (New Orleans, 1873), 98–102. Later the period of redemption changed to two years in Louisiana and one year in Mississippi. In Mississippi the state could sell forfeited land at public auction, but the original owner retained the right of redemption even if the property was purchased. James O. Fuqua to Lizzie Hamilton, April 27, 1868, in C. D. Hamilton Papers; Adams County Record of Lands Sold for Taxes.

35. E. D. Farrar to Kate D. Foster, March 24, 1873, in James Foster Papers, Department of Archives and Manuscripts, Louisiana State University, Baton Rouge.

**Table 15.** REDEMPTION OF LAND IN ADAMS COUNTY SOLD TO THE
STATE BY ANTEBELLUM ELITE FOR NONPAYMENT OF TAXES, 1872–74

| Owners Who Redeemed Their Land | Acres Forfeited | Tax and Charges |
|---|---|---|
| A. F. Alexander | 850 | $ 173.29 |
| E. R. Bennett | 2,000 | 492.99 |
| H. Bennett | 665 | 169.50 |
| Mary C. Bradley | 1,110 | 225.23 |
| Mrs. C. Brandon | 1,800 | 452.95 |
| Richard Chotard | 75 | 123.00 |
| Thomas T. Davis | 650 | 132.60 |
| D. S. Farrar | 700 | 143.12 |
| F. T. Ford | 500 | 123.00 |
| William Holliday | 5,840 | 1,432.89 |
| William Holmes | 3,000 | 364.50 |
| E. S. Irvine | 80 | 98.75 |
| Est. of H. L. Metcalfe | 1,133 | 306.93 |
| Robert Pipes | 2,815 | 569.72 |
| Heirs of Stephen Pipes | 1,000 | 203.50 |
| John Robson | 2,000 | 427.58 |
| A. J. Rowan | 718 | 151.51 |
| Aaron Stanton | 3,700 | 479.45 |
| Anna E. Stanton | 3,000 | 424.87 |
| Est. of Robert Stanton | 1,700 | 344.37 |
| Est. of S. Duncan | residence | 687.25 |
| W. R. Gilreath | 2 town lots | 246.00 |
| Owners Who Failed to Redeem Their Land | | |
| Mrs. C. Brandon & children | 1,700 | 344.36 |
| John Grafton | 700 | 157.36 |
| James H. Rowan | 978 | 250.32 |
| Louis Winston | 840 | 171.30 |
| A. & S. W. Stanton | 1 town lot | 346.75 |

SOURCE: Adams County Record of Lands Sold for Taxes.
NOTE: The antebellum elite includes the large slaveholders, their spouses and children.

"almost unsalable," particularly on the Mississippi side of the river, where much of the soil was shallow. T. J. Chamberlain and his sister Pauline, for example, were able to continue operating their two forfeited Jefferson County plantations, The Mound and Liverpool, into the 1880s, although they owed taxes dating back to 1874.[36]

In the final analysis, then, the single most important factor behind the persistence of the old elite was almost certainly the general deterioration in the real estate market. Many former slaveowners held on to their land only because no one else with capital wanted it. Those with opportunities to sell their property were unable to get anything approaching a satisfactory price. Edward King, who passed through the district in 1874, told of a Madison Parish plantation that had originally cost $30,000 and now was being offered for $700. The situation was much the same elsewhere. That the old elite remained economically ascendant in the district points not to their own prosperity but to the relative impoverishment around them[37] (see, for example, Table 16). (See Appendix I.) They were lords of the realm still, but in plainly diminished circumstances.

In the 1880s, economic conditions improved nationally. But now the Natchez district started to lose its preeminent position in the cotton South. For the first time locally but in a familiar regional pattern, significant numbers of planters began to abandon their estates for newer, more fertile lands elsewhere, in the Mississippi Delta especially, but also in Arkansas and east Texas. Left behind were members of the old elite who were heavily burdened with debts and could not raise the capital to relocate. Ironically, the continued persistence of this group in the Natchez aristocracy came increasingly to signify their comparative weakness. In a word, they were land-poor. "Mr. West cannot go to Texas as he ex-

36. Nordhoff, *The Cotton States*, 78; R. G. Dun & Co. Collection, Mississippi XI, 353. See also Roger W. Shugg, *Origins of Class Struggle in Louisiana: A Social History of White Farmers and Laborers During Slavery and After, 1840–1875* (Baton Rouge: Louisiana State University Press, 1972), 261; Orlando Dorsey to Mrs. C. D. Ventress, March 8, 1875, in Trask-Ventress Family Papers, Folder 191.

37. King, *The Great South*, 276; Shugg, *Origins of Class Struggle*, 51; Theodore Saloutos, "Southern Agriculture and the Problems of Readjustment, 1865–1877," *Agricultural History*, XXX (1956), 61; James L. Roark, *Masters Without Slaves: Southern Planters in the Civil War and Reconstruction* (New York: Norton, 1977), 173–75.

**Table 16.**   VALUE OF REAL ESTATE, CLAIBORNE COUNTY

| Total Value of Land | | |
|---|---|---|
| 1857 | 1866 | 1879 |
| $2,065,999 | $784,272 | $917,054 |

| Value of Land Owned by Large Planters | | |
|---|---|---|
| 1857 | 1866 | 1879 |
| $1,316,327 | $504,880 | $465,918 |

| Average Value of Land Owned by Large Planters | | |
|---|---|---|
| 1857 | 1866 | 1879 |
| $15,130 | $4,950 | $6,131 |

SOURCES: Claiborne County Land Rolls, 1857, 1866, 1879.
NOTES: Value is measured in constant 1860 dollars. The large planters are all those with 1,000 or more acres, not just those who had belonged to the antebellum elite.

pected," wrote Susan Sillers Darden of her son-in-law, "there is a mortgage on his Mother's place that will have to be raised before he can leave for $2,000."[38] Such men and women were bound to their acres. Of necessity they had to learn to content themselves with the prerogatives of power and influence in a declining regime.

During the fifteen years or so following the war, most large land-owners had roots in the old elite. But a word should be said about the newcomers. Although evidence on these individuals is some-what scanty, a few observations can be made. In each county or parish, there were likely to be a handful of large landholders who had belonged to the class of small planters before the war. Of the seventy-six property owners with 1,000 or more acres in Claiborne County in 1879, five had owned between thirty-five and forty-nine slaves in 1860. William McD. Sims, for instance, with 4,717 acres, had held forty-seven slaves.[39]

38. There was some movement of planters out of the district during Reconstruction (see, for example, Darden Diary, II, December 10, 1866, January 14, 1869, January 7, 1872). Darden Diary, II, October 24, 1874.
39. Claiborne County Land Rolls, 1879; U.S. Bureau of the Census, MS Slave Schedules for Claiborne County, 1860, p. 13. Jonathan Wiener (*Social Origins*, 22–28) reached a similar conclusion for Alabama.

Other new planters came from diverse backgrounds. H. H. Harris, who amassed considerable property in Concordia Parish, was a former tax collector from New Orleans. Levi Fields, a butcher, and James Orr, a wagonmaker, each acquired a plantation in Adams County. J. E. Slicer, following a more traditional route, earned enough money practicing medicine to purchase an estate in Tensas Parish.[40]

Certain commercial interests from other localities bought acreage in the district, although presumably mainly for purposes of speculation. A. Miltonberger of New Orleans acquired Chevy Chase in Concordia Parish from the estate of R. D. Percy in 1871. Three years later, Brandeis & Crawford, a Louisville firm, purchased a half interest in Union Point, another Concordia Parish plantation.[41]

Finally, among the new large landowners was a significant number of local merchants. Meyer Eiseman and Louis Kiefer, to name only two, acquired extensive holdings in Jefferson and Claiborne counties, respectively. The activities of such men played a conspicuous role in the history of the old elite after the war. The nature and full extent of that role will be discussed at length later.

IV

As in the past, economic ascendancy translated into social authority for the antebellum gentry. They remained in positions of leadership in established local institutions—the church, for example, and schools.[42] And they took control of various organizations that emerged after the war to deal with the needs of the new regime. The Grange provides a good example. When a chapter of the organization was formed on Pine Ridge in Adams County in 1873, James F. McCaleb and Samuel H. Lambdin were appointed mas-

40. R. G. Dun & Co. Collection, Louisiana IV, 240.2, Mississippi II, 138, 121, Louisiana XXII, 16.

41. Lease, February 8, 1871, in Concordia Parish General Mortgages, Vol. P, p. 65; sale of property, January 9, 1874, in Concordia Parish Conveyance Records, Vol. P, p. 407.

42. See, for example, list of trustees, in Minute Book of Port Gibson Female Academy (Z 1331) (MS in Mississippi Department of Archives and History, Jackson), 81; lists of trustees, in Jefferson College Papers, VI, passim; "Register of Members and Probationers in Woodville Station, Methodist Episcopal Church, South," in Woodville Methodist Church Records, Z 993, Mississippi Department of Archives and History, Jackson.

ter and secretary, respectively. Both had been prominent planters before the war, and Lambdin had held two large plantations and 275 slaves. Later, the office of master passed to J. C. Stowers, a member of one of the oldest and most influential families in the county. When the Natchez Grange opened a store in 1877 with capital of about $2,000, the principal backer was George W. Baynard, still one of the most successful planters in the region and, prior to the war, owner of well over 1,500 acres. Finally and most notably, Put Darden, who became head of the State Grange in Mississippi and later national master, belonged to an extended Jefferson County clan whose considerable wealth traced back to eighteenth-century Georgia. His father, John Darden, had held 70 slaves in 1860. His brother Thomas would rise to prominence in the Farmers' Alliance.[43]

Indeed, extant membership lists for local chapters of the Patrons of Husbandry read like excerpts from an antebellum social register. The gentry came not only to dominate the organization but to treat it as something of an exclusive private club. Josie Ker wrote to her sister-in-law, Mary Ker, in September, 1875, "Miss Katie Bennet & Mrs. Percy were here Monday, and they were quarreling about Nell. Mrs. P. wanted her to join the Pine Ridge Grange & Miss Kate wanted her in the Natchez Grange." As this comment suggests, for reasons that were apparently largely social, women played a major role in the emergence of the Grange in the district. In May, 1876, Josie Ker wrote to Mary Ker again, this time to report, "I have joined the Grange—what do you think of that? Will attend next Sat. if nothing happens, for the first time. Hope I will get Mr. Ker in before long." It surely says something about the pretensions of the membership that the Pine Ridge Grange elected, along with other officers, a "Ceres," a "Pomona," and a "Flora."[44]

In a variety of ways the life of the old elite remained unchanged

---

43. Pine Ridge Grange, "Book for Information" (MS in possession of Mrs. Waldo Lambdin, Natchez); R. G. Dun & Co. Collection, Mississippi II, 90; *Goodspeed's Biographical and Historical Memoirs of Mississippi, Embracing an Authentic and Comprehensive Account of the Chief Events in the History of the State and a Record of the Lives of Many of the Most Worthy and Illustrious Families and Individuals* (2 vols.; Chicago: Goodspeed Publishing Co., 1891), Vol. I, Pt. 1, pp. 616–18. See also membership list of the Phoenix Grange No. 516, May 23, 1874, in Darden Family Papers, Box 1, Folder 9.

44. Josie C. Ker to her sister[-in-law], September 29, 1875, May 7, 1876, both in Ker

after the war. Each "season" a number of families left the district for the healthful spas of Virginia and Arkansas or for the North (more often the Midwest now; less frequently New England). A few members of the gentry even continued to enjoy the occasional vacation abroad. John R. Ayres, for example, did the Grand Tour of Europe in 1871. Five years later, Rosalie Quitman Duncan took a trip across the Continent with her young son William.[45]

Still, the changed economic situation had an obvious effect. Even those who could afford to travel had to keep an eye on expenses. While in Europe, the aforementioned Rosalie Duncan received a cautionary note from her brother-in-law and benefactor, William S. Lovell: "I cannot possibly see how I can send you but £300 more, that is £100 in Jay—£100 in Feby and £100 March. . . . Matters was never harder with me, now what I mean is this—I can only send you £300 & at the rate you were spending it you would have to leave by 15th April. Of course if you economize you could stay longer. . . . I am truly sorry I am not able to do more."[46] As it was, most planters simply remained at home now, even during the oppressive summer months.

The one area in which almost no one was prepared to make sacrifices was education. If anything, the commitment to learning intensified as economic prospects declined. Lewis B. Ker of Huntley informed his sister in September, 1874, that he had recently released his cook "for want of money to pay her." He continued:

> Another reason for our trying to do as much of our own work as we can is, I am going to try to send Johnie to Natchez to school this winter to Hallie Eustis, who has offered to teach him & board him free of

---

Papers; Pine Ridge Grange, "Book for Information." For examples of other activities and organizations in which the old elite took the lead, see [Mrs. A. M. Farrar?] to My dear Child, June 13, 1876, in Richardson-Farrar Papers, Southern Historical Collection, University of North Carolina, Chapel Hill; Darden Diary, II, January 9, 1871; diploma, South Mississippi and East Louisiana Agricultural and Live Stock Association, October 28, 1887, in Trask-Ventress Family Papers, Folder 275.

45. See, for example, [Antonia Quitman Lovell] to Posie, July 23, 1880, in Quitman Family Papers, Southern Historical Collection, University of North Carolina, Chapel Hill; Dunbar Hunt to his brother, September 2, 1868, in Archer-Finlay-Moore Papers, Box 1, Folder 6, Mississippi Department of Archives and History, Jackson. [Ayres] Diary, 1871 (MS in possession of Ayres and Emily Haxton, Natchez); Quitman Family Papers, XXI; Stephen Duncan Correspondence, II, Department of Archives and Manuscripts, Louisiana State University, Baton Rouge.

46. Wm. S. Lovell to Rose, January 12, 1877, in Quitman Family Papers.

charge. It will take every cent I can get, to buy him some clothes and what books he needs. He is going to sell his gun and a nice yearling, to get money to buy his clothes. He seemed to be very anxious to go, and I hope he may do well. I feel extremely anxious about him, but I believe he is as good a boy for his age and opportunities as I ever saw. If he goes, I shall be at a great loss to get along without him. If I possibly can, I will try to have him take writing lessons in the afternoons.

Similar hopes and concerns can be seen in a communication from Joseph D. Shields to his son Bayard, away at school in Virginia in 1867: "We are living on half rations. I am overwhelmed with debts & can not tell how long I can keep you going to College. I tell you this not to discourage you but to spur you on to extraordinary diligence."[47]

Unfortunately, sometimes a willingness to sacrifice was not enough. "How we wish Sister could be sent off to school for two years," remarked Kate Stone of Brokenburn with evident regret in 1868, "but it has been impossible. No money." "My own boys are growing up without any advantages," confessed Levin Wailes to a friend some years later, "I have not the means to send them to school—every cent that I make being turned over yearly to pay off old debts. They have but a half year schooling, and that when they were in Md. five years ago."[48]

For those in more fortunate circumstances, education followed relatively familiar paths. Lizzie Hamilton of Claiborne County hired a tutor for her children in 1869 at the cost of $50 a month plus board. Various members of the elite opened private schools in their homes. Clara Walworth, for instance, conducted classes at The Burn. Thomas Henderson offered instruction to about fifty boys at his father's mansion in Natchez.[49]

47. Lewis B. Ker to his sister, September 25, 1874, in Ker Papers; Jo. D. Shields to Bayard F. Shields, August 24, 1867, in Joseph D. Shields Papers, Department of Archives and Manuscripts, Louisiana State University, Baton Rouge.

48. John Q. Anderson (ed.), *Brokenburn: The Journal of Kate Stone, 1861–1868* (Baton Rouge: Louisiana State University Press, 1972), 376; L[evin] W[ailes] to W. N. Whitehurst, September 17, [c. 1872], in William N. Whitehurst Papers, Z 15, Box 1, Folder 10, Mississippi Department of Archives and History, Jackson.

49. Claire Duval to Mrs. [Lizzie Hamilton], September 1, 1869, in C. D. Hamilton Papers; W.P.A. Records, RG 60, for Adams County, Folder: Schools and Colleges, Mississippi Department of Archives and History, Jackson.

There existed a handful of private academies in the region, the best known being Jefferson College near Natchez, which in 1873–1874 had an enrollment of eighty-eight students, most of whom came from the vicinity. None of the local institutions was particularly distinguished, however, and despite its name, Jefferson College was little more than a preparatory school. As a result, a number of planters elected to send their children outside the district for their education. Sue Inman attended a boarding school in New Orleans in 1869, as did Annie Lovell a decade later. The sons of George Wilson Humphreys went to the Kentucky Military Institute, while several boys from Wilkinson County attended the Collegiate Institute in Baton Rouge, a highly regarded academy run by W. H. N. Magruder.[50]

As for those children of the elite who went on to college, very few went to the North now; most enrolled at schools in Virginia. James A. Ventress and his brother Willie attended the University of Virginia in the 1870s, as did Sargent Prentiss Nutt, son of Haller Nutt, and perhaps ten other scions of prominent antebellum families. Another dozen or so went to Washington and Lee University. As in the past, such students normally pursued a liberal education, although from time to time the opinion would be offered—perhaps by a student, perhaps by his parents—that practical training might be more suited to a slaveless world.[51]

To some extent conspicuous consumption continued after the war. Successful planters still bought luxury items in the North and in Europe, still kept expensive racing horses, still dined regally, and still threw lavish parties. Four hundred guests attended the wedding of James Surget and Catherine Boyd at Natchez in 1873, a union of two of the most powerful and affluent clans in the lower Mississippi Valley. The bride ordered her trousseau from a famous

50. Jefferson College Papers, VI, 273; report cards, November, 1869, February, 1871, both in Inman Papers; report card, May 1, 1879, in Quitman Family Papers; B. E. Humphreys to his mother, September 29, 1869, Leon Humphreys to his sister, December 29, 1869, both in George Wilson Humphreys and Family Papers, Z 29, Folder 10, Mississippi Department of Archives and History, Jackson; James Stewart McGehee Papers, III, 38–42, Department of Archives and Manuscripts, Louisiana State University, Baton Rouge.

51. *Catalogues of the University of Virginia*, 1870–80; *Catalogues of Washington and Lee University*, 1870–80; J. A. Montgomery to his wife, April 2, 1870, in Montgomery Papers.

Parisian milliner; the duty on it and other materials imported from France for the occasion amounted to over $500. Entertainment at the reception was provided by a band from New Orleans, and dinner was catered by a firm from the same city. For a wedding gift Surget gave his bride a cluster of diamonds "so arranged as to be separated into parts and detached: and so formed bracelets, earrings, necklaces—Tiara—buttons—pins—rings . . . and all conceivable jewelry."[52]

Still, such displays were clearly exceptional. Laura Turpin of Richland wrote to her daughter Beck regarding the wedding arrangements of another daughter, Ellen, "It is useless to say I would love her to have all of her friends if she wishes, but she knows your Fathers circumstances as well as I can tell her & I'm sure will act accordingly." Indeed, the continuing extravagance of the few served to draw attention to the difficulties of other members of the aristocracy and underline the disparities created by the war. In late 1868, Jenny Ralston attended an affair at the residence of William Ogden in Natchez. Afterward, she wrote of the evening to Kate Foster, describing in particular detail the attire and manner of a mutual acquaintance, Mrs. Dunbar Hunt: "She *treated* her elegant silk dress & superb diamonds with what appeared to *my poverty struck eyes*, unaccountable indifference and *disdain*—the skirt dragged *yards* upon the floor & I thought *without* covetousness, there is enough material in *that* dress of *splendid* silk, to make *me* with a *little* more added, quite a *magnificent* one—I *wonder*, Katie, if I'll *ever* have a silk dress again." Others at the party wore calico.[53]

The attendance of individuals of varying fortunes at the same affair points to one unchanged characteristic of the old elite after the war: their essential unity. Former slaveowners socialized only

52. See, for example, Elgin Journal, 1879–80 (MS in possession of Mr. and Mrs. Hyde D. Jenkins, Natchez), July 16, October 5, 1879; Tonie [Lovell] to Posie, February 22, 1878, in Quitman Family Papers; "Inventory of Race Stables at Farmland," in possession of Mrs. Douglas MacNeil, Natchez; receipts, August 3, 1870, August 30, 1871, both in William Newton Mercer Papers, Department of Archives and Manuscripts, Louisiana State University, Baton Rouge. F. W. Boyd to Katy Boyd, February 23, 1873, in possession of Mrs. Douglas MacNeil, Natchez.

53. L. S. T[urpin] to Beck, April 14, 1869, in Drake-Satterfield Papers, Box 2, Folder 18; Aunt Jenny [Ralston] to Kate [Foster], December 16, 1868, in Foster Papers.

with each other and a handful of wealthy newcomers. Further-more, (both the successful and the struggling among the gentry continued to exhibit the class consciousness that had become espe-cially evident in the years leading up to the war.) "The boys here are just the best fellows that ever lived," wrote John Q. Lovell to his mother from the Virginia Military Institute in March, 1876, "& I like them very much, of course there are some who are not my equals & with them I will not associate." His brother, William S. Lovell, Jr., revealed a like cast of mind after a visit to friends in Sewanee, Tennessee: "What struck me most was their perfect contentment, so far out in the country and surrounded by a very inferior class of people." Such elitism came naturally to the grand-sons of John A. Quitman, but others from less distinguished back-grounds shared their opinions. Alex Stacy, for example, remarked to Mary Ker in 1875 that he hoped her brother would consider a return to Mississippi from his plantation in the swamplands of Louisiana. "Then his daughters instead of being thrown in contact with boors would be able to associate with ladies and gentlemen of their own station."[54]

As before, class consciousness manifested itself most clearly in patterns of marriage. To be sure, financial considerations played a larger role in marital decisions now than they had in the days prior to the war. But it was still expected that members of the gentry would wed within their rank. "I was sorry to hear there are any prospects of Sallie Fort marrying Jack Redhead," commented James A. Ventress to a brother in the fall of 1872. "Altho: he may be a very clever fellow, yet I think, were I her, I should endeavor to marry someone of a little better family."[55]

54. For evidence of occasional social contact between the old elite and well-to-do mer-chants during Reconstruction, see Darden Diary, II, *passim*; Louisa Tweed Diary (MS in Robert Tweed Papers, Southern Historical Collection, University of North Carolina, Chapel Hill); "The Sportsman's Note Book" (MS in possession of Mr. and Mrs. Hyde D. Jenkins, Natchez). J. Q. Lovell to his mother, March 7, 1876, W. S. Lovell, Jr., to his mother, Janu-ary 4, 1880, both in Quitman Family Papers; Alex. Stacy to Mary [Ker], May 6, 1875, in Ker Papers.

55. J. A. Ventress to L. T. Ventress, November 24, 1872, in Trask-Ventress Family Pa-pers, Folder 238.

## V

It would be difficult to ignore the element of continuity in the story of the old elite. Despite very real problems with debt and taxation, they continued to serve as leaders of the community. And within the admittedly narrow limits imposed by their financial difficulties,  they endeavored to hold to the style of life they had known before the war.

And yet something had changed, something fundamental—something beyond the general decline in economic prospects. It found expression in a new attitude toward planting itself. Formerly a plantation had been the "*ne plus ultra* of every man's ambition." "You could not have a better investment . . . than a plantation," Mrs. John Quitman had advised a daughter in 1859. "Houses will burn down, stocks will break and fly to the winds, but a plantation is a solid thing, it is always there." But now increasing numbers of former slaveowners began to direct any surplus capital into other enterprises. On the advice of her brother, Lizzie Hamilton of Claiborne County purchased stock in various southern railroads. So did a neighbor, Clarissa Young, who also bought an interest in an insurance company. A. D. Rawlings acquired 100 shares of the New Orleans Gas Company in 1880, while the entry on Frederick A. W. Davis for 1879 in the Adams County ledgers of the Dun Agency noted, "Owns larger prop[erty] in Calif & large investments in Bonds & other securities."[56]

At the same time, certain members of the gentry began to show a limited yet discernible interest in the development of local manufacturing. A. D. Rawlings purchased $5,000 worth of stock in the Rosalie Yarn Mills Company in Natchez. Stephen Duncan, A. C. Britton, and Wilmer Shields joined with a number of merchants in 1877 to form the Natchez Cotton Mills, capitalized at $70,000. Three years later, the venture was "flourishing." "They

56. E. Quitman to Louisa, April 15, 1859, in Quitman Family Papers; Richard Nugent to Lizzie Hamilton, August 24, September 27, 1869, James [Belknap] to Lizzie Hamilton, October 5, 1869, June 16, 1870, all in C. D. Hamilton Papers; M. E. Musson to Clarissa Young, April 30, 1870, August 2, 1874, both in William Hughes and Family Papers, Z 68, Folder 8, Mississippi Department of Archives and History, Jackson; receipt, April 10, 1889, in Baker Papers, Box 3, Folder 31; R. G. Dun & Co. Collection, Mississippi II, 183.

have increased their capl to 225m$," observed the local representative of the Dun Agency. Britton was also instrumental in the formation of the Natchez Ice Company in 1882.[57] All this is not to suggest that the very restricted impetus given to manufacturing in the district during this period was solely the responsibility of the gentry; mercantile interests played perhaps a larger role. But the fact remains that, for the first time, a representative element of the landholding elite was looking for investments beyond the plantation.

For the first time, too, members of the gentry were giving serious thought to alternative professions, especially for their children. "It is a pity to have these two boys grow up without any business habits," wrote Amelia Montgomery of Belmont to her husband, regarding their sons Tom and Walter. "If I had a home for them in N[ew] O[rleans] I should say put Tom in a business house & let him learn to make a living & learn to depend upon himself as soon as possible, & break him from the poluting [sic] society he is exposed to on a plantation." Johnny Stewart informed his parents from the University of Virginia that he had no desire to return to the family estate in Wilkinson County; he intended, he said, to become a merchant.[58]

Obviously, economic considerations had something to do with such decisions. But as the above remarks of Amelia Montgomery indicate, the former slaveowners were also becoming increasingly disenchanted with the broader way of life that the plantation had come to represent. Those who could afford to do so spent more and more time away from their estates. And there were frequent complaints about the dispiriting nature of planting and the unsatisfying quality of day-to-day existence. "I am willing to live on

57. Receipt, December 2, 1882, in Baker Papers, Box 2, Folder 30; articles of copartnership, April 17, 1877, in Stephen Duncan and Stephen Duncan, Jr., Papers, Department of Archives and Manuscripts, Louisiana State University, Baton Rouge; R. G. Dun & Co. Collection, Mississippi II, 169; "Industries," Supplement (Typescript in W.P.A. Records for Adams County, Folder: Industry).

58. A. F. Montgomery to her husband, December 27, 1866, in Montgomery Papers; Willie [Ventress] to Charlotte D. Ventress, January 19, 1873, in Trask-Ventress Family Papers, Folder 239. See also Roark, *Masters Without Slaves*, 151; Thomas D. Clark, *Pills, Petticoats, and Plows: The Southern Country Store* (Norman: University of Oklahoma Press, 1964), 10.

this dreary plantation, submitting to any privations, and studying the most rigid economy," observed one young woman in 1871, "if by any means I can have my maternal inheritance disentangled from its present embarrassments." James A. Ventress reported to his mother in early 1873 that Olivia Hollingsworth, daughter of the prominent planter Robert Semple, would soon be moving back to Wilkinson County from New Orleans. Her return, he suggested, "tends to confirm the rumor of [her husband] having no business qualifications; certainly if he was doing very well Miss Olivia would never consent to return to a plantation to live, having already tasted the sweets of plantation life."[59]

Not only were the gentry growing disillusioned with planting; worse, they were beginning to see in themselves values that they had long decried in northerners, bourgeois values. Henry Swayze spent all his time "hunting . . . for the almighty dollar that is always larger to his eye than his conscience," grumbled F. W. Ford to Alexander K. Farrar in 1874. "He will work when one is in sight—and be as liberal as any body if he can take in two dollars and put out one." The Reverend Joseph B. Stratton pronounced:

> The children of the present require to be instructed in the value and utility of all right undertaking, irrespective of the material gains or rewards that may follow them. In other words, they should be taught that an honorable life has not been lost if it has not issued in the acquisition of wealth or fame. The question "what will it pay" has come to be so currently asked in this mercenary age, that the use of it has bred a disposition to make literal "pay" the motive to every exertion, and to swell the appetite for "pay" to such inordinate bounds that contentment has become an impossible virtue.

Fanny Conner spoke similarly some years earlier, though perhaps with more despair: "What has become of the gentlemen of the country? The men of the 'old Regime'? What a complete revolution. Do you observe how *money* is worshipped now? More than ever before the men of high character—of sterling worth and integrity—without wealth, have no influence."[60]

59. M. C. Thornhill to Mr. Estlin, October 21, 1871, in William J. Pattison Papers, Southern Historical Collection, University of North Carolina, Chapel Hill; J. A. Ventress to Mrs. C. D. Ventress, February 8, 1873, in Trask-Ventress Family Papers, Folder 239. See also Roark, *Masters Without Slaves*, 201–202.

60. F. W. Ford to A. K. Farrar, May 13, 1874, in Alexander K. Farrar Papers, Depart-

No doubt, this widespread disaffection was partly a product of the generally unpromising economic situation. And yet, in truth, the prevailing feeling reflected something more profound. It reflected real changes in the fundamental organization of the plantation, changes in the relationship between former master and former slave. In short, planting had been transformed, and to their great unease the planters found that they were being transformed along with it.

ment of Archives and Manuscripts, Louisiana State University, Baton Rouge; Jos. B. Stratton, D.D., *Address Delivered July 23rd, 1875, Before the Trustees, Professors and Students of Jefferson College, Washington, Adams County, Miss.* (Natchez: Democrat Book and Job Print, 1875), 9–10; Fanny E. Conner to her husband, March 10, 1869, in Conner Papers.

# CHAPTER FIVE

# Transformation of the Plantation

Return to 1865. The freedman has taken to the road and thereby introduced the marketplace into the labor settlement. Now begins what C. Vann Woodward has described as "a more or less automatic and simultaneous withdrawal of master and slave from the more burdensome obligations of the old allegiance: duties on the one side, responsibilities on the other."[1] The paternalistic organization of the plantation starts to break down—but gradually and unevenly. Planter and, to a far lesser extent, freedman bring attitudes to the marketplace that inhibit immediate and unambiguous change.

That the gentry were cautious is understandable. Any elite has cause to be skeptical of a radical alteration in the status quo. In the case of the former slaveowner, such inherent conservatism was compounded by those ideological concerns that we have already noted. Then, too, there was the sheer physical separateness of the plantation itself. As Edgar T. Thompson has ably demonstrated, geographic isolation abetted that intense psychological and emotional interdependence that slavery bred between master and bondsman.[2] Under the circumstances, many planters and even some freedmen found it difficult coldly to disavow traditional obligations. But perhaps the main obstacle to change was simple self-interest. It is one thing to abandon duties; it is something quite different to relinquish rights and privileges. Neither side was inclined to sacrifice advantages enjoyed under the old system.

It should come as no surprise, then, that initially at least, many

1. C. Vann Woodward, *American Counterpoint: Slavery and Racism in the North-South Dialogue* (Boston: Little, Brown, 1971), 252.

2. Edgar T. Thompson, "The Plantation: The Physical Basis of Traditional Race Relations," in Edgar T. Thompson (ed.), *Race Relations and the Race Problem* (Durham, N.C.: Duke University Press, 1939); Edgar T. Thompson, "The Plantation" (Ph.D. dissertation, University of Chicago, 1932).

old responsibilities survived. For one reason or another, these were assumed to be enduring and unamenable to negotiation. Visitors to the district in 1866 found a regime similar in many essentials to that which had existed before the war. Changes were taking place, but slowly at first. In time the distinctive social and economic conditions of free labor would produce a fundamentally new and different plantation order; but the process took several years because of the attendant problem of undoing the past.

I

The principal objectives of the former slave at the end of the war were unquestionably land, education, and a secure family life. But in the first flush of freedom he also seemed determined to secure and expand his limited antebellum rights. After all, such rights had represented the more benevolent side of his life in bondage. He had little cause to renounce them now. Take the matter of gifts, for example. Slaveowners had occasionally favored their hands with clothes or small amounts of whiskey, tobacco, or cash. Blacks had come to expect these presents and to look upon them as deserved compensation, especially for extra or superior labor. Amelia Montgomery of Belmont in Claiborne County wrote to her husband in May, 1866, "Bartlett . . . thinks you ought to send him a present now that he has finished the disagreeable job of ginning that dusty cotton." Thomas W. Knox, a northern lessee, remarked perceptively, if somewhat critically, "Whatever little advantage the old system might have [the freedmen] wished to retain and ingraft upon their new life. To be compensated for labor was a condition of freedom which they joyfully accepted. To receive 'presents' was an apparent advantage of slavery which they did not wish to set aside."[3]

Nor were they inclined to relinquish their traditional holidays. On a trip through the region in 1865, J. T. Trowbridge encoun-

3. A. F. Montgomery to her husband, May 10, 1866, in Joseph A. Montgomery and Family Papers, Department of Archives and Manuscripts, Louisiana State University, Baton Rouge; Thomas W. Knox, *Camp-Fire and Cotton-Field: Southern Adventure in Time of War* (New York: Blelock, 1865), 411.

tered several Mississippi planters who had been to Memphis to "buy Christmas" for their hands. Wilmer Shields, manager of William Newton Mercer's four estates in Adams County, wrote to his employer on December 19 of that same year that the freedmen "seem now to have their heads full of Xmas, & propose to do but little after they have had their Xmas holy day. I presume they will knock off somewhere about Friday and we will see but little of them until after the New Year."[4]

Too, the former slaves sought to extend the leisure time they had customarily been allowed on weekends. "Saturday was fair," noted Amelia Montgomery in early 1866, "but we could not get any thing done that holliday if the whole Affrican race had to starve, they will not do any work on Saturday." Four years later, Susan Sillers Darden observed indignantly, "The negroes dont work any of Sat. hardly."[5]

Such behavior drove the Yankee lessees to distraction. Committed to the essential rightness of a system of thrift and hard work, they could not understand the apparent "laziness" of the freedman. Isaac Shoemaker, who was renting a place near Vicksburg, noted in his diary that "as they have been used in Slavery to have Saturday to themselves, I have given it; so that I have but 5 days of their work in a week and yet have to feed them 7 and cloth [sic] them."[6]

Furthermore, as products of a laissez faire society, the Yankees showed little willingness to provide those services that had been the responsibility of the planter under the old regime and that, in these early days at least, the former slave still expected: medical attention, care during old age, food, clothing. Whitelaw Reid ob-

4. J. T. Trowbridge, *The South: A Tour of Its Battlefields and Ruined Cities* (New York: Arno Press, 1969), 348; Wilmer [Shields] to Doctor [William N. Mercer], December 19, 1865, in William Newton Mercer Papers, Department of Archives and Manuscripts, Louisiana State University, Baton Rouge.

5. A. F. Montgomery to her husband, May 7, 1866, in Montgomery Papers; Susan Sillers Darden Diary (MS in Darden Family Papers, Z 82, Mississippi Department of Archives and History, Jackson), II, September 17, 1870.

6. Isaac Shoemaker Diary (MS in Manuscript Department, William R. Perkins Library, Duke University, Durham, N.C.), 28. For a thorough treatment of the reactions of the Yankees, see Lawrence N. Powell, *New Masters: Northern Planters During the Civil War and Reconstruction* (New Haven: Yale University Press, 1980), esp. Chap. 7.

served in early 1866, for example, that "Northern lessees feel all their notions of conducting business on business principles outraged at the idea of having to support all the old negroes, in addition to hiring the young ones." Reid defended his fellow Yankees, contending that in the end they generally allowed their "feelings" to get the better of their "business habits," but this was a generous assessment. Ben Montgomery, the articulate former slave who took over the Warren County estates of Joseph Davis after the war, testified that he was inundated with elderly blacks who had been forcibly removed from their homes "because they were not serviceable to the lessees of those plantations." The story was much the same in the area of medical care. Indeed, during the occupation, military authorities had to resort to a temporary levy on both freedmen and lessees to support the ailing and otherwise dependent.[7]

For their part, the old elite were considerably less surprised than the Yankees at the actions of the former slave; if anything, their ideology had prepared them for more widespread evidence of irresponsible behavior. At the same time, habit and an enduring sense of obligation led the gentry to continue to carry out many of their traditional duties, even after it began to become apparent that blacks would not be satisfied with an order structured along antebellum lines. Care for the aged provides a good example. "You must not turn the old folks on the place off," wrote Jacob Surget from his self-imposed exile in New York to his nephew James. "Let them remain and take good care of them, as long as they behave themselves." Lest it be suspected that Surget was simply humanitarian or somehow of a uniquely sensitive bent, note that he also remarked, "It is a pity the blacks were not all driven out of the country."[8]

7. Whitelaw Reid, *After the War: A Southern Tour* (Cincinnati: Moore, Wilstach & Baldwin, 1866), 534; deposition by B. T. Montgomery, [1865], in Joseph E. Davis and Family Papers, Z 1028, Box 1, Folder 1–ii, Mississippi Department of Archives and History, Jackson; John Eaton, *Grant, Lincoln and the Freedmen: Reminiscences of the Civil War with Special Reference to the Work for the Contrabands and Freedmen of the Mississippi Valley* (New York: Longmans, Green, 1907), 127, 141, 150–51; Powell, *New Masters*, 86.

8. Jacob [Surget] to Jimmy [Surget], December 8, 1868, January 18, 1869, both in possession of Mrs. Douglas MacNeil, Natchez. Leon F. Litwack, *Been in the Storm So Long: The Aftermath of Slavery* (New York: Knopf, 1979), 197, offers a different interpretation.

If they can be taken at their word, some former slaveowners were quite generous with the elderly. Wilmer Shields reported to his employer, William Newton Mercer, in early 1867, "I will not fail to attend to Christian and the old ones—They get all they want and ask for." James Gillespie observed that on his Hollywood place "many are old & infirm: All are fed & cared for & paid in money: have ground to cultivate and many other advantages."[9]

Nevertheless, instances of liberality were clearly exceptional. Most planters gave their former chattels no more than the free use of a small plot of land and perhaps a little food and some clothing. As in the past, aged hands were expected to perform certain tasks around the plantation. Men were required to care for livestock or mend broken equipment, women to help around the house or in the garden; members of both sexes served as domestics. The following passage from a letter by Amelia Montgomery to her husband shows how one planter dealt with the problem posed by an elderly former slave and his family:

> Old Sams family are a necessary evil, we dont pay them any wages & they do all the house work, that is milking, working in the patches, going to town, wood cutting, driven up stock [sic], washing & part of the ironing, scouring, & helping Statira, & making a sweet potatoe patch for me besides the Boys patch & Old Sam is a kind of watcher for the boys, for which services they get no wages, only for their living, & a chance to make a little corn for themselves, & I am oblige [sic] to give them bread & a little meat once a day. Vegetables & milk also help along. Old Sam takes care of the Hogs and mends pickets & c. & c.[10]

Certain former slaveowners took the opportunity afforded by Emancipation to disclaim responsibility for the medical expenses of their hands; but many did not—at least not immediately—and almost all continued to offer personal care and attention to the sick. In addition, as in the past, places were found for the infirm and physically handicapped. James Gillespie created simple tasks

---

9. Wilmer [Shields] to Doctor [William N. Mercer], April 27, 1867, in Mercer Papers; list of hired hands on Hollywood, July 12, 1865, in James A. Gillespie and Family Papers, Department of Archives and Manuscripts, Louisiana State University, Baton Rouge.

10. Reid, *After the War*, 507–508, 533; Wm. Phillips to Mrs. [Lizzie] Hamilton, May 8, 1869, in Charles D. Hamilton and Family Papers, Mississippi Department of Archives and History, Jackson; A. F. Montgomery to her husband, May 4, 1868, in Montgomery Papers.

around his house and garden at Hollywood in 1865 for Hannah, who was blind, and Louiza, "infirm." Four years later, William Newton Mercer was still supporting two blind freedmen at Laurel Hill.[11]

As for those infants and young black children orphaned or abandoned during the war, most were taken in by other former slaves or turned over to Federal asylums. It is noteworthy, however, that at least some remained on the plantations, where they were cared for by their former masters and presumably put to work at the age of five or six. Here, for what it is worth, is the recollection of one former Jefferson County bondsman as reported by a white W.P.A. interviewer in the 1930s: "When peace was declared my mother and father went to Vicksburg with the Yankees and left four of us poor little children behind. Old marster brought us up to the Big House and was good to us. Lots of children were there who had been deserted by their parents, and marster took care of them all."[12]

There is no need to exaggerate the benevolence of the former slaveowners. Their humane actions—humane by comparison with the actions of the northerners—derived from a perceived self-interest and an ideology deeply rooted in the old regime. If this ideology told them to care for the aged, it also told them that they were entitled to unquestioning obedience from all blacks. In any case and for whatever reason, through 1865 and into 1866 the gentry continued to acknowledge an obligation to their hands.

These were curious times, the first months after the war. The marketplace was tentatively introduced, with freedmen beginning to move from place to place seeking to improve their condition. But because there was still near unanimous agreement among the gentry that blacks could not be trusted with any meaningful degree of freedom or responsibility, and because, to repeat, planters were willing to carry out many of their traditional duties, bargaining

---

11. Memorandum, March 10, 1865, in Gillespie Papers; Wilmer [Shields] to Doctor [William N. Mercer], November 8, 1869, in Mercer Papers.

12. Litwack, *Been in the Storm So Long*, 191; J. Eaton, *Grant, Lincoln and the Freedmen*, 201; Herbert G. Gutman, *The Black Family in Slavery and Freedom, 1790–1925* (New York: Pantheon Books, 1976), 226–28; W.P.A. Records, RG 60, for Jefferson County (Typescript in Mississippi Department of Archives and History, Jackson), Vol. XXXII, Pt. 1, p. 264.

was confined to very limited and particular kinds of issues. Prospective laborers were offered, in addition to higher wages, not control over their own labor or the opportunity to lease land, but the extension of existing privileges: more free time on Saturday, for example, liberal gifts of whiskey, and larger garden patches. Representative was the situation on William Newton Mercer's Laurel Hill, where, at the end of 1865, negotiations revolved around the demand of the hands that they be allowed to go to Natchez on occasion to market their potatoes, chickens, and eggs.[13]

The freedmen, themselves somewhat oriented toward past objectives and as yet unaware of the full extent of their potential influence under the new conditions, did not at first effectively press to broaden the range of issues open to bargaining. For a variety of reasons, then, the initial impact of the marketplace on the plantation was not so much to upset existing relations as to modify them. For the black, freedom was not confirmed; rather, slavery was ameliorated.

Had the freedman, like the planter, believed in the essential justness of a patriarchic order, in the years to come negotiations would no doubt have remained narrowly circumscribed. Blacks would have sought improved medical care, increased security for old age, more leisure time, and larger rations of food and clothing. But, in fact, except in the first months after the war, the former slaves showed little interest in the preservation of their traditional rights. They learned quickly that by moving around they could secure not only gardens and whiskey but social autonomy and a measure of economic independence. They started to push harder for substantive changes, and as the united resistance of the gentry gradually broke down, a new plantation system began to emerge.

II

The war that freed the slave also cast him as a wage laborer. With few exceptions, Federal authorities assumed that the future of the black lay as a hired hand on the plantation of his former owner.

13. Wilmer [Shields] to Doctor [William N. Mercer], December 19, 1865, in Mercer Papers.

Accordingly, during the occupation, officials in the lower Mississippi Valley implemented minimum wage rates intended to ease the process of adjustment by ensuring the freedmen acceptable compensation for their labor. In the spring of 1865 the prescribed figures stood at ten dollars per month for a first-class male hand, eight dollars for a second-class hand, and six dollars for a third. The corresponding scale for women was eight, six, and five dollars. Boys under fourteen were to receive three dollars, and girls, two. In addition, employers were expected to provide their laborers with rations and clothing.[14]

Although the government did indeed regard these as *minimum* rates, former slaveowners and lessees rarely offered more than the specified figures during the occupation or in the first days after the war. Through the following months, however, perceptible changes began to take place. J. T. Trowbridge reported in early 1866 that the majority of planters were paying over twelve dollars per month and rations. J. Floyd King wrote from Natchez at the beginning of the year that "wages for field hands vary from $8 to $15—women the former and men (wagoners) the latter—mostly the men hands receive $12 pr month with rations."[15]

In some sections, compensation climbed even higher. Whitelaw Reid observed disapprovingly that, by the end of 1865, "competition had driven the planters who needed hands the worst to offering extravagant wages. Twenty dollars per month, with rations, lodging, etc." The landowner who lived far from a major town or back from the river found that he had to make substantial financial concessions to overcome the disadvantage of his location. The former slaves on Brokenburn in Madison Parish threatened to move on unless Amanda Stone agreed to wages of twenty to twenty-five dollars per month plus their usual rations. Even when she ac-

14. Bell Irvin Wiley, *Southern Negroes, 1861–1865* (New Haven: Yale University Press, 1965), 222–29; Regulations of Provost Marshals of Freedmen, in James S. Allen and Family Papers, Z 14, Box 3, Folder 27, Mississippi Department of Archives and History, Jackson.

15. See, for example, Alden Spooner Forbes Diary (MS in Mississippi Department of Archives and History, Jackson), II, October 28, 1865; "Calculations About Planting with Free Nigers [*sic*]" (MS in possession of Mr. and Mrs. Boyd Sojourner, Natchez). Trowbridge, *The South*, 366; J. Floyd King to Mallery [King], January 18, 1866, in Thomas Butler King Papers, Southern Historical Collection, University of North Carolina, Chapel Hill.

ceded to their demands, many chose to try their luck elsewhere. Most planters would have sympathized with Wilmer Shields of Adams County, who complained in early 1867, "They demand exorbitant wages. And the more the white owner of the soil yields, the more they require."[16]

The freedmen also used their newly found mobility to undermine the power of the lash. The overseer on A. C. Britton's Eutaw reported to his employer at the end of 1865, "Sally tells me that Janie Willis and perhaps others with them, will be here about Christmas to pay us a visit kill hogs & c. I should like they would defer their visit, since they were here I hear no other talk in the kitchen but Civil Law. They say they were told by *them* that in Natchez no one dares hit you ('without the law being put to you'). I should not wonder if another visit did not make them, leave here to go where they can find Civil Law." Although Federal officials were disinclined to interfere in the daily operations of the plantation or to question the authority of the planter, they generally supported the efforts of the freedmen to put an end to physical coercion. A mate on a steam packet in early 1866 griped to J. T. Trowbridge, "You can't hit a nigger now, but these d——d Yankees sons of b——s have you up and make you pay for it." Of course, instances of beatings can be found during Reconstruction and long afterward; but violence ceased to be central to the economic organization of the plantation. Ten years after the war, Edward King claimed that he could discover no trace of forced labor in the district.[17]

Pressure from freedmen was only one factor determining labor arrangements in the aftermath of the war. The economic distress

16. Reid, *After the War*, 561; John Q. Anderson (ed.), *Brokenburn: The Journal of Kate Stone, 1861–1868* (Baton Rouge: Louisiana State University Press, 1972), 368; Wilmer [Shields] to Doctor [William N. Mercer], January 9, 1867, in Mercer Papers. For a discussion of the wage system, see Robert Higgs, *Competition and Coercion: Blacks in the American Economy, 1865–1914* (New York: Cambridge University Press, 1977), 43–45.

17. James W. Melvin to A. C. Britton, December 1, 1865, in Audley Clark Britton and Family Papers, Department of Archives and Manuscripts, Louisiana State University, Baton Rouge; Trowbridge, *The South*, 389; Edward King, *The Great South* (New York: Arno Press, 1969), 299. One planter told Trowbridge in early 1866 that he had a contract with his former slaves that allowed him "to whoop em when I pleased." Needless to say, his claim is highly suspect. Trowbridge, *The South*, 390.

accompanying the short crops of 1866 and 1867 temporarily depressed wages and, more important, led to a shift in the nature of
compensation. Most planters now took to paying their hands with
shares, not cash. In part, the gentry simply wanted a valid excuse
for withholding disbursements until after the crop had been marketed.[18] But their principal objective was to limit their own financial risks while, at the same time, giving the freedmen a vested interest in the efficient operation of the plantation. Working for
cash, the former slave had evinced little concern for the ultimate
success of the growing cotton. "You are in error when you suppose
[the freedmen on Laurel Hill] have an equal interest in the crop,"
complained Wilmer Shields to his employer in the summer of 1867.
"They get their monthly wages in money and have, unfortunately,
*no* interest in the crop."[19]

     Under the share system the landowner normally gave his freed-
men one-third of the harvest plus rations. However, as might be
expected of a fluid situation, there was some variation in agreements. Thomas T. Davis of Beechland, for example, allowed his laborers one-third of the crop plus rations and, in addition, permitted them one-half day off on Saturday with the understanding that
they would be charged for provisions "used by them when not at
work." Samuel Postlethwaite of Louisiana contracted to give his
hands two-thirds of the potatoes and hogs and one-third of the
cotton on Westmoreland while requiring them to procure their
own supplies. But as he acknowledged, his was an untypical case.
"I have quite an advantage on my neighbors this year," he informed an uncle, "as they are generally giving one third of cotton
& corn & feeding & clothing besides or one half & they feed &
clothe themselves. I look upon a man as losing money that gives a
third & feeds & clothes, & I think they ought to be run out of the

     18. A. F. Montgomery to her husband, January 2, 1868, in Montgomery Papers; Vernon
Lane Wharton, *The Negro in Mississippi, 1865–1890* (New York: Harper & Row, 1965),
68; Roger L. Ransom and Richard Sutch, *One Kind of Freedom: The Economic Consequences of Emancipation* (New York: Cambridge University Press, 1977), 60. For a discussion of antebellum precedents for sharecropping, see Theodore Saloutos, "Southern
Agriculture and the Problems of Readjustment, 1865–1877," *Agricultural History*, XXX
(1956), 70–71.
     19. J. Floyd King to Lin [Caperton], September 8, 1866, in King Papers; Wilmer [Shields]
to Doctor [William N. Mercer], June 26, 1867, in Mercer Papers.

Parish as they destroy the chances of others." It is suggestive of the marketplace power of the freedman that within three years Postlethwaite was operating under the same terms that he so unreservedly discredited in 1867: rations plus one-third of the crop—and, incidentally, half of Saturday off, private garden patches, and the free use of plows and mules.[20]

Still, the system of share wages scarcely satisfied the former slaves. While it did allow them a measure of control over their own economic destiny, it left them vulnerable to short crops or a depressed cotton market. After the disastrous harvest of 1867, many freedmen concluded that the necessary risks far outweighed the potential benefits. Then, too, because the share laborer only received his pay at the end of the year, he could not avail himself of the higher wages regularly offered at harvesttime. Nor could he usually find the means to make cash purchases. Merchandise bought on credit invariably cost 25 to 100 percent more than goods paid for with cash. The freedman who accepted his wages in shares was liable to find, like the share-tenant who came later, that he was deeply in debt at the conclusion of the year.[21]

In the end, however, the blacks were simply opposed to any system built around wages, and with good reason. As slaves they had worked in gangs under the direction of a driver or overseer; as hired hands they worked under conditions that, to their way of thinking, were not significantly different. When Whitelaw Reid traveled through the region in early 1866, he discovered that the big estates were being run much as they had been before the war: laborers worked in large units under close and constant supervision. Reid himself concluded that the system was efficient, acceptable to the former slaves, and entirely necessary to the successful operation of the plantation,[22] and the vast majority of planters

20. Account for 1867, Sam Postlethwaite to Uncle [James] Gillespie, March 27, 1867, January 20, 1870, all in Gillespie Papers.

21. For a discussion of the freedman's preference for cash, see Wharton, *The Negro in Mississippi*, 65. By contrast, Joe Gray Taylor (*Louisiana Reconstructed, 1863–1877* [Baton Rouge: Louisiana State University Press, 1974], 373) contends that blacks, in fact, favored sharecropping.

22. Reid, *After the War*, Chaps. 47 and 48.

would have agreed. Through 1866 and 1867, they held determinedly to the routine that had served them so well in the past.

But, in fact, the freedmen were far from content. They resented strict regulation and were quick to make their dissatisfaction manifest. In the fall of 1865, for instance, the former slaves of Lemuel P. Conner walked off his Rifle Point plantation in Concordia Parish in protest over the continued employment of their old overseer. One planter assured J. T. Trowbridge in early 1866:

> I should get along very well with my niggers if I could only get my superintendent to treat them decently. Instead of cheering and encouraging them, he bullies and scolds them, and sometimes so far forgets himself as to kick and beat them. Now they are free they won't stand it. They stood it when they were slaves because they had to. He can't get the notion out of his head that they are still somehow slaves. When I see things going right badly, I take him, and give him a good talking to. Then for about three days he'll use 'em better, and everything goes smooth. But first I know there's more bullying and beating, and there's more niggers bound to quit.

Another former slaveowner confided to Whitelaw Reid that many of the overseers "thought they could knock and cuff niggers about as they used to; and by the time they discovered their mistake, the niggers were leaving, and keeping others from coming in their places." Prudent landowners hired black men to run their operations or, like David P. Williams of Adams County, allowed the laborers to pick a foreman from among themselves. A black planter in Louisiana told Stephen Powers in 1871 that he worked in the fields alongside his hands and "they do twice the labor they would for a white overseer."[23]

Still, the real problem, as far as the freedman was concerned, was not that some overseers were vicious, but that there were overseers at all. Strict supervision was incompatible with his vision of

23. Fanny E. Conner to her husband, October 21, 1865, in Lemuel Parker Conner and Family Papers, Department of Archives and Manuscripts, Louisiana State University, Baton Rouge; Trowbridge, *The South*, 367; Reid, *After the War*, 572; agreement, February 4, 1870, in Adams County Deed Records, Vol. QQ, p. 50, Adams County Courthouse, Natchez; Stephen Powers, *Afoot and Alone: A Walk from Sea to Sea by the Southern Route* (Hartford: Columbian Book Co., 1872), 96.

the future. Not that the former slaves were lazy, as so many of their white contemporaries charged. But they wanted the flexibility to adjust their labor to the rhythms and demands of family life. "Andy wants to stay with his family," reads an entry in the diary of Susan Sillers Darden for 1866, "but Betsey is not willing to work in the field. Hester will not stay. Ria says she is going to get a home."[24] For such freedmen, "getting a home" had very definite connotations. Ultimately it meant time for husbands, wives, and children to be together, and the opportunity to work for themselves in whatever way they should choose. It also meant having land of their own.

At the end of 1865, blacks throughout the South refused to hire out for the coming year, believing that Congress was about to partition the plantations of the gentry. In the Natchez district the situation was aggravated by speculators seeking to unsettle the labor situation and thereby drive down the price of real estate. Only economic necessity and repeated appeals by the Freedmen's Bureau induced the former slaves to contract for wages again.[25]

So hopeful were the blacks, and so convinced of the justice of their cause, that rumors of imminent land redistribution continued to surface long after any realistic chance for radical congressional reform had disappeared. Alvan C. Gillem, commissioner of the bureau in Mississippi, complained in December of 1867, "There seems to be a wide spread belief, which is daily increasing among the freedmen, that the land in this state is to be divided among them, and in some sections of the state this illusion is assuming a practical form by the freedmen refusing to contract

24. Darden Diary, II, January 2, 1866. Observers were struck by the determination of black women to spend more time with their children and fewer hours in the fields. See, for example, Reid, *After the War*, 488; "The Cotton Trade of the World," *De Bow's Review*, After the War Series, VI (July, 1869), 609. On the ramifications of this development, see, especially, Ransom and Sutch, *One Kind of Freedom*, 44; Higgs, *Competition and Coercion*, 40; Litwack, *Been in the Storm So Long*, 244–45, 340–42.

25. *Senate Executive Documents*, 39th Cong., 1st Sess., No. 2, p. 31; James Wilford Garner, *Reconstruction in Mississippi* (New York: Macmillan, 1901), 134; Glyde [Swain] to his father, January 11, 1866 (microfilm copy from Wisconsin Historical Society), in Samuel Glyde Swain Papers, Mississippi Department of Archives and History, Jackson. The determination of the freedmen to secure land is described in depth in Edward Magdol, *A Right to the Land: Essays on the Freedmen's Community* (Westport, Conn.: Greenwood Press, 1977), esp. Chap. 6.

for the next year, or to leave the premises they have cultivated this year."[26]

Nonetheless, while blacks placed hope in the Federal authorities, they prudently withheld faith. On the contrary, they indicated a willingness—indeed, a determination—to seek land on their own, through the marketplace. When Dr. Joseph Warren, superintendent of freedmen's schools in Mississippi, warned a former slave in early 1866, "The whites intend to compel you to hire out to them," he was answered bluntly. "What if we should compel them to lease us lands?" Freedmen pressed this issue each year at contract time, much to the annoyance of the gentry. Samuel Postlethwaite of Westmoreland in Louisiana observed unhappily to an uncle in Mississippi in 1869, "The general idea amongst our freedmen is to buy or lease, as with you."[27]

In the first few years after the war, however, the former slaves made little headway. Most members of the gentry were opposed to attempts of any kind to break up the plantation, even when white purchasers could be found. As for the sale or leasing of land to blacks, that was regarded as out of the question. Whitelaw Reid observed in early 1866, "In many portions of the Mississippi Valley the feeling against any ownership of the soil by the negroes is so strong, that the man who would sell small tracts to them would be in actual personal danger. Every effort will be made to prevent negroes from acquiring land, and even the renting of small tracts to them is held to be unpatriotic and unworthy of a good citizen." There were notable exceptions. The brother of Jefferson Davis sold his two estates in Warren County to a former servant. But, as Reid suggested, such transactions were rare.[28]

Gradually, however, conditions began to change. The continuing labor shortage abetted the efforts of the freedman to put an

26. Alvan C. Gillem to Major General E. C. C. Ord, December 10, 1867 (typescript), in W.P.A. Records, RG 60, for Warren County, Folder: Reconstruction, Mississippi Department of Archives and History, Jackson. On the question of land confiscation and redistribution, see Claude F. Oubre, *Forty Acres and a Mule: The Freedmen's Bureau and Black Land Ownership* (Baton Rouge: Louisiana State University Press, 1978).

27. Trowbridge, *The South*, 362; Sam Postlethwaite to Uncle [James] Gillespie, March 14, 1869, in Gillespie Papers.

28. Reid, *After the War*, 564–65; bill of sale, November 15, 1866, in Davis Papers, Box 1, Folder 8.

end to the gang system and acquire some land to work on his own. Here and there, to secure hands, a planter agreed to dispense with his overseer or to experiment with some sort of leasing arrangement. The relative success of these ventures broke the ideological consensus that blacks would act responsibly only when under the constant supervision of a white man. Those former slaveowners who remained doubtful found that they had to make concessions of their own in order to remain competitive in the labor market.

"I look upon this as the last year [the freedmen] will work in gangs," remarked Samuel Postlethwaite with evident disappointment in early 1869. In place of the old system emerged a form of "squad" labor in which, as *De Bow's Review* noted in the summer of 1869, "from two to eight hands only work together, in many instances a single family."[29] Squads not only were considerably smaller than gangs but they normally operated without an overseer and were comprised of freedmen who had at least agreed, if not chosen, to work together.

Jesse Darden of Jefferson County began to organize his hands in squads as early as 1868. Other planters followed in later years. In 1870, Antonio Yznaga del Valle leased his Ravenswood plantation in Concordia Parish to several squads of former slaves. The following year, John H. Thorne rented his Adams County estate to nine squads, varying in size from three to seven laborers. Not all places were organized in this manner. Many freedmen contracted individually; and in some corners of the district, gangs and overseers could be found into the 1880s. Charlotte D. Ventress, for example, continued to employ an overseer on her Wilkinson County plantation. And while William S. Lovell of Palmyra in Warren County called his labor units "squads," the units were quite large—the plowing "squad" had twenty-six hands—and operated under a foreman.[30] But the fact remains that, by about 1870, squads had become prevalent on plantations in the district.

29. Sam Postlethwaite to Uncle [James] Gillespie March 14, 1869, in Gillespie Papers; "The Cotton Trade of the World," 609. See also Ralph Shlomowitz, "The Transition from Slave to Freedman: Labor Arrangements in Southern Agriculture, 1865–1870" (Ph.D. dissertation, University of Chicago, 1978), 65–66.

30. Darden Diary, II, January 1, 1870; contract, January 1, 1870, in Concordia Parish General Mortgages, Vol. O, p. 679; contract, February 10, 1871, in Adams County Deed

This development, if not dependent on the rise of leasing—wage laborers too preferred to work in small, family-oriented groups— was clearly facilitated by it. Squad labor and tenancy appeared and spread together. In 1868, for the first time, a significant minority of planters in the district agreed to rent to freedmen. Within a year, perhaps two, most plantations were being run in this way. As for the terms of rental, initially the general preference was for a shared distribution of the crop, just as there had been under wage labor. Indeed, this element of continuity between wage and leasing arrangements has led many historians to overlook basic differences between the two systems and thereby underestimate the period of labor adjustment after the war. Under share wages the freedman was a hired hand. His labor belonged to the landowner, who retained major authority over the process of production. Gang labor persisted on many plantations where there were share wages, as did the overseer. Under share-renting, on the other hand, the freedman's labor was, within limitations, his own. He secured the use of some property and maybe a few implements. While usually subject to general contractual directives, he was often free to make daily operational decisions. Perhaps more significant, he had the satisfaction of knowing that, for one year at least, he had some right to a piece of land.[31]

In the Natchez district, share-rents tended to be one-half of the crop if the landowner provided operating expenses and feed for the stock, or one-quarter or one-third if he provided only land. There was, however, considerable variation. Nancy Pinson of Wilkinson County agreed in 1867 to give her hands "lands, mules, and half of the farming utensils necessary to carry on the planta-

Records, Vol. QQ, p. 519; Charlotte D. Ventress to C. Gallagher, December 31, 1870, in Trask-Ventress Family Papers, Z 607, Folder 211, Mississippi Department of Archives and History, Jackson; William S. Lovell Plantation Records (MSS in Southern Historical Collection, University of North Carolina, Chapel Hill), II, 30, 42, 44; "Old Fell" [William S. Lovell] to his wife, April 4, 1875, in Quitman Family Papers, Southern Historical Collection, University of North Carolina, Chapel Hill.
    31. For a recent and pointed discussion of this issue, see Harold D. Woodman, "Sequel to Slavery: The New History Views the Postbellum South," *Journal of Southern History*, XLIII (1977), 551. On the rise of tenancy, see Ransom and Sutch, *One Kind of Freedom*, 68–70; Joseph D. Reid, Jr., "Sharecropping as an Understandable Market Response: The Post-Bellum South," *Journal of Economic History*, XXXIII (1973), 109–120.

tion, also feed the mules six months, and have any repairs necessary done to the Cotton Press." In return, they paid her one-half of the produce raised on the plantation. Robert Cox contracted to bear one-half of the operating costs on his Jefferson County plantation in 1871 and to provide his tenants with teams and one-quarter of the necessary feed; he too received one-half of the crop. On the other hand, the freedmen on the neighboring plantation of Bisland Shields undertook to pay all expenses themselves and rented for one-third. Two years later, the tenants on John M. Marshall's Concordia Parish plantation leased under similar terms for one-quarter of the crop.[32]

Robert Fogel and Stanley Engerman have argued that former slaves who elected to lease rather than to hire themselves out made a major financial sacrifice. The earnings of wage laborers, they contend, were more than 100 percent higher than those of share-tenants.[33] Although this figure is difficult to substantiate, it is easy to identify the crux of the issue. Wages were generally for one-third of the crop plus rations. The renter retained two-thirds of the crop but had to pay operating expenses and acquire food for his family. Given the costly nature of credit in the region, it is understandable that many tenants may have fared worse than did the average wage laborer. All the same, it would probably be wrong simply to ascribe this circumstance to the price the former slave was willing to pay for liberation from gang labor, as Fogel and Engerman have suggested. Because the share-renter normally retained a substantially greater portion of the crop than did the hired hand, he had a better opportunity to avail himself of the benefits of a single good crop. Most freedmen were willing to make certain financial sacrifices to secure favorable working conditions. But there seems little reason to believe that they were willing to pawn the future.

32. Contract, January 10, 1867, in Mrs. Nancy Pinson Papers, Department of Archives and Manuscripts, Louisiana State University, Baton Rouge; mortgage, January 21, 1871, lease, January 8, 1871, both in Jefferson County Deed Records, Vol. BB, pp. 656, 707, Mississippi Department of Archives and History, Jackson; lease, February 18, 1873, in T. Otis Baker Papers, Z 72, Box 3, Folder 25, Mississippi Department of Archives and History, Jackson.

33. Robert William Fogel and Stanley L. Engerman, *Time on the Cross: The Economics of American Negro Slavery* (Boston: Little, Brown, 1974), 238.

In any event, share-renting was relatively short-lived in some sections of the Natchez district. During the 1870s many planters began to lease their property for a specified quantity of cotton. Under this system, rents tended to vary according to the capabilities of the individual laborer and the productivity of the land to be cultivated.[34] Charles Nordhoff contended in 1875 that most tenants were paying about 80 pounds of "clean" cotton per acre. Edward King, who visited the district at about the same time, suggested that the usual figure was 430 pounds for six acres, or about 10 pounds per acre less than Nordhoff claimed. The Nordhoff estimate was probably more accurate. Most agreements fell between the 67 pounds per acre charged by Celestina A. Page on her Concordia Parish plantation in 1878 and the 90 pounds per acre charged by John F. Jenkins on Demarcation the following year. Still, there were exceptions. Jenkins rented his land at Elgin for 250 pounds per acre in 1879. Alternatively, Eli C. Briscoe leased a portion of his Claiborne County plantation in 1871 for 30 pounds of cotton and 17 bushels of corn per acre.[35]

A few planters rented for cash, usually for anywhere from four or five dollars per acre inland to ten or eleven dollars per acre on or near the Mississippi. Katherine Minor, for instance, let out property on her Carthage and Blackburn estates in Adams County for between eight and eleven dollars per acre each year from 1870 to 1874. During the same period, her neighbor James Surget leased Linwood at from four to eleven dollars per acre, the lower rents falling to those tenants who took the largest tracts. However, there were serious obstacles to cash agreements. To protect his interests the landowner wanted payment early in the year; yet very few tenants could come up with cash before their cotton had been marketed. Contracts between Katherine Minor and the tenants on Carthage in 1870 called for half of the rent to be paid when the

34. On the fixed rent system, see Higgs, *Competition and Coercion*, 50–51.

35. Charles Nordhoff, *The Cotton States in the Spring and Summer of 1875* (New York: D. Appleton, 1876), 72; King, *The Great South*, 276; agreement of lease, January 23, 1878, in Concordia Parish General Mortgages, Vol. T, p. 547; "Lease of Demarcation," in Elgin Journal, 1879–80 (MS in possession of Mr. and Mrs. Hyde D. Jenkins, Natchez); lease with mortgage, March 24, 1871, in Claiborne County Deed Records, Vol. II, p. 325, Mississippi Department of Archives and History, Jackson.

agreement was signed and the remainder by September 1. Within two years, economic realities had forced deferral of any payment until after the first harvest.[36] Furthermore, cash rentals clearly did not apportion risks or potential benefits evenly. The freedman's profit or loss was closely tied to annual fluctuations in the cotton market. Few landlords felt comfortable with such an unpredictable and uncontrollable situation.

A fixed rent in kind distributed risks more equitably. When cotton prices were high, both planter and tenant would benefit; when low, both would suffer. Of course, share-renting provided the same protection and in addition ensured that neither party would bear the full brunt of a short crop. But that may explain why some landlords apparently preferred to lease for a set quantity of cotton; they could claim their rent out of the first harvest and leave the freedman to suffer the consequences of a crop failure. On the other hand, tenants too had something to gain from a fixed rent in kind. Observers noted that land in the district was likely to produce between one-half and one bale of cotton per acre, with property in Louisiana being somewhat more fertile than that in Mississippi.[37] The tenant who leased for one bale per five or six acres had a potential advantage over the share-renter who took home two-thirds of the crop. Imagine, for instance, a freedman who worked six acres and produced one bale per acre. If he leased for shares, he would pay his landlord two bales and keep four for himself. If however, he rented the land at one bale per five acres, he would retain four and one-fifth bales, if one bale per six acres, five bales. In terms of average financial return, the two renting systems were approximately similar—most freedmen in the district would have made about the same if they rented for shares as they would leasing for a specified amount of cotton. But the exceptional worker could benefit from the latter arrangement and undoubtedly favored it.

36. See, for example, various leases, 1870–74, in Adams County Deed Records, Vol. PP, pp. 712, 714, 773, Vol. QQ, pp. 422, 489, 505, Vol. RR, pp. 274, 280, 321, Vol. SS, pp. 263, 256, 251, Vol. TT, pp. 87, 416.

37. Nordhoff, *The Cotton States*, 72; King, *The Great South*, 275. See also Ransom and Sutch, *One Kind of Freedom*, esp. Chap. 3; Reid, "Sharecropping as an Understandable Market Response," 120–27.

Leasing under any terms represented something of a triumph for the freedman. It ensured an end to aspects of the old regime that he had particularly resented. And it facilitated his efforts to organize his life and labor around his family. But the triumph, while impressive, was incomplete. For reasons to be explored, most blacks found it difficult to save enough money to acquire farms of their own. Those who did try to purchase land faced the lingering, if diminished, opposition of the white community. Too, tenants only rarely secured as much independence as they would have liked. Squads were formed through negotiation and compromise. On occasion, the planter surrendered to the wishes of his hands; in 1872, for example, Lewis Ker reluctantly agreed to the dissolution of a productive squad when two members of the group declined to continue working with a third. But it was not always the landowner who gave ground. The manager of the Madison Parish estate of Judge John Perkins reported at the end of 1878 that "Jim and York had to be sepeated [*sic*], they have gathered very little over their rent. Youngsters like them have to have a leader. Jim is located between Abe Thoms & Ashwood. York is with Bob Miles who raised him. Zed I dont know what will become of him, but some settled man, or tenant will take him." Planters were careful to ensure that each squad had a responsible leader. And they occasionally demanded that squads pledge to assist each other in times of need.[38]

Like Judge Perkins, some planters—mostly absentee landowners—thought it necessary to hire managers to look after their estates. Antonio Yznaga del Valle employed a superintendent on Ravenswood in Concordia Parish in 1870. Five years later, James Surget arranged to have J. F. Moriarty run his several Adams County plantations for $1,800. The duties of the manager varied from place to place, but often they were theoretically broad. Consider, for example, the following clause in the 1870 contract for Ravenswood: "Since the common interest requires and intelligent

38. Lewis B. Ker to his sister, February 1, 1872, in Mary Susan Ker Papers, Southern Historical Collection, University of North Carolina, Chapel Hill; J. Stanbrough to Judge [John Perkins], December 16, 1878, in John Perkins Papers, Southern Historical Collection, University of North Carolina, Chapel Hill; Darden Diary, II, December 5, 1870.

heads direct that [the tenants] will obey all lawful orders and directions of the manager and upon failure to do so and if any of the contracting parties become profane, insolent, drunk or Refractory, he or they shall be discharged." On many plantations where managers were not employed, landlords reserved a like authority for themselves. The freedmen on James C. Brandon's Adams County place agreed to work under his "direction and control" during 1873. Alfred V. Davis of Sycamore in Concordia Parish secured the right in 1876 to expel any tenant who became "refractory, quarrelsome, disorderly, lazy, negligent, or refuses to obey the orders of said Davis."[39]

But contractual provisions notwithstanding, it was difficult for the planter or his representative to exercise strict control without the whip. The superintendent of the New South plantation was not a latter-day overseer. His principal responsibilities were financial, and only occasionally did he make decisions regarding the organization of labor. Those managers who attempted to take a more active role complained repeatedly that the former slave adhered to a schedule of his own. "It is almost an impossibility to get ground broken up," lamented F. K. Winchester in late May, 1879. "It appears to be too hard work for this season of the year. Kelly 'bucks against' it and Alec shirks it. If you get ½ of what you direct to be ploughed, broken up, you may count yourself lucky."[40]

Such independence of action on the part of the freedmen had important consequences for the everyday operation of the plantation. Landowners found that they could not count on the hands to do routine work related to the general maintenance of property. As

39. Contract, January 1, 1870, in Concordia Parish General Mortgages, Vol. O, p. 679; account for 1876, in possession of Mrs. Douglas MacNeil, Natchez; lease, March 15, 1873, in Adams County Deed Records, Vol. SS, p. 277; various agreements, March 25, 1876, in Concordia Parish General Mortgages, Vol. S, pp. 385–408.

40. M. B. Hammond observed in the 1890s that, on some big plantations in Mississippi, "authority little short of compulsion is often exercised by the managers" (*The Cotton Industry: An Essay in American Economic History* [New York: Johnson Reprint Corp., 1966], 186); Vernon L. Wharton (*The Negro in Mississippi*, Chap. 5) has argued that planters were unable to maintain rigid control over their laborers. For two recent views, see Reid, "Sharecropping as an Understandable Market Response," 109–120, 126; Jay R. Mandle, *The Roots of Black Poverty: The Southern Plantation Economy After the Civil War* (Durham, N.C.: Duke University Press, 1978), 19. Elgin Journal, 1879–80, May 26, 1879.

Thomas Clark and Albert Kirwan have noted, tenants "approached the land with the objective of getting as much income as possible in one crop season. It was an unusual tenant who looked upon his relationship to the land as more than a one year's investment."[41] Why bother, then, to tend to livestock or repair fences?

Some landlords tried to circumvent this problem by legally binding renters to do ordinary chores. The contracts for Ravenswood in 1872, for example, obligated the freedmen to perform "a due proportion of the plantation [labor] necessary . . . to carry on the General work of the plantation." But stipulations of this kind were not easily enforced. Most planters found that they had to pay their tenants to do maintenance work or, alternatively, bring in wage laborers. In 1872, for instance, Alexander K. Farrar agreed to reimburse the freedmen on Commencement one dollar for each day spent at work not directly related to production of the crop— cutting wood, say, or repairing fences. The previous year, Jesse Darden gave his hands seventy-five cents each time they split one hundred rails. The records of Washington Ford for 1887 include a payment of ten cents to a tenant for sharpening an implement.[42]

With good reason, historians are increasingly turning to contracts between landowners and freedmen to understand the economic reorganization of the plantation after the war. Here, better than anywhere else, can be found the trial and error that characterized labor arrangements into the 1870s. Consider, for a moment, the experiences of James Gillespie of Adams County. In 1865 he bound his entire labor force to one brief agreement in which he promised to provide cash wages, clothing, and rations in return for "faithful" service. Like the vast majority of his fellow planters, he hope-

41. Thomas D. Clark and Albert D. Kirwan, *The South Since Appomattox: A Century of Regional Change* (New York: Oxford University Press, 1967), 93. Even as wage laborers the former slaves had resisted the more disagreeable tasks around the plantation. James L. Sellers, "The Economic Incidence of the Civil War in the South," *Mississippi Valley Historical Review*, XIV (1927–1928), 189.

42. Agreements, January 1, 1872, in Concordia Parish General Mortgages, Vol. P, pp. 490–98; statement, March 3, 1872, in Alexander K. Farrar Papers, Department of Archives and Manuscripts, Louisiana State University, Baton Rouge; Darden Diary, II, September 7, 1871; estate of Wash. Ford, in Baker Papers, Box 2, Folder 21; Gillespie Papers, XVI, April 12, 24, 1875.

fully imagined that the labor question had now been settled; and like the vast majority of his fellow planters, he discovered that adjustment had only begun. In 1866 he experimented with share wages—in this case one-third of the crop and provisions—and spelled out in detail the duties that he expected his hands to perform. In 1867 he contracted to pay his laborers one-half of the crop and charged them for provisions. In 1868 he leased to individual squads for one-third of their produce, the freedmen bearing all operating costs. In 1869 he again leased for shares but this time contributed one-half the operating expenses plus two teams of mules and received, in return, one-half of the crop. The contract for 1870 is unavailable, but in 1871 he rented to squads for a specified quantity of cotton. Here, finally, was a lasting arrangement. After 1871 the Gillespie contract, altered annually since 1865, remained unchanged except in details.[43]

Not all planters took the same course as James Gillespie, and yet his story is suggestive. The four or five years following the war represented a period of adjustment for just about everyone. Planters experimented, exchanged ideas, negotiated with their hands, and experimented once more. Not until about 1870 did squad labor emerge and wages fully give way to tenancy. Not until about 1870 do we see the beginnings of an enduring labor settlement.

III

Historians tend to measure the impact of Emancipation on the plantation in terms of economic questions. Did the pattern of land tenure change? How was labor organized, and by whom controlled? But the slaves had resented the social manifestations of their subservience no less than the economic. They desperately wanted an unmonitored family life. And they longed for the opportunity to develop their recreational, religious, and educational

43. Contracts, July 12, 1865, January 1, 1866, January 4, 1867, January 10, 1868, January 5, 1869, January 12, 1871, January 10, 1873, January 29, 1874, January 22, 1875, January 7, 1876, all in Gillespie Papers. Ransom and Sutch (*One Kind of Freedom*, 89–90) argue that, after about 1868, negotiations shifted from the size of the share to the number of acres allotted to the tenant.

interests away from the stifling attention of their owners. One reason why the freedmen moved around in the years after the war was to secure these objectives.

The most volatile issues were those centering on the family. The former slaves insisted that, for their emancipation to have meaning, they would have to be given complete control over all matters relating to home life. Yet the planter was convinced that any surrender of authority on his part could only lead to social dislocation and, by implication, economic chaos. In March of 1867, for instance, Wilmer Shields wrote to his employer William Newton Mercer, owner of four estates in Adams County but resident of New Orleans, "Anna is not only willing to go to you but says she is anxious to do so—but has no one here with whom to trust her two children. Times have changed, fathers, mothers, husbands, wives, brothers & sisters do not care to assist each other or their *own* children, much less the children of others. She says she will go at any moment you say so, but must be allowed to take her children with her—to leave them here would be, under this new regime, equivalent to abandonment."[44]

Doubtless there were troubled slave families that did not long survive Emancipation; their experiences were unrepresentative, however. Most blacks saw liberation as a glorious opportunity to stabilize relationships rendered fragile by slavery. Many left home to seek near or distant relatives. Their sense of joy was evident in the words of a woman whom J. T. Trowbridge encountered on the road: "De best ting de Yankees done was to break de slavery chain. I shouldn't be here to-day if dey hadn't. I'm going to see my mother."[45]

The freedmen also acted quickly to remove their marriage arrangements from the jurisdiction of their former owners. True, some blacks—invariably servants close to their white employers—continued to solicit and receive advice. Ibby Barnes recalled that her marriage was sanctioned by her former master, Edwin Bennett, and celebrated in the Big House. And if the somewhat romantic

44. Wilmer [Shields] to Doctor [William N. Mercer], March 27, 1867, in Mercer Papers.
45. Trowbridge, *The South*, 393.

reminiscences of Julia Tigner Noland can be trusted, two of her father's freedmen "petitioned," as of old, to be wed. Still, such postbellum gestures by the blacks were largely acts of courtesy. Almost from the moment of liberation they proved more than ready in affairs of the heart to disregard the wishes and ignore the interests of their former owners. In February, 1864, Louisa Quitman Lovell of Monmouth, in Natchez, wrote with exasperation to her husband, "To cap the climaxes of annoyance Lutt has taken it into her head to get married & refuses to leave Yankeedom too, so when I go I must hunt me up a nurse. Upon whom do you think she has cast her regards? You would never guess that it was old *Harry*—Yes, she has turned the old fellow's head & as he hinted to me last night something about 'making something for himself' to prevent another exodus possibly, I agreed to give him some wages monthly.—Oh! deliver me from the 'citizens of African descent.'"[46]

Such instances only increased after the war. In June, 1866, Maryanne, a servant on the Darden plantation in Jefferson County, became engaged to a hand on a neighboring estate. Apparently the Dardens had no initial objections to the union, for they were among the few white guests invited to the ceremony. Their approval gave way to shock and dismay, however, when they discovered that Maryanne intended to leave them in order to live with her new husband. "William came in a buggy for Maryanne," observed Mrs. Darden with disgust, "she did not ask to go—said he had come for her & she wanted her Silk Dress I had fixed for her— It has come to a high pass that they can go when they feel like it without asking."[47]

Unfortunately for the freedmen, improvement in their marriage arrangements was not initially accompanied by increased privacy. They had lived in quarters before the war and continued to do so

---

46. George P. Rawick, Jan Hillegas, and Ken Lawrence (eds.), *The American Slave: A Composite Autobiography,* Supplement, Series 1 (12 vols.; Westport, Conn.: Greenwood Press, 1977), IX, 1854; Julia Tigner Noland and Blanche Connelly Saucier, *Confederate Greenbacks: Mississippi Plantation Life in the 70's and 80's* (San Antonio: Naylor Co., 1940), 103–105; Louisa [Quitman Lovell] to Capt. Joseph Lovell, February 17, 1864, in Quitman Family Papers.

47. Darden Diary, II, June 20, July 15, 20, 1866. Similarly, Leon Litwack observes that, after Emancipation, freedmen demanded "the exclusive right to manage and discipline their own children" (*Been in the Storm So Long,* 238).

for several years afterward. Typical was the housing observed by Whitelaw Reid on a plantation near Vidalia, Louisiana. The hands resided in two rows of frame, one-story buildings. Each cabin had two rooms, a garden, and a projecting roof that covered an earthen porch floor.[48]

Right from the beginning, blacks raised objections to perpetuation of the quarters. *De Bow's Review* commented in 1869 that the former slave exhibited "great anxiety to have his little home, with his horse, cow, and hogs separate and apart from others." But many planters successfully resisted change into the 1870s. It was not until 1873, for instance, that James Gillespie agreed to give serious consideration to the request of his tenants on Indian Village that their cabins be segregated one from the other. And it was another year still before he acceded to their wishes.[49] Like his fellow planters, he found it hard to believe that increased privacy for the black family would benefit the operation of the plantation.

Education of the freedman was introduced to the district during the occupation, when philanthropic agencies, working under the direction of the military, established schools in a number of the more heavily populated communities. However, attempts by Federal officials to extend formal instruction to the individual plantations met the active opposition of northern lessees. As Colonel John Eaton wryly observed in his memoirs, "It was intended that on the leased plantations schools and teachers should be located and maintained, but here experience soon taught us that men who entered upon cotton cultivation with the intention of making a great fortune in a single year were not to be expected voluntarily to meet our expectations in this regard."[50]

In no sense did the actions of the lessees reflect the attitudes of their laborers. On the contrary, visitors to the district repeatedly testified that blacks showed intense commitment to learning. It

48. Reid, *After the War*, 483.
49. "The Cotton Trade of the World," 609; Wm. Jett & Co. to Jas. A. Gillespie, August 28, 1873, agreement, October 1, 1874, both in Gillespie Papers. See also King, *The Great South*, 300–301; Nordhoff, *The Cotton States*, 72.
50. John Stanford Coussons, "The Federal Occupation of Natchez, Mississippi, 1863–1865" (M.A. thesis, Louisiana State University, 1958), 59; J. Eaton, *Grant, Lincoln and the Freedmen*, 195. Compare Wiley, *Southern Negroes*, 275.

was not simply that the former slave recognized the practical advantages of being able to read and write, although that was true enough. But as Thomas Clark and Albert Kirwan have noted, "Education became the symbol of his freedom, and large numbers of freedmen sought this confirmation of freedom with some diligence."[51]

Contrary to what one might expect, planter resistance to the education of blacks, though pronounced, did not last long. For one thing, the gentry discovered that laborers would work more industriously when their children had access to a school. Then, too, the former slaveowner had every reason to conclude that he would be able to exercise personal control over the education process. The stated objective of the Federal authorities was to have children taught in schools on the plantations. "I am thoroughly convinced," remarked General Thomas J. Wood, head of the Freedmen's Bureau in Mississippi in 1866, "that the great work of educating the freed people can only be accomplished by the hearty, vigorous, general efforts of the entire white population which inhabits the same soil with the negroes." Build schools on your estates, he advised the gentry.[52]

The plantation school had obvious advantages for both freedman and planter. It allowed blacks easy access to the education that they so earnestly desired; and it permitted the former slaveowner to keep a watchful eye on what was being taught and by whom. Most members of the old elite would have agreed with Wilmer Shields, who, when faced with a demand for a school of some sort from hands not yet under contract, remarked, "I think well of the school, if we can get a proper school master."[53]

As the planter understood it, then, educational developments would be under his jurisdiction. It would be his responsibility to provide a classroom, but it would also be his prerogative to dictate

51. *Senate Executive Documents*, 39th Cong., 1st Sess., No. 2, p. 75; J. Eaton, *Grant, Lincoln and the Freedmen*, 208; Clark and Kirwan, *The South Since Appomattox*, 165.

52. Quoted in Clifton Ganus, "The Freedmen's Bureau in Mississippi" (Ph.D. dissertation, Tulane University, 1953), 342–43; *Senate Executive Documents*, 39th Cong., 2nd Sess., No. 6, p. 75. See also Litwack, *Been in the Storm So Long*, 238.

53. Wilmer [Shields] to Doctor [William N. Mercer], December 12, 1866, in Mercer Papers.

the hiring and firing of teachers. Problems arose because, in the long run, blacks were unwilling to leave their education in the hands of their former owners. "The freedmen have had a Yankee by the name of Kinstry teaching school here at nights without Mr. Darden's permission," complained Susan Sillers Darden in late 1867. And her assessment of this instructor? "He is of Bad Character."[54]

Gradually the educational authority of the planter declined. Conversely the number of public schools for black children increased. In 1865, there were four in Adams County; by 1867, there were eleven; by 1869, fourteen. In Claiborne County, there were two in 1866, four in 1867, five in 1868, and eight in 1869. While admittedly most of these schools were in the cities and therefore inaccessible to the vast majority of children on the plantations, a few institutions were built in the rural areas. In any case, the implication of this development could not have been lost on the former slave. His school was to be separate from the plantation; and his education was to be free from the restrictive oversight of his employer.[55]

Similar changes took place in other areas. Blacks created their own fraternal clubs and social organizations—Edward King, for instance, commented on the many brass bands formed by freedmen throughout the South. Most important perhaps, they took steps to free their spiritual affairs from the supervision of their former owners. The gentry viewed this last development with particular alarm. George Torrey of Jefferson County wrote to his friend, Governor Benjamin G. Humphreys, in early 1866 to urge legislation outlawing preaching by Negroes, as "it is now doing more harm in the country to freedmen than any thing else." A segment of the old elite sought to circumvent the problem by continuing to offer those services that they had provided before the war. George

54. Darden Diary, II, November 1, 1867.
55. "Number of Schools Open" (Typescript in Records of the Auditor of Public Accounts, Box 83, Mississippi Department of Archives and History, Jackson); "Negro Schools" (Typescript in W.P.A. Records, RG 60, for Adams County, Folder: Races and Nationalities, Mississippi Department of Archives and History, Jackson); "Educational and Religious Adjustment" (Typescript in W.P.A. Records, RG 60, for Claiborne County, Folder: Reconstruction, Mississippi Department of Archives and History, Jackson).

Ralston arranged to have Joseph B. Stratton, the prominent pastor of the First Presbyterian Church in Natchez, preach to his freedmen in 1870. Alexander K. Farrar of Adams County erected a chapel on his plantation and brought in a black minister whom he proudly described as "of 25 years standing in the African Methodist Church."[56]

Some planters contributed financially toward the establishment of separate black congregations, presumably expecting to secure some influence over policy decisions; the Rose Hill Church in Jefferson County, for instance, was built with donations from local freedmen and their former owners. A few landowners attempted to exercise authority through the contract. The 1873 agreement between Spencer Wood and the tenants on Spokan in Concordia Parish included the provision, "Preaching and prayer meeting to stop at 9 o'clock at night and not to be held on work days."[57]

But as in the area of education, blacks were increasingly able to escape white surveillance. At least in one respect this goal was compatible with the aims of the gentry. As much as the planter wished to reserve patriarchic authority, he was inclined to limit his social contact with the freedman beyond the plantation. In 1866, for example, the aristocratic Pine Ridge Presbyterian Church in Adams County removed ninety-five former slave communicants from its rolls. Such actions only encouraged the appearance and growth of black congregations. There were seven in Adams County in 1865; by 1870, there were eighteen. In Claiborne County, there were only two black churches in 1865. Four years later, there were ten. Nor do these figures speak to the many freedmen who lacked church facilities and had to meet in their homes or, for safety, in the woods.[58]

56. King, *The Great South*, 611; Geo. Torrey to B. G. Humphreys, March 29, 1866, in Governors' Correspondence, Box 65, Mississippi Department of Archives and History, Jackson; Stratton Diary (Typescript in Joseph B. Stratton Papers, Department of Archives and Manuscripts, Louisiana State University, Baton Rouge), II, 299; A. K. Farrar to Captain McDonald, January 9, 1867, in Farrar Papers.

57. W.P.A. Records for Jefferson County, Vol. XXXII, Pt. 2, p. 56; lease, December 31, 1873, in Concordia Parish General Mortgages, Vol. Q, p. 547.

58. "The History of the Pine Ridge Presbyterian Church" (MS in possession of Mrs. Waldo Lambdin, Natchez), 9; "Part of a Report Probably for the Census of 1870," "Number of Churches" (MSS in Records of the Auditor of Public Accounts, Box 117); Nordhoff,

To the extent that the new congregations were moderate and not activist, the gentry raised few objections. But certain developments left them uneasy. Planters complained that tenants neglected their duties to attend allegedly trivial services and prayer meetings. Furthermore, the former slaveowners found fault and were frequently at odds with many of the new black ministers. Finally, in some communities, there was evidence that freedmen were turning from Christianity to traditional folk religion. The former slave, concluded one planter, had given in "to what might almost be termed a rule of superstition." James Stewart McGehee of Wilkinson County recounted an incident that, for him, illustrated the sheer folly of this development:

> As late as 1878 there was an intelligent negro man about twenty five years old working on my father's place. He was a descendant of one of my grandfather's leading slave families and had had the benefit of being with white people all his life. On several occasions I knew him to give $3 of his hard-earned money to old "Aunt" Malinda Lanus to "unconjure" him. When he consulted that good dame she told him he was full of snakes and scorpions, for which she charged him $3 and required him to bring three more at the end of seven days, by which time she prepared for him a decoction guaranteed to remove the spell.[59]

Whether, in fact, the influence of the conjurer expanded after the war or merely became public knowledge is a moot point. To the planter who now occasionally unearthed glass jars filled with roots, herbs, lizards, and snakes, however, it seemed obvious that without constant white guidance, blacks were slipping into some form of African barbarism.

The old elite reached a similar conclusion about the freedman's general morality. At the end of the war and for a brief period thereafter, many planters demanded the contractual authority to police the conduct of their hands. An agreement between the landowner and tenants on one Claiborne County plantation in 1868 called for the latter "to be obedient to the regulations of the place, having

---

*The Cotton States*, 73; Rawick, Hillegas, and Lawrence (eds.), *The American Slave*, Supp., Ser. 1, Vol. VII, p. 567.

59. Darden Diary, II, January 21, 1872; James Stewart McGehee papers, III, 32–33, Department of Archives and Manuscripts, Louisiana State University, Baton Rouge.

no meetings, or gathering on the place & to attend to their religion in a quiet way, & take in no straglers [*sic*] or loungers about their homes."[60]

Sometimes freedmen were subject to fines or dismissal for conduct that their employers deemed immoral or irresponsible. But such was the nature of the times that the former slave was usually able to ignore rules governing his social activities. "Our neighbors' negroes have dances and revels almost nightly," moaned Wilmer Shields in the summer of 1866. "Of course under the circumstances it is impossible to keep some of ours from joining them." It seemed apparent to the gentry that such behavior was merely the first step to dissipation and ruin. "The Negroes are having glorious times sundays shouting & jumping," observed an appalled Amelia Montgomery in late 1867. "The women were jumping & pitching & hollowing & the men holding them. I believe they will go back to barbarism in a few years if allowed to go on as they do."[61]

Such outbursts of dismay are revealing. They suggest the full extent to which the freedmen had managed, by pressing their interests in the marketplace, to undermine the authority of the individual planter. Especially in matters not directly related to the narrow economic purposes of the plantation—matters pertaining to the family, religion, recreation, and education—the former slaves had effectively challenged the primacy of plantation law and laid claim to responsibility for their own lives.

## IV

The efforts of the former slave to secure social autonomy and economic advantage produced a predictable response on the part of the gentry: they began to disavow those obligations that they had accepted under slavery and that, for the most part, they had continued to acknowledge in the immediate aftermath of Emancipa-

---

60. A. F. Montgomery to her husband, January 23, 1868, in Montgomery Papers. See also memorandum of agreement, October 14, 1869, in Concordia Parish General Mortgages, Vol. O, p. 403.

61. Wilmer [Shields] to Doctor [William N. Mercer], July 10, 1866, in Mercer Papers; A. F. Montgomery to her husband, November 18, 1867, in Montgomery Papers.

tion. Take the matter of gifting, for example. Laborers learned that they could no longer expect presents from their employers, even on special occasions or for superior labor. In 1870, Susan Sillers Darden noted almost wistfully in her diary, "Not one of the freedmen have been up to say Christmas gift—something so unusual."[62]

More significant, the gentry began to curtail support for the elderly, some planters now denying a responsibility for their own former slaves. James Belknap wrote to his sister, Lizzie Hamilton of Claiborne County, "I am satisfied from observation and information that the Old Servants on a place are a nuisance, and ought to be driven off." A few former slaveowners eventually decided to act on this principle, although not without evident misgivings. Amelia Montgomery reported to her husband in the summer of 1867 that her sons had decided to dismiss "Old Austin, he not being competent to do what he undertook." The following year, she wrote sadly, "Old Joe hated to leave but the boys would not let him stay on any terms, he had so many useless ones." And there was a chilling postscript: "The boys had to haul some of the families to the Road, or we would not yet have been clear of them." The costs of growing old on the plantation now fell solely on the black family—and in more ways than one. The financial records of James Gillespie of Hollywood for 1866 indicate that Eliza owed him $21.66 for labor missed "waiting on her mother."[63]

Indeed, all time off, for whatever reason, now became expensive for the freedman. In 1867, Thomas T. Davis agreed to use the hands on Beechland only half-time on Saturday. But he charged them thirty-five cents apiece for the half day they were not required to work. The previous year, James Gillespie docked delinquent laborers forty cents per day plus rations. The implications of this development were not lost on the former slaves. "Sometimes in fact," observed Whitelaw Reid in 1866, "they went to the fields when really too sick to work, lest they should lose their wages for the day." James Lucas recollected, "Sometimes I b'leeves I worked

62. Darden Diary, II, December 25, 1870.
63. James [Belknap] to Lizzie Hamilton, August 30, 1870, in C. D. Hamilton Papers; A. F. Montgomery to her husband, July 15, 1867, July 9, 1868, both in Montgomery Papers; financial statement, January 27, 1866, in Gillespie Papers.

harder en if us got sick . . . well, de boss shore could hire some-
body else."[64]

For that matter, ailing hands also found that they could no
longer count on the health care they had received before the war.
To be sure, many members of the old elite continued to provide at
least some personal assistance to the sick and infirm. But almost all
now declined to bear responsibility for the medical expenses of
their freedmen. In an early contract with the laborers on Hollywood, for instance, James Gillespie pledged, "I will attend to them
as usual when sick but will not pay Dr Bills." Eventually, under the
new conditions, many planters came to serve as middlemen between the former slave and his physician. The planter would pay
the doctor, the freedman would reimburse the planter. Alexander K. Farrar of Adams County gave Dr. Thomas Cosby ninety-
eight dollars in 1866 for services rendered to laborers from March
to June. This included fifty dollars for sixteen visits to one William
Carter. Whether Carter recovered sufficiently to liquidate his obligation to Farrar is unclear; his experience does indicate, however,
that some landowners were prepared to go to significant lengths
on behalf of their hands.[65]

Planters also intervened between doctors and freedmen in less
formal ways. Dr. Hercules Sanche of Port Gibson wrote to Wilson
Humphreys in late 1883 to secure his aid in collecting two outstanding bills:

> I hold a claim of the amount of $18.50 against James McKay Col., and
> an other to the amount of $23 against Thomas Richardson Col. both
> of whom I understand to have been croping [sic] this year with you, or
> one of your sons. Both amounts have been due me a long time, and I
> feel that now is my best time to get them, but that I can only get them
> by your assistance. Both are acting crooked and McKay twice made
> himself liable to prosecution. Please have the kindness to take the mat-
> ter in hand and keep such part as you find necessary to compensate
> you.[66]

64. Account notice between Thomas T. Davis and his laborers, 1867, and Vol. XIV,
both in Gillespie Papers; Reid, *After the War*, 488; Rawick, Hillegas, and Lawrence (eds.),
*The American Slave*, Supp., Ser. 1, Vol. VIII, p. 1347.

65. Contract, July 12, 1865, in Gillespie Papers; bill, [?], 1866, in Farrar Papers.

66. Dr. Hercules Sanche to Wilson Humphreys, December 17, 1883, in George Wilson

Evidently, in the eyes of at least some members of the professional community, the gentry remained to a degree responsible for the actions of their laborers.

At the same time, planter intervention was scarcely a foregone conclusion. Consider, for a moment, an incident on the Alexander Farrar plantation in the summer of 1868. One of Farrar's hands, a woman named Relda, became ill and sent for Thomas Cosby, regular physician for freedmen on the estate. Dr. Cosby came as requested and dutifully prescribed some medicine. Later, however, when Relda became worse and summoned him again, he refused to return. "I cannot attend such cases," he sent word, "unless some one is responsible."

When Farrar learned what had happened, he was furious. "If you had made known your fears at the first I would have had no hesitation in saying that I would be responsible," he wrote the doctor bitterly. "By your course you have placed the patient's life in jeopardy. . . . If you have decided to abandon her, I think it is due her to say so, at once, giving her thereby an opportunity of knowing that her only chance for her life is to make arrangements, to get another Doctor."

But Cosby remained unapologetic. "Let me assure you," he replied, "that I have reflected well on the course I have taken. I had no right to presume that Relda had means and even if I had known that she had, it would certainly have been a very foolish conclusion in one to think that left to herself she would have used those means in paying me."[67]

Dr. Cosby's ethics were arguably deplorable; his business instincts, on the other hand, were quite acute. Although many planters, Farrar among them, were prepared to serve as middleman for the physician, their services were not something he could afford to take for granted. Too often the planter, like the doctor, showed

---

Humphreys and Family Papers, Z 29, Folder 9, Mississippi Department of Archives and History, Jackson. Sometimes as a last resort a planter agreed to liquidate the outstanding debts of his laborers. Tonie [Lovell] to Posie, April 17, 1874, in Quitman Family Papers.

67. A. K. Farrar to Thomas R. Cosby, August 1, 1868, T. R. Cosby to A. Farrar, August 1, 1868, A. K. Farrar to Dr. Thomas R. Cosby, August 2, 1868, all in Farrar Papers.

himself to be principally interested in those freedmen likely to meet their financial obligations.

The burden of health care, then, fell to the former slaves, as did its cost, which could be prohibitive. Not surprisingly, many freedmen ceased to call on white physicians. Charlie Davenport, who had lived on Gabriel Shields' Aventine before the war, recalled that, following Emancipation, "I show had to pay my own way or do wid out. Long ez I kep well hit wuz purty nice but when I got sick I wuz just like a animal what crawled off to his hole. Marse wuz good but he wuzn't sponsible fur me en my fambly no mow." Ailing freedmen increasingly turned to members of the black community for assistance, usually to elderly women versed in traditional folk remedies. In view of the state of medicine at the time, the quality of health care may not have diminished significantly. Still, on occasion, there must have been tragic consequences. In late 1868, Perry Drake of Claiborne County wrote with obvious irritation to his brother Steele, "Two weeks ago we lost our servant Amanda, who died in child-birth. She was taken on Saturday night and died Sunday evening, could have been saved if the Doctor had been sent for in time, but they depended on old negro grannies till it was too late."[68]

Developments in the area of law enforcement took a similarly doubtful turn as far as the former slave was concerned. With the power of the planter declining, the state took over responsibility for the administration and execution of the laws. Although punishment of offenders now became less discretionary than it had been in the past, it was arguably no less severe and in certain instances was clearly more inhumane. The way in which theft was dealt with provides a good illustration.

Petty stealing continued after the war, indeed increased as a result of the economic distress of 1866 and 1867. "The negroes are so destitute they will keep stealing," complained Amelia Mont-

68. Rawick, Hillegas, and Lawrence (eds.), *The American Slave*, Supp., Ser. 1, Vol. VII, p. 568, Vol. VIII, pp. 1347–48. Credit charges for a doctor's visits were sometimes more than cash charges. Darden Diary, II, December 18, 1874. Perry [Drake] to Steele [Drake], November 30, 1868, in Drake-Satterfield Papers, Z 96, Box 2, Folder 17, Mississippi Department of Archives and History, Jackson.

gomery of Belmont in April, 1866. "They think, the last one of them, that they have a right to what belongs to their former owners." Of course, the planter could charge the suspected guilty party for the goods taken, and invariably he did.[69] But correction often went beyond fines. If the planter reckoned that he could afford to dispense with the services of the presumed offender, he might well dismiss him and then turn him over to the local authorities for prosecution. For the petty criminal, retribution had just begun. As Charles Nordhoff observed some ten years after the war, "Formerly a negro thief received thirty-nine lashes from the overseer, and there an end; now a constable catches him and a prison holds him for trial, a grand jury indicts him, a petit jury hears evidence for and against him, a judge sentences him if he is guilty, and thereupon a penitentiary receives him." The process was painful and the punishment long-lasting. And among its victims were laborers who worked for people once considered the most dedicated of paternalists. Wilmer Shields wrote to William Newton Mercer, a man of conscience and respectability, to report in December of 1866:

> To day I have sent Charles up to N[atchez] to get out a warrant to arrest Viney—whom he caught in the act of stealing a large shoat—She had just knocked it in the head and had it in a basket—Her children, two of them, are at Hutchins' and starving—that is to say they get nothing from him to eat—If I can induce the officers of the law to come so far, she shall be arrested and prosecuted, if not I will drive her from the place, first making her pay for the 40 lb. hog?[70]

It was not just that the new form of punishment could be severe, which was true enough. But in escaping the arbitrary authority of his master, the freedman of necessity forfeited the protection of a patriarch. This was a development that he did not anticipate and that at first, it seems, he did not fully appreciate. A local justice of the peace complained to Whitelaw Reid in 1866 of one suspected thief who "can't see why a word from his employer isn't enough

---

69. A. F. Montgomery to her husband, November 18, 1867, in Montgomery Papers. Fining left a lot of discretionary power in the hands of the planter. See, for example, Gillespie Papers, XIV.

70. Nordhoff, *The Cotton States*, 24; Wilmer [Shields] to Doctor [William N. Mercer], December 19, 1866, in Mercer Papers.

now to release him, as it would have done while he was a slave. He doesn't comprehend the fact that he has committed an offense against the State, as well as against his master."[71]

Occasionally a planter took steps to protect his hands from the impersonal justice of the legal system. In 1866, for instance, Alfred Vidal Davis arranged for several of the more prominent members of the Natchez gentry to testify to the good character of a former slave charged with theft of a mule. Similarly, a year earlier, fifty-seven Wilkinson County planters came to the defense of two blacks who had been jailed for allegedly helping a white man steal some cotton.[72]

Often, however, the landowner who intervened on behalf of an accused or convicted freedman had some overriding personal interest in securing his release. To be sure, when James D. Wood wrote to Governor Benjamin G. Humphreys to seek clemency for one Levi Robinson charged with assault and battery, he included assurances as to Robinson's "good & faithful" character. But the core of his appeal was somewhat different: "It is now late in the season & planters are generally unwilling to hire [out] negroes."[73] In short, he needed laborers. Many freedmen found, as Robinson evidently did, that the extent of their protection came to vary roughly with the demands of the cotton culture.

This specific development in the area of law enforcement only illustrates a broader development in the general situation of the black laborer after the war. Formerly he had been able to look to the planter for protection—from the state, from other whites, from other blacks. Now, as a direct consequence of his decision to press his interests in the marketplace, he was largely on his own. To suggest that he had highly regarded the limited security slavery had provided would be a substantial exaggeration. Bondage had rendered life precarious, not sure. And yet undeniably slavery had

71. Reid, *After the War*, 516.

72. See various letters from A. L. Bingaman, D. L. Rivers, A. K. Farrar, Edward Sparrow, Spencer Wood, and Lemuel P. Conner to Benjamin G. Humphreys, November, December, 1866, in Governors' Correspondence, Box 67; petition, 1865, in Governors' Correspondence, Box 65, Folder: Correspondence 1865—not dated.

73. James D. Wood to Benjamin G. Humphreys, September 25, 1866, in Governors' Correspondence, Box 67.

offered certain safeguards, and these the freedmen did not happily surrender. "We was nigh scared out of our wits," observed one former slave, recalling a particularly threatening time during Reconstruction, "living on a new place, and working for money, and didn't have no one to protect us."[74] Such fear was real enough. For blacks, it was the price of freedom.

### V

The plantation that emerged out of Reconstruction was, in a very real sense, a different institution from the plantation that had existed under slavery. Two fundamental changes had taken place. First, paternalism had collapsed, giving way to a more impersonal form of interaction between planter and black laborer. Second, plantation law had lost much of its force.

The latter point is clear enough, although its implications have never received the attention they deserve. Prior to the war, the slaveowner had been the dominant figure in the lives of his hands. Now he had to share authority not only with the black family, strengthened by Emancipation, but with a wide variety of new organizations—churches and schools, clubs and mutual aid societies—and with the state, above all with the state. During the decades immediately following Reconstruction, some freedmen must have occasionally had second thoughts about this development. The state, in its own way, could be as repressive as the individual master. And the social separation that blacks perceived as a means to independence became, in the hands of their enemies, a weapon for discrimination. But in the long run, if perhaps in ways not apparent at the time, the destruction of plantation law significantly furthered the interests of racial democracy in the Black Belt. It put an end to the legal autonomy of the plantation, thereby undermining the institutional basis for authoritarianism in the region. And it held out to blacks the promise, though long deferred, of full and equal citizenship in the society.

74. Rawick, Hillegas, and Lawrence (eds.), *The American Slave*, Supp., Ser. 1, Vol. VIII, p. 991.

As for paternalism, some observations made many years ago by the sociologist Robert E. Park are well to the point: "When the Negro moved off the plantation upon which he was reared, he severed the personal relations which bound him to his master's people. It was just at this point that the two races began to lose touch with each other. From this time on the relations of the black man and the white, which in slavery had been direct and personal, became every year, as the old associations were broken, more and more indirect and secondary." Not that the gentry ceased to perform acts of genuine humanity. Antonia Quitman Lovell wrote to her sister from Palmyra in 1874, "I have been quite worried about Charlotte. She has really been very ill, & is now so weak, that I have to employ Winnie as a regular nurse to her. She is however better to day [sic] and has begun to take a little nourishment, which for some days she would not touch, till she became so weak, from want of sustenance that we really feared the old woman could not stand it—I feed her daily on milk punches & chicken broth." The diary of Susan Sillers Darden of Jefferson County mentions numerous trips to the quarters to look in on sick laborers. But such displays of kindness must be placed in perspective. Under slavery the planter had been obligated to provide various services to all his hands. Now he bestowed benefits, if and when he chose, on particular freedmen toward whom he was favorably disposed. Christmas, 1879, on the Noland plantation in Wilkinson County provides a case in point. Three of the tenant families were invited to the Big House for eggnog and presents. The remaining families were ignored, however. "They moved about from year to year, and were not considered our colored folks," explained Julia Tigner Noland. "But those faithful few who had stayed with us through the hectic war days and the reconstruction period which followed were dear to our hearts."[75]

More was involved here than simply a decline in bonds of affec-

75. Robert E. Park, "Racial Assimilation in Secondary Groups," *Publications of the American Sociological Society*, VIII (1913), 76. See also James L. Roark, *Masters Without Slaves: Southern Planters in the Civil War and Reconstruction* (New York: Norton, 1977), 145–46, 197–98. Tonie [Lovell] to Posie, March 26, 1874, in Quitman Family Papers; Darden Diary, II, *passim*; Noland and Saucier, *Confederate Greenbacks*, 76–77.

tion. The social organization of the plantation had itself under-
gone a radical transformation. A cash nexus now intervened between planter and laborer, with rights and responsibilities taking
on a specific monetary value. Traditional tasks were performed
and services provided, but, more often than not, for a price. If a
tenant whitewashed a fence he normally demanded compensation;
if a landlord arranged for the services of a doctor he expected to
be paid. No wonder that critical observers complained of an en-
croaching bourgeois ethic. That individual acts of a paternalistic
nature persisted during these years and long afterward only under-
scores the fact that the general tendency of the new system—its
internal logic—lay in a different direction. The road to the New
South plantation ran through the marketplace.

# CHAPTER SIX

# Planter and Merchant

A general shortage of labor persisted in the district through the 1870s, and there is evidence of continuing competition among planters for the services of available freedmen.[1] In April, 1873, for instance, the manager of Indian Village informed his employer, James Gillespie, "We have lost eight hands this year by other plantter coming in and swarring to theme and tell theme that I will [give] you a better Bargin than you have." Efforts by the gentry to regulate hiring practices and leasing arrangements proved no more successful than they had in the past. "There is too much the feeling among us of bravado in the implied threat and action 'Every man for himself and the devil for the hindermost,'" complained William R. Brandon in 1874. This lack of cooperation, he suggested, had made "capital subservient to labor where as the reverse should be the case."[2]

And yet, such testimony can be highly misleading. It is true that a decade after the war the gentry were still largely unable to act collectively. But acting individually, each seeking leverage over his own laborers, they had learned how to protect their interests by exploiting the cash nexus that now mediated relations on the plantation. In particular they had learned that by allying themselves

1. The shortage of labor became so acute during the middle of the 1870s that many planters recruited freedmen from Alabama and Georgia. C. W. Howard, "Condition of Agriculture in the Cotton States," in U.S. Department of Agriculture, *Report of the Commissioner of Agriculture for the Year 1874* (Washington, D.C.: Government Printing Office, 1875), 222; Charles Nordhoff, *The Cotton States in the Spring and Summer of 1875* (New York: D. Appleton, 1876), 21, 78.

2. William Jett to Jas. A. Gillespie, April 8, 1873, in James A. Gillespie and Family Papers, Department of Archives and Manuscripts, Louisiana State University, Baton Rouge; penciled notes, [1874], on the flyleaf of *American Agriculturalist*, VII (1847), in Brandon Account Books (MSS in Department of Archives and Manuscripts, Louisiana State University, Baton Rouge).

with local merchants to control the sale of supplies to their tenants and hired hands, they could both increase their own profits and maneuver the freedman into a state of material dependence that effectively reduced his opportunities in the marketplace.

To understand fully this further stage in our story, however, it is necessary to look beyond the plantation. More specifically, it is necessary to examine a restructuring in the supply system of the region which took place during Reconstruction, a restructuring involving the collapse of traditional provisioning arrangements whereby planters furnished their laborers with goods secured through commission merchants in New Orleans, and the rise to prominence of an element of local storekeepers whose newfound authority over the freedmen represented a challenge to the standing of the gentry. It was only when the planters had accommodated themselves to these changes that their long-term interests were secured. We return once more to the end of the war.

I

The Federal occupation of New Orleans in April, 1862, resulted in two hundred to three hundred commission merchants closing their offices. Many fled the city. Had Confederate loyalties been of a higher order, this disruption of trade might have had serious implications for the planting community. As it was, most factors returned soon after the introduction of Federal currency into the captured territories. Although the wartime blockade and subsequent inability of planters to pay outstanding debts had left quite a few firms without the necessary operating capital, loans were available in the North and in Europe. Indeed, some Yankees, hoping to take part in the anticipated windfall, opened their own agencies. By the end of the war, New Orleans commission houses were advancing credit optimistically and impulsively, and they continued to do so into 1866.[3]

3. R. G. Dun & Co. Collection, Louisiana IX, 259, 281, Baker Library, Harvard Graduate School of Business Administration, Boston; John Q. Anderson (ed.), *Brokenburn: The*

The majority of enterprises dealing with the Natchez district in 1865 were resurrected antebellum establishments or new operations put together by members of old houses. On the eve of the war, Buckner, Stanton & Newman had been one of the wealthiest firms in the city. With peace restored, the two surviving partners went their separate ways. Henry S. Buckner set up business in 1864 with an investment of approximately $500,000. By September, 1866, the firm of Buckner & Co. had a branch office in Natchez and an expanding trade that was to make the concern worth $1 million by 1870. Meanwhile Samuel B. Newman began operations after the war with $200,000 in capital. Like Buckner, he opened a branch office in Natchez, where he carried on an extensive business. Other former merchants also fared well. Nalle & Cammack paid off its antebellum obligations and rapidly built a small investment into a substantial enterprise. Richard Nugent, unable to liquidate his own debts, allied himself with R. McDowell, who contributed $20,000 toward the establishment of a new house.[4]

Naturally it was to their old clients that the factors first turned, in an effort to patch together a postwar trade. "I returned to the City on 8th Inst. in excellent health," wrote Richard Nugent in August, 1865, to his former customer and close friend, Charles D. Hamilton of Claiborne County, "and will commence my occupation in a few days & so soon as I can select an office." He suggested that the two proceed with business as usual. "As one of our oldest and most esteemed personal friends," S. B. Newman & Co. wrote to Alexander K. Farrar, "we cannot but feel the assurance of your interest in our behalf and beg your influence for us as we make a new venture in life after the disasters of the last four or five years."[5]

---

*Journal of Kate Stone, 1861–1868* (Baton Rouge: Louisiana State University Press, 1972), 368; M. B. Hammond, *The Cotton Industry: An Essay in American Economic History* (New York: Johnson Reprint Corp., 1966), 142; Ross H. Moore, "Social and Economic Conditions in Mississippi During Reconstruction" (Ph.D. dissertation, Duke University, 1937), 77–78, 83; Charles A. Pilsbury, "Farming in the South," *De Bow's Review*, After the War Series, V (April, 1868), 363; Joe Gray Taylor, *Louisiana Reconstructed, 1863–1877* (Baton Rouge: Louisiana State University Press, 1974), 392.

4. R. G. Dun & Co. Collection, Louisiana IX, 183, 281, 286K, Louisiana X, 160, Louisiana XII, 77, Louisiana XIII, 122, Louisiana XIV, 178.

5. Richard Nugent to C. D. Hamilton, August 10, 1865, in Charles D. Hamilton and

The close relationship that had existed between factor and slave-holder ensured that such solicitation would receive a favorable response from those with the inclination to resume planting. Hamilton, already in contact with the New Orleans market, did return his patronage to Nugent. James Archer was shipping cotton to his old agent Payne, Huntington & Co. by 1866. When an individual discovered, as one Madison Parish planter did, that his old factor had not reopened business, it proved a simple matter to locate another willing house.[6]

The gentry needed the commission merchant principally for two reasons. First, to secure an outlet for their cotton. Second, and more important for our purposes, to gain access to goods for their hands. Of course, the postbellum planter was free of the legal obligation of the slaveowner to provide for his laborers. But it appears that at the end of the war the old elite gave little thought to alternative methods of supplying. For reasons already discussed, planters assumed that they would continue to carry out most of their traditional duties. Consequently, they contracted to provide the freedman with food and sometimes clothing, either as a stipulated compensation for his labor or at cost.[7]

Rations were much as before the war, usually three to five pounds of pork and a peck of cornmeal per individual each week. Flour was occasionally thrown into the bargain as was sugar or molasses. More frequently the planter included coffee. Clothing allotments normally consisted of two simple outfits, one for summer, one for winter, as well as one or two pairs of shoes or a pair of boots.[8]

Family Papers, Z 98, Mississippi Department of Archives and History, Jackson; S. B. Newman & Co. to A. K. Farrar, September 1, 1866, in Alexander K. Farrar Papers, Department of Archives and Manuscripts, Louisiana State University, Baton Rouge.

6. A. F. Dunbar to C. D. Hamilton, August 14, 1866, McDowell & Nugent to C. D. Hamilton, September 29, 1866, both in C. D. Hamilton Papers; account of sales, December 20, 1866, in Archer-Finlay-Moore Papers, Mississippi Department of Archives and History, Jackson; Anderson (ed.), Brokenburn, 368; receipt, November 18, 1865, invoice, October 10, 1865, both in George Wilson Humphreys and Family Papers, Z 29, Mississippi Department of Archives and History, Jackson.

7. Whitelaw Reid, After the War: A Southern Tour (Cincinnati: Moore, Wilstach & Baldwin, 1866), 475. See, for example, agreement with freedmen, March 23, 1865, in Archer-Finlay-Moore Papers.

8. Vernon Lane Wharton, The Negro in Mississippi, 1865–1890 (New York: Harper &

Even after the freedmen began moving around, many former slaveowners did not appreciably mark up prices on goods furnished. As late as the summer of 1867, a touring correspondent for the Louisville *Journal* discovered that the standard practice was to supply at "a slight advance upon the original cost." Yet, as J. T. Trowbridge observed, "The better class of planters admitted that the system was liable to gross abuse."[9] White southerners soon discovered that facing uneducated buyers in an imperfect marketplace opened the way for all manner of exploitative practices. If they learned this lesson too quickly and too well, it was because they had formidable teachers, the Yankee invaders.

The acquisitive impulses of the northerners were apparent from the moment the first wave of lessees reached the Natchez district. More than elsewhere in the occupied South, the Mississippi Valley seemed to attract the speculator and fortune hunter, a situation with ominous implications for the emancipated slave. Military authorities took some steps to control the provisioning arrangements of the lessees—for instance, limiting the price of clothes charged to laborers to cost in 1863, then to cost plus 15 percent a year later. But there is little reason to believe that the new planters obeyed such regulations. In a survey of one hundred lessees taken in 1864 by Colonel Samuel Thomas, superintendent of freedmen in the Vicksburg district, fully one-quarter acknowledged that they were turning over a profit of at least 25 percent, a startling admission in view of the fact that those interviewed had every reason to exaggerate their generosity. Some Yankees marked up nearly 200 percent, and Thomas Knox, himself a failed lessee, claimed bitterly that few of his fellow northerners had paid the freedmen for their labor "except in furnishing them small quantities of goods for

---

Row, 1965), 72; Reid, *After the War*, 490; Pierce Butler, *The Unhurried Years: Memoirs of the Old Natchez Region* (Baton Rouge: Louisiana State University Press, 1948), 166; Alden Spooner Forbes Diary (Z 752) (MS in Mississippi Department of Archives and History, Jackson), September 14, 15, 1865; "Time Book for Lynwood Plantation" (MS in John Snodgrass and Family Papers, Z 624, Mississippi Department of Archives and History, Jackson).

9. "Department of Commerce," *De Bow's Review*, After the War Series, IV (July, August, 1867), 106; J. T. Trowbridge, *The South: A Tour of Its Battlefields and Ruined Cities* (New York: Arno Press, 1969), 366.

which they charged five times the value." As for the local Federal officials, they identified their interests, more often than not, with those of the lessees at the expense of the former slave.[10]

With the end of hostilities, Yankees institutionalized their operations in the form of plantation stores. In theory these enterprises facilitated the furnishing of necessities, but once the lessees discovered that there were certain cheap, inessential goods that the freedman was anxious to purchase almost regardless of cost, they stocked up on such items. Colorful baubles and trinkets, handkerchiefs, tobacco, and whiskey became conspicuous features on the shelves of most Yankee stores, including the following operation that Whitelaw Reid visited on a plantation south of Natchez in 1865. "Its business was done entirely for cash, and its sales averaged over fifty dollars a day—all made at an average profit of one hundred per. cent. Calicoes, cottonades, denims, shoes, hats, brass, jewelry, head handkerchiefs, candy, tobacco, sardines, cheese, and whiskey were the great staples. The latter was always watered down by at least one-fourth, and the fine was kept up by a liberal introduction of pepper pods."[11]

Lessees showed little inclination to curb extravagance on the part of the freedman or to provide much-needed guidance in purchasing decisions. Driven by the desire to turn a rapid, substantial profit, they offered at best only mild admonitions of the sort overheard by Reid at another plantation: "If you would let me give you a little advice, I'd tell you all not to waste your money on fish, and candy, and rings, and breastpins, and fine hats. If you will have them, we'll sell them to you, but you had better not buy so freely."[12] Under the circumstances, the freedmen learned little from their al-

10. Lawrence N. Powell, *New Masters: Northern Planters During the Civil War and Reconstruction* (New Haven: Yale University Press, 1980), 11; *The American Annual Cyclopaedia and Register of Important Events of the Year 1863* (14 vols.; New York: D. Appleton, 1865), III, 428–29; James E. Yeatman, *Report to the Western Sanitary Commission, in Regard to Leasing Abandoned Plantations, with Rules and Regulations Governing the Same* (St. Louis: Western Sanitary Commission Rooms, 1864), 14; Bell Irvin Wiley, *Southern Negroes, 1861–1865* (New Haven: Yale University Press, 1965), 240; Thomas W. Knox, *Camp-Fire and Cotton-Field: Southern Adventure in Time of War* (New York: Blelock, 1865), 316.

11. Powell, *New Masters*, 87–93; Reid, *After the War*, 498–99.

12. Reid, *After the War*, 528.

leged benefactors about the subtleties of the marketplace or the potential sorts of leverage available to the buyer.

Such lucrative examples of how to exploit the new order soon helped persuade a few former slaveowners to open stores themselves in an effort to recoup diminished fortunes. And when the crop failures of 1866 and 1867 made planting itself a precarious venture, the district witnessed a small rush to merchandising by the antebellum elite. Not all who opened stores did so with the intention of making a profit. William Newton Mercer charged a 10 percent markup on all goods, reckoning that his net gain would just cover the expense of providing for the old and infirm remaining on his plantations. But few followed Mercer in having a systematic pricing policy, and probably still fewer restrained their greedier inclinations. When, in early 1868, A. J. Kelly applied to Charles D. Hamilton for a managerial position on Allendale, he found it prudent to promise a profit of 30 to 50 percent at the plantation store. Wilmer Shields, superintendent of Mercer's Adams County estates, observed a neighbor ruefully: "As for Hutchins, he seems, from what I hear, to be more of a negro hotel keeper than a planter, and in addition to the supplies with which he furnishes the negroes, he keeps whiskey—from his store he does a good business & he seems to do better, at *present*, under the new than he did under the old regime."[13]

For those planters who opened stores, exorbitant profits might be the difference between survival and collapse in a period when cotton crops were failing. And yet, despite the ostensible financial benefits, comparatively few former slaveowners took up merchandising in the first years after the war. This is not hard to understand. The Yankee lessee looked at life through the eyes of the speculator. He was willing to take extensive risks in a quick strike for wealth. But the former slaveowners viewed the Natchez district

13. J. Brickell to Lem [Conner], September 21, 1866, in Lemuel Parker Conner and Family Papers, Department of Archives and Manuscripts, Louisiana State University, Baton Rouge; Wilmer [Shields] to Doctor [William N. Mercer], February 6, 1867, in William Newton Mercer Papers, Department of Archives and Manuscripts, Louisiana State University, Baton Rouge; A. J. Kelly to C. D. Hamilton, March 28, 1868, in C. D. Hamilton Papers; Wilmer [Shields] to Doctor [William N. Mercer], May 22, 1867, in Mercer Papers.

as home and, expecting to remain there through success or failure, were sensitive to long-term considerations. They were unconvinced that exploitative merchandising would provide immediate riches and were dubious about the lasting benefits of such practices. Their concern was heightened by the realization, quickly brought home in the first months after the war, that Emancipation had so changed the conditions of supplying that they could not take for granted the advantages of continuing to furnish their own laborers, let alone of entering into full-scale merchandising.

Individual freedmen and their families expected individual attention. This upset the traditional predisposition of the planter to purchase and distribute goods in bulk. Furthermore, the former slaveowner could not be sure that his hands would fulfill their immediate contractual obligations or, even if they did, hire for the following year. To top it off, the freedmen seemed unmindful of their debts and thought that they should be allowed to purchase goods at all times. Jesse Darden of Jefferson County refused to make an advance to one of his hands, only to see the freedman in question run away. "They are wanting things all the time," complained Darden's wife, "& when it comes time to pay they make a fuss."[14]

Those members of the old elite who tried to capitalize on the freedman's ignorance of the marketplace occasionally confronted unexpected problems. Colonel Fall was a Delta planter with a scheme worthy of a Yankee. He ordered large quantities of bright handkerchiefs, combs, prunella shoes, red-topped boots, calico gloves, cheap yet brilliant jewelry, and "perfumes of every odor, all strong," intending to sell them to his hands at exorbitant prices as soon as he paid them their wages. When the goods arrived he swaggered off to brag to friends of his impending coup. Here let his kinsman Elisha Greenlee pick up the story:

> We were resting and enjoying the fire. Colonel Fall came in pretty drunk. Aunt Bettie arose and said, "Old man, we have sold all the goods." "Well Dollie let me see the money. Let's count the cash." "Money. I

14. Susan Sillers Darden Diary (MS in Darden Family Papers, Z 82, Mississippi Department of Archives and History, Jackson), II, October 19, 1872.

ain't got no money." "My god, you have ruined me." "Well, man, why don't you attend to your own business? You go up and get drunk with Sam Taylor—man, and you want me to do your work. I won't do it no more, Mun. You didn't tell me to sell the goods for money."

Fall was frantic, but finally he said, "Greenlee, let me see the book." He read and lamented, "Old Fosey—$150.00, My God!; Club-fisted Jim—$75.00. Oh God! Old Frank—$94.00, the Lord help us!!!" He read and commented down the line. His strength failed him and as the tears came into his eyes he said, "Cotton gone, money gone, goods gone. Old Lady we are dead broke."[15]

Few suffered the fate of Colonel Fall. Yet his story does highlight a feature of merchandising that made it distasteful to so many former slaveowners—it was unpredictable. Too many unexpected contingencies could turn the arrangement against the planter. The colonel's misadventure also points to another more significant problem, namely, a profit on the books was often no profit at all. The likelihood of his ever collecting $150 from Old Fosey was obviously slim. In hard times in particular it benefited the planter very little to have scores of freedmen indebted to him. Their financial obligations would not help him pay his own creditors. A bad crop was felt painfully right down the line.

There were other constraints against merchandising as well. At the end of the war, the ethos of paternalism rested too heavily on the shoulders of many planters to allow them to take advantage of the financial inexperience of the freedman. By the same token it seemed unnecessarily demeaning to engage in commercial transactions with former slaves—demeaning to face them as equals in the marketplace, demeaning to match wits with an obviously inferior race simply in the interest of material gain. Consequently, when her friend and neighbor, Cicero Stampley, opened a store in January, 1866, Susan Sillers Darden observed the situation with the discomfort of one who has seen her life take an unavoidably undignified turn. She was not alone. In the first few years following the war, community feeling in general, and the feeling of the gentry

---

15. A. J. Paxton, Sr., "Reminiscences" (MS, Z 555, in Mississippi Department of Archives and History, Jackson), 16.

in particular, held in low esteem indeed those who made a livelihood by trading with blacks. As the Adams County representative of the R. G. Dun Agency said of Allen & Co., a concern that appeared at the end of the war, "Dg a gd bus, trade a gd deal with Negroes which prejudices people vs them."[16]

Ironically, it was the Yankee lessees—the same lessees who had demonstrated the potential profitability of merchandising—who convinced most former slaveholders that there were more elevated ways of surviving in a slaveless world. The observations of J. Floyd King of Concordia Parish reflect the kinds of unflattering associations that members of the gentry came to make between northerners and storekeeping:

> Those Yankees and abolitionists who throng this country to avail themselves of the production of cotton and other staples, show to the black man no kindness, no friendliness, no justice. They hire him to work for them, and, by selling them the necessaries of life, when the pay day comes the laborer is almost always in debt to his employer. As in an instance I witnessed this other evening myself; the lessee was rendering up his accounts with the negroes, in tobacco and the smaller articles of merchandise, he brought them almost invariably in debt to him—this was done by charging 50 & 100 pr cent on articles and also by charging for things which the negroes never received. The accounts and pay lists had been standing for three months, it was the end of the year, and not one man received more than four dollars—mostly they were paid 10–15–25 & 30 cents![17]

If this was the way to make a fortune under free labor, it is no wonder that so many planters left the field of storekeeping to the invaders from the North. Such rapacious materialism might be suitable for a Yankee, but surely never for a Southern gentleman or lady.

Still, constraints of conscience proved relatively short-lived. The most enduring obstacle to merchandising in the late 1860s was of a more practical nature. The planter's traditional source of credit

---

16. Darden Diary, II, January 17, 1866; R. G. Dun & Co. Collection, Mississippi II, 99.
17. J. Floyd King to Lin [Caperton], January 1, 1866, J. Floyd King to Mallery [King], January 18, 1866, both in Thomas Butler King Papers, Southern Historical Collection, University of North Carolina, Chapel Hill.

was failing. Operating a plantation store and even supplying basic rations came to involve greater financial sacrifices than most former slaveowners were willing or able to take.

The immediate problem lay in New Orleans, with the factors. Although they had reopened enthusiastically at the end of the war, they remained dependent on northern and European capital. Some, like Samuel B. Newman and Henry S. Buckner, bore their burdens well. But for every successful house, there were a number of failures. A majority struggled through 1865, expecting to recover their lost position in the years ahead. They were to be disappointed. The short crops of 1866 and 1867 proved catastrophic. Most of the new concerns fell away, as did many of the old ones. Northern financiers, no doubt appalled at the insecurity of their original investments, removed their backing. New capital was scarce. "Everything is going to the devil here in a hard gallop," wrote J. W. Labouisse from New Orleans in January, 1868, "and I can see no light ahead. Nearly all the Factors are broke, and all other branches of trade must sympathise."[18]

The difficulties in New Orleans had severe repercussions in the countryside. Commission houses were forced to deny many of the normal requests of their clients. J. U. Payne wrote to Joseph E. Davis of Warren County in early 1868, "The old resource to raise money by discounting paper predicated upon the growing crop is exploded: and at this season it is very difficult to procure the means to fill the small orders for pork & corn to feed the people untill [sic] they can raise something at home, which they have failed to do in sufficient quantity for the last two years. This kind of orders [sic] has so completely exhausted our resources that we

18. Roger W. Shugg, *Origins of Class Struggle in Louisiana: A Social History of White Farmers and Laborers During Slavery and After, 1840–1875* (Baton Rouge: Louisiana State University Press, 1972), 194; J. P. Harrison to Governor Sharkey, August 10, 1865, in Governors' Correspondence, Box 62, Mississippi Department of Archives and History, Jackson; A. F. Montgomery to her husband, January 20, 1868, in Joseph A. Montgomery and Family Papers, Department of Archives and Manuscripts, Louisiana State University, Baton Rouge; B. F. Nourse, "Report on Cotton," *De Bow's Review*, After the War Series, VI (September, 1869), 785; Taylor, *Louisiana Reconstructed*, 392–93; Harold D. Woodman, *King Cotton and His Retainers: Financing and Marketing the Cotton Crop of the South, 1800–1925* (Lexington: University of Kentucky Press, 1968), 363; J. W. Labouisse to Will [Ker], January 28, 1868, in Mary Susan Ker Papers, Southern Historical Collection, University of North Carolina, Chapel Hill.

are run out of means & credit to raise money." It was the same for many other factors who served the lower Mississippi Valley. Despite considerable success during the first two years after the war, John Hardin had to discontinue advancing by late 1867. The firm of McDowell & Nugent regretfully informed Charles D. Hamilton in the spring of that same year that it lacked the capital to relieve him of financial difficulties brought on by the flooding of his Louisiana plantation.[19]

Alternative sources of credit were almost nonexistent. Federal banking legislation prohibited loans secured by mortgages on real estate. This policy effectively precluded the growth of national banks in the planting regions. There were only two such institutions in Mississippi in 1867, only three in Louisiana. Long-term loans were "usually very difficult to come by and always very expensive." The severity of the planters' distress led *Harper's* to suggest that the government itself take the unorthodox step of providing credit.[20]

The disastrous crops of 1866 and 1867 had a lasting effect on the supply system of the South. Bereft of slaves and with land values at unprecedentedly low levels, planters found that advances could no longer be obtained on terms as favorable as before the war. Credit was available, but factors insisted that their additional risks be met by additional security.

Robert M. Davis reported in 1871 that planters had to pay commission houses at least 14 to 25 percent, often more, for advances in money and supplies. Furthermore, factors increasingly began to ask for mortgages on real estate to secure loans, a recourse only occasionally adopted before the war. When the firm of

19. J. U. Payne to J. E. Davis, June 10, 1868, in Joseph E. Davis and Family Papers, Z 1028, Mississippi Department of Archives and History, Jackson; John Hardin to Capt. Wm. Hughes, January 16, 1868, in William Hughes and Family Papers, Z 68, Folder 7, Mississippi Department of Archives and History, Jackson; McDowell & Nugent to C. D. Hamilton, April 9, 1867, in C. D. Hamilton Papers.

20. William C. Harris, *Presidential Reconstruction in Mississippi* (Baton Rouge: Louisiana State University Press, 1967), 159; "Miscellany," *De Bow's Review*, After the War Series, III (January, 1867), 92; Roger L. Ransom and Richard Sutch, "Debt Peonage in the Cotton South After the Civil War," *Journal of Economic History*, XXXII (1972), 644–46; Richard W. Griffin, "Problems of the Southern Cotton Planters After the Civil War," *Georgia Historical Quarterly*, XXXIX (1955), 110.

Meyer, Deutsch & Weis advanced $2,730 to James Foster in 1867, it demanded a mortgage on his Woodland place. When Foster subsequently failed to liquidate the debt, the company foreclosed and took over the property.[21]

More widely requested than mortgages on land, however, were pledges to ship cotton or outright mortgages on the crop. Before the war it was commonplace for a planter to sell his cotton through the commission house that supplied him. But this arrangement was rarely formalized in a contract, and most slaveholders felt free to market their bales through any number of houses during the same season. Not so after 1867. "All who make advances do so in the express stipulation that the whole crop shall be shipped," observed a factor in that year. J. W. Champlin carried this policy even further, agreeing to ship pork and flour to Lewis Clarke of Claiborne County "on a pledge of shipment of your cotton and influence."[22]

Crop mortgages were still more binding. To secure an advance of $4,500 in 1865, Carrie Nutt had to mortgage her share of the bales produced on Longwood, near Natchez. Meyer, Deutsch & Weis required P. K. Montgomery of Jefferson County to guarantee a loan of $1,000 in 1868 with a deed of trust on the crops of Lochnagan. Often factors asked their clients to mortgage both land and crops. In 1866, Benjamin Galtney had to give his commission merchant, Samuel B. Newman, one mortgage on his 800-acre Adams County plantation and another on all his cotton and corn. Jurey & Harris agreed to furnish Nancy Pinson of Wilkinson County only after she signed a deed of trust on her lands, implements, stock of all kinds, and crops.[23]

21. Robert M. Davis, *The Southern Planter, the Factor and the Banker* (New Orleans: n.p., 1871), 4–5; mortgage, April 29, 1867, in Jefferson County Deed Records, Vol. L, p. 507, Mississippi Department of Archives and History, Jackson.

22. Lewis A. Atherton, *The Southern Country Store, 1800–1860* (Baton Rouge: Louisiana State University Press, 1949), 28; Woodman, *King Cotton and His Retainers*, 64, 68; J. A. Montgomery to his wife, April 26, 1870, in Montgomery Papers; J. W. Champlin to Lewis Clarke, July 2, 1870, in Lewis Clarke Papers, Manuscript Department, William R. Perkins Library, Duke University, Durham, N.C.

23. Mortgage, October 3, 1865, in Adams County Deed Records, Vol. NN, p. 512, Adams County Courthouse, Natchez; deed of trust, March 4, 1868, in Jefferson County Deed Records, Vol. L, p. 641; note from the Final Record of the Adams County Chancery Court, in possession of Mrs. Waldo Lambdin, Natchez; Jurey & Harris to Mrs. N. and

To continue supplying their hands under these adverse conditions or, more ambitious, to expand into storekeeping seemed too hazardous to most planters. For those already deeply in debt, it was out of the question. The close personal relationship between planter and factor wavered in these troubled times.[24] The former slaveowners were deeply disappointed in the new credit arrangements and some curtailed their business dealings with New Orleans. Into the 1880s, most planters continued to rely on commission houses to market their cotton and handle their finances. But many turned over to the laborer the responsibility for procuring his own provisions. For these the freedman turned to local sources. The storekeeper, once on the periphery of the plantation economy, now came center stage.

II

Merchants in the river counties and parishes enjoyed only limited influence before the war. Except for a few factors who lived in Natchez and Vicksburg and successfully competed with New Orleans for the trade of the interior, no one rivaled the economic and social position of the planters. In the more important towns—Port Gibson, for example, and Woodville—some storekeepers fashioned an impressive trade. The most prosperous did business in excess of $25,000 a year. But the average enterprise was capitalized at under $10,000 and at best provided its owner with a comfortable town subsistence. Stores in the smaller towns or at the crossroads carried on a still more restricted trade; most involved an investment of no more than $500 to $2,000.[25]

Outside the plantation South—and in frontier regions, in particular—local merchants exerted a powerful influence. Their dealings with the many small farmers and laborers whose resources were too limited to warrant the attention of coastal commission

S. A. Pinson, July 6, 1870, in Mrs. Nancy Pinson Papers, Department of Archives and Manuscripts, Louisiana State University, Baton Rouge.

24. Edward King, *The Great South* (New York: Arno Press, 1969), 53.

25. Atherton, *The Southern Country Store*, 205; R. G. Dun & Co. Collection, Mississippi II, 22, Mississippi VI, 135, 138, Mississippi XXI, 35.

houses effectively gave them control over the economic affairs of the communities in which they lived. The storekeeper of the Black Belt had a less prominent role, however. He still served the farmers, laborers, and townsmen, but these were often fewer in number and, at any rate, depended themselves on the plantation economy. Significantly, the local merchant relied on the planter for the major part of his business. He supplied the cheap groceries and coarse goods that the large slaveholders did not buy through commission merchants and he took care of the incidental needs that arose on the plantation from day to day. Equally important, he acted as middleman for planter and factor, providing storage facilities and shipping services.[26]

Many planters had a financial interest in their local merchants. The credit ledgers of the R. G. Dun Mercantile Agency suggest that historians have insufficiently noted the extent to which the antebellum gentry had a hand in the operations of town and crossroads stores. Some large landowners, James H. Maury of Claiborne County, for instance, owned property that they rented out to merchants. Others provided necessary financial assistance. John D. Kaigler, a Wilkinson County planter with real estate worth $100,000, held a hidden interest in the successful Woodville concern of L. Loeb & Brother. J. B. Palmer's store at nearby Percy Creek received financial backing from W. B. Davis, owner of 170 slaves.[27]

In the overall scheme of things, the local merchant was simply another element of secondary importance in a society dominated by the landholding elite and the plantation economy. Those with aspirations of wealth and status looked upon their merchandising ventures as stepping-stones to planting. Yet the storekeeper of the antebellum period was very surely the precursor of the influential

26. See Atherton, *The Southern Country Store*, Chap. 3. The following items give some idea of the nature of local purchases by planters: bill, October 7, 1853, in Thomas Freeland Papers, Z 774, Folder 1, Mississippi Department of Archives and History, Jackson; receipt, February 2, 1856, in Trask-Ventress Family Papers, Z 607, Folder 267, Mississippi Department of Archives and History, Jackson; receipts, January 2, February 28, 1854, both in Benajah R. Inman and Family Papers, Department of Archives and Manuscripts, Louisiana State University, Baton Rouge.

27. James H. Maury to James Fontaine Maury, September 18, 1863 (handwritten copy), in Eunice J. Stockwell Papers, Z 629, Mississippi Department of Archives and History, Jackson; R. G. Dun & Co. Collection, Mississippi XXII, 147, 155, Mississippi XI, 311.

figure of the New South. To a limited extent in the Black Belt and to a significant extent elsewhere, he existed to fill the needs of small producers and laborers. The war, in liberating the slaves, flooded the plantation South with just such individuals. When old patterns of supply broke down, it was the local storekeeper who stood best prepared to deal with the material needs of the freedmen.[28]

Table 17 documents the rapid expansion of the merchant class during Reconstruction. In those counties and parishes of the Natchez district that were predominantly rural, there were 130 merchants in 1860, 218 in 1870, and, despite the depression from 1873 to 1879, 283 in 1880.[29] Some communities actually enjoyed greater growth during the 1870s than they had during the immediate postwar years. Concordia Parish, for example, burdened with devastated levees and flooding in the 1860s, had only 11 merchants in 1870, an increase of but 2 over the course of a decade. By 1880, however, there were 31 in the parish. Jefferson County, on the other hand, from 1860 to 1870, saw its merchant class grow almost 100 percent before experiencing a falling off, presumably in part attributable to the decline of Rodney as an active trading center and the increasing prominence of Port Gibson storekeepers in neighboring Claiborne County. Nevertheless, beyond these local variations the overriding characteristic was that of growth. And, worth noting, it was growth that took place in the face of occasionally heavy taxation on mercantile enterprises.

The merchant class of the Reconstruction era included a handful of local storekeepers who had survived the war, even turned it to their advantage. The sons of Jacob Mayer serve as a good illustration. While one went off to fight for the Confederacy, the other

28. Thomas D. Clark, *Pills, Petticoats and Plows: The Southern Country Store* (Norman: University of Oklahoma Press, 1964), 12; Ransom and Sutch, "Debt Peonage," 651; "Changes in Marketing the Great Staple," *Bradstreet's*, April 10, 1886, p. 226.

29. Because changes in Adams and Warren counties would reflect conditions in Natchez and Vicksburg rather than in the countryside, Table 17 is confined to rural counties and parishes. It is worth noting, however, that circumstances were conducive to a significant increase in the number of merchants in the two shipping centers of the district as well. There were 101 storekeepers in Natchez in 1850, 95 in 1860, 115 in 1870, and 138 in 1880. The growth of the Vicksburg merchant class was explosive, reflecting the rapid expansion of that city.

**Table 17.**   MERCHANTS IN THE RURAL COUNTIES AND PARISHES, 1850–1880

|  | 1850 | 1860 | 1870 | 1880 |
|---|---|---|---|---|
| Claiborne County | 51 | 45 | 53 | 67 |
| Jefferson County | 25 | 25 | 48 | 36 |
| Wilkinson County | 30 | 16 | 40 | 49 |
| Concordia Parish | 2 | 9 | 11 | 31 |
| Madison Parish | 18 | 23 | 26 | 47 |
| Tensas Parish | 11 | 12 | 40 | 53 |
| Total | 137 | 130 | 218 | 283 |

SOURCES: U.S. Bureau of the Census, MS Population Schedules for Claiborne County, Jefferson County, Wilkinson County, Concordia Parish, Madison Parish, Tensas Parish, 1850, 1860, 1870, 1880.

remained in Natchez, where he speculated in cotton and dealt with the Yankees. At the end of hostilities, the brothers were sufficiently prosperous to earn the jealous scorn of the returning gentry. "They are now just looking over the front steps of the crem de la crem (?) [*sic*]," snorted a young planter, "they themselves having but recently become of the consolidated milk of this society."[30]

Few antebellum storekeepers were nearly so fortunate, however. In fact, by 1870, most had disappeared from the local census rolls.[31] The vast majority of merchants in the decade following the war were new to the district or the profession, in some cases both. They came from a wide variety of occupational backgrounds and represented a diversity of geographic and ethnic origins.

Northerners made up a conspicuous element of the wave of the 1860s but were notably unsuccessful in establishing themselves, especially outside Natchez and Vicksburg. They tended to blame their difficulties on southern vindictiveness, and not without some justification. J. H. Price & Co. struggled for several years to overcome community hostility in Milliken's Bend, Louisiana. Despite sound financial backing, the firm was never able to gain credibility,

30. J. Floyd King to Lin [Caperton], January 24, 1866, in King Papers.
31. Michael Stuart Wayne, "Ante-Bellum Planters in the Post-Bellum South: The Natchez District, 1860–1880" (Ph.D. dissertation, Yale University, 1979), 236–40.

finally closing up operations in 1869. Nevertheless, it would probably be a mistake to attribute most northern failures to sectional prejudice. While resentment did exist, the popularity enjoyed by a few Yankee entrepreneurs suggests that southerners were prepared to deal with those individuals who had a reputation for reliability and honest financial practices. E. W. Wilson and H. M. Gastrell, for example, each built up a profitable enterprise in Natchez and eventually gained social respectability. It seems likely that most of those who attributed their problems to antinorthern sentiment were merely covering up their own recklessness or incompetence. Rickey, Shelton & Co. complained repeatedly of ill-treatment by Adams County residents. But the ambitious partners far overextended themselves, borrowing from street brokers at .25 percent per day. It was of little surprise when, in 1867, heavy speculation in cotton toppled the shaky enterprise. The state eventually sued the associates for nonpayment of taxes, but by then they had fled north with their stock.[32]

Former Confederate soldiers also opened stores, as did many farmers and even some planters ruined by the war. Perhaps the most successful newcomers were the Europeans, particularly the Jews. The census reveals that over 40 percent of the merchants in the rural counties of the region in 1870 were born abroad (see Table 18). There is no way of knowing how many of these men and women came to the South after the war, although clearly many did. It seems likely that those immigrants who were most successful in establishing themselves had help from friends or relatives already living in the community. A large group of Bavarian Jews settled in Jefferson County. Pockets of Irishmen and Frenchmen appeared here and there throughout the district.

Ironically, the one figure who is conspicuously absent in the postwar rush to merchandising is the freedman himself. There were some attempts by blacks to service their own, but these were largely unsuccessful (See Table 19). This is scarcely surprising. Except for those few free Negro shopkeepers of antebellum times, blacks lacked the experience and credit necessary to build a signifi-

32. Reid, *After the War*, 481; R. G. Dun & Co. Collection, Louisiana VII, 14, Mississippi II, 99, 101, 106, 107.

**Table 18.**   GEOGRAPHIC ORIGINS OF MERCHANTS IN THE RURAL
COUNTIES AND PARISHES, 1870

|  | North | South | Europe |
|---|---|---|---|
| Claiborne County | 8 | 21 | 24 |
| Jefferson County | 4 | 23 | 21 |
| Wilkinson County | 4 | 18 | 18 |
| Concordia Parish | 0 | 3 | 8 |
| Madison Parish | 6 | 14 | 6 |
| Tensas Parish | 9 | 20 | 11 |
| Total | 31 | 99 | 88 |

SOURCES: U.S. Bureau of the Census, MS Population Schedules for Claiborne County, Jefferson County,
Wilkinson County, Concordia Parish, Madison Parish, Tensas Parish, 1870.
NOTE: A southerner is someone born in one of the states that belonged to the Confederacy. Merchants
born in Canada are included in the European category.

cant trade and compete with whites. Most of their stores were cap-
italized to only $500 or $1,000 and, like white stores of the same
size, carried on a small local business.[33]

The surge of merchandising was dominated by men of limited
capital if perhaps high aspirations. A significant majority of the
postbellum merchants were landless, in marked contrast to the
situation before the war, as Table 20 shows (see Appendix I). In
Claiborne County in 1860, 53 percent of the mercantile enterprises operated on rented property. By 1868, this figure had risen
to 62 percent, by 1879 to 66 percent. In Adams County, the difference was more striking. Only 32 percent of the firms were landless in 1861. This figure had climbed to 70 percent by 1870. Concordia Parish had eight mercantile concerns in 1860, of which six
owned their own stores. Twenty years later, there were twenty-five
enterprises, fully seventeen operating on rented property. These
figures say much about the new merchants. They were, by and
large, men of modest means. Some were simply interested in carv-
ing a subsistence out of a cash trade with the former slaves. But

33. R. G. Dun & Co. Collection, Mississippi VI, 162, Louisiana XXII, 34, Louisiana
IV, 229.

**Table 19.** STORES OPERATED BY BLACKS IN ADAMS AND CLAIBORNE COUNTIES, 1865–1870

|  | 1865 | 1866 | 1867 | 1868 | 1869 | 1870 |
|---|---|---|---|---|---|---|
| Adams County | 4 | 23 | 34 | 19 | 15 | 11 |
| Claiborne County | 1 | 1 | 1 | 2 | 4 | 5 |

SOURCE: "Number of Stores," in Records of the Auditor of Public Accounts, Box 117, Mississippi Department of Archives and History, Jackson.

**Table 20.** MERCANTILE ENTERPRISES

|  | Total Enterprises | Landless | Percentage Landless |
|---|---|---|---|
| *Adams County* |  |  |  |
| 1861 | 93 | 30 | 32% |
| 1870 | 114 | 80 | 70% |
| 1879 | 135 | 77 | 57% |
| *Claiborne County* |  |  |  |
| 1860 | 45 | 24 | 53% |
| 1868 | 47 | 29 | 62% |
| 1879 | 62 | 41 | 66% |
| *Concordia Parish* |  |  |  |
| 1860 | 8 | 2 | 25% |
| 1871 | 10 | 4 | 40% |
| 1880 | 25 | 17 | 68% |

SOURCES: U.S. Bureau of the Census, MS Population Schedules for Adams County, Claiborne County, Concordia Parish, 1860, 1870, 1880; U.S. Bureau of the Census, MS Agricultural Schedules for Claiborne County, Concordia Parish, 1860; Adams County Land Rolls, 1861, 1870, in Mississippi Department of Archives and History, Jackson; Adams County Land Rolls, 1879, in Adams County Courthouse, Natchez; "Report of State Tax, 1868," in Records of the Auditor of Public Accounts, Box 85; Claiborne County Land Rolls, 1879, in Mississippi Department of Archives and History, Jackson; Concordia Parish Assessment Rolls, 1871, 1880, in Louisiana State Capitol, Baton Rouge.
NOTE: The total figures on merchants in Table 17 do not correspond precisely with the figures here. This is because the census listed individuals according to occupation, while the tax rolls listed firms where appropriate. Inasmuch as some merchants belonged to partnerships, the figures here are slightly smaller than those in Table 17. Since the tax rolls do not list landless individuals, I have assumed that each merchant without real estate was an enterprise unto himself or herself. This supposition will marginally overstate the landless element, but the bias is inconsequential, being small and presumably applicable to both the antebellum and postbellum periods.

others were men of ambition, anxious to convert extensive credit sales into control of the cotton crop and great wealth.

Those who took up storekeeping after the war faced substantial risks, and, for most, there was little to fall back on. The observation made by a credit agent about the prospects of Moses Dreyfus of Tensas Parish could easily be applied to others throughout the region: "He does not own anything more than the stock of goods say 15c$ in his store. If the crop turns up well, of wh. there is now every prospect, he will do well—if there be disasters in the Cotton Crop he as well as most of the mrchts in the South wd be almost ruined." There were disasters frequent enough to imperil the business of many merchants far more secure than Dreyfus. And men of his stature were constantly going under, victims of armyworms, bad weather, levee overflows, and any variety of unanticipated catastrophes that nature or man might fashion.[34]

Hard times for the plantation invariably led to desperate scrambling by merchants. Edward King found that bad crops left the former slave loath to settle his accounts even when he had the funds. "He seems to think his debt has been outlawed."[35] More often the problem was not intransigence but simply lack of means. In depressed periods, few were the tenants white or black who had the wherewithal to cover their indebtedness.

Even in good times, there were substantial risks. Year in and year out a significant minority of freedmen failed to pay their accounts in full or ran off without attempting a settlement. Typical of the class was Thomas Wallace, who, in the summer of 1870, disappeared from the Snyder plantation in Tensas Parish, owing Winter & Hunter of Waterproof $42.40. Seven of the tenants whom George W. Montgomery supplied on Montrose in Madison Parish in 1876 absconded by September 1. Their outstanding accounts of $231.14 represented one-tenth of his disbursements to the plantation. Charles Otken complained with exaggeration that there was not a merchant in the South "whose losses from this source have not amounted to thousands of dollars."[36] The difficulties of the

34. R. G. Dun & Co. Collection, Louisiana XXII, 45, 49, 22.
35. King, *The Great South*, 274.
36. Winter & Hunter Ledger (MS in Hunter Brothers Business Records, Department of

storekeeper were complicated by his dependence on outside capital. Some merchants relied heavily on northern money. Jacob Wertheimer of Rodney secured advances in New York, for example, as did the prominent Natchez concern Fleming & Baldwin. But the majority of enterprises continued to look to New Orleans commission houses for backing. This was true both of small firms, such as Dobyns & Hunt of Jefferson County, which operated on just $300 advanced by John Chaffe & Son, and large companies, such as that of C. L. Holden of Natchez, which in 1881 received a loan of $10,000 from Nalle & Cammack.[37]

Some New Orleans factors built up a large clientele of merchants. John Burnet & Co. controlled many of the storekeepers in and around Port Gibson, as did J. W. Person. On a wider scale, Meyer, Deutsch, & Weis had customers throughout the region, ranging from small crossroads traders to the major concerns in Natchez. By the late 1870s the company was the largest receiver of cotton in New Orleans, with a worth variously estimated at $750,000 to $1 million. The scope of its dealings with both planters and merchants gave the firm unequaled economic influence in the cotton areas of the lower Mississippi, and to a significant extent its policies determined regional credit arrangements.[38]

His indebtedness and the uncertain prospects of his customers left the local merchant in an enormously vulnerable position. The ledgers of the R. G. Dun Mercantile Agency contain entries on numerous stores in the area that the company would not recommend to its subscribers. Not surprisingly, the storekeeper faced very high, if not prohibitive, interest rates.[39]

---

Archives and Manuscripts, Louisiana State University, Baton Rouge), I, 37; George W. Montgomery Account Books (MSS in Department of Archives and Manuscripts, Louisiana State University, Baton Rouge), VI; Charles H. Otken, *The Ills of the South: Or, Related Causes Hostile to the General Prosperity of the Southern People* (New York: G. P. Putnam's Sons, 1894), 24.

37. R. G. Dun & Co. Collection, Mississippi XI, 310C, 328; deed of trust, December 28, 1869, in Adams County Deed Records, Vol. PP, p. 670; pledge of shipment, May 26, 1881, in T. Otis Baker Papers, Z 72, Box 2, Folder 22, Mississippi Department of Archives and History, Jackson.

38. J. H. Danjean and Co., Ltd., Records, Z 917, Vols. I and II, *passim*, Mississippi Department of Archives and History, Jackson; R. G. Dun & Co. Collection, Mississippi VI, 170, 144S, 144E, Mississippi XI, 319, Louisiana XXII, 40, Mississippi II, 153.

39. Woodman, *King Cotton and His Retainers*, 357–58.

To minimize the risks in advancing, merchants sought protection in two potent weapons: the crop lien system—which was also used to effect by landlords—and a pricing policy that differentiated sharply between cash and credit purchases. It was standard practice in the South to require low-risk customers to shoulder the burden of unreliable ones. As Charles Otken observed, "Every honest man must help pay his *pro rata* of the bad man's debts." Storekeepers observed this dictum by charging substantially higher prices for goods bought on credit. In a society in which as much as 90 percent of a merchant's business was likely to be in the form of advances and most of those receiving supplies were poor, propertyless tenants, the reliable customer paid a heavy price indeed. Historians agree that credit charges ranged from 10 to well over 100 percent above cash prices. The average markup was probably in excess of 60 percent.[40]

Without doubt, this system produced its shameful share of abuse. Storekeepers rarely followed a systematic approach to price increases, and the vulnerability of the freedman tempted many into flagrantly exploitative practices. The former slaves were ill-equipped to identify and expose exorbitant markups. In a competitive environment they might have been able to play off merchant against merchant to secure lower prices. As it was, the crop lien effectively precluded this eventuality.

The lien system has earned considerable criticism for the damaging effects it had on the economy of the New South. But at the end of the war, observers regarded it as a necessity, and not an evil one at that. It seemed a very efficient way to get credit to the small producer without creating prohibitive risks for the supplier.[41]

The lien itself was simply a pledge of the forthcoming crop. It

40. Otken, *The Ills of the South*, 24, 70; Roger L. Ransom and Richard Sutch, *One Kind of Freedom: The Economic Consequences of Emancipation* (New York: Cambridge University Press, 1977), 129–31; Fred A. Shannon, *The Farmer's Last Frontier: Agriculture, 1860–1897* (New York: Farrar & Rinehart, 1945), 91; Clark, *Pills, Petticoats and Plows*, 175, 273–74. Ransom and Sutch contend that although merchants had severe financial burdens, their credit charges were exorbitant and exploitative. See also Robert Higgs, *Competition and Coercion: Blacks in the American Economy, 1865–1914* (New York: Cambridge University Press, 1977), 57.

41. C. Vann Woodward, *Origins of the New South, 1877–1913* (Baton Rouge: Louisiana State University Press, 1971), 180; Woodman, *King Cotton and His Retainers*, 298.

legally obligated the individual receiving an advance to forward his produce for the season to his supplier, with the supplier taking all marketing responsibility. Once the indebtedness had been paid out of the proceeds of the crop, the lien fell void.

Precedents for this system existed before the war. Antebellum merchants commonly required their farmer and small planter clients to secure advances with mortgages on the coming crop. And factors occasionally asked large slaveholders to make similar commitments, although these tended to be verbal, informal, and only loosely enforced. Roger Shugg has found that crop pledges were sanctioned by the legislature of Louisiana in the 1840s and enforced by the state courts. Familiarity with the device clearly facilitated the enactment and public acceptance of postbellum lien laws in 1867 in Mississippi and in 1874 in Louisiana. Indeed, both merchants and landlords were securing freedmen's debts with crop pledges before the legislatures of the two states gave formal approval to such arrangements.[42]

Although a few merchants encumbered their contracts with elaborate and complicated provisions, there was little variation in substance between one lien and the next. The following agreement between a Jefferson County freedman and his supplier stands as representative.

Know all men by these presents that I Peter Brunson of the county of Jefferson and state of Mississippi for and in consideration of supplies, goods and merchandise furnished and agreed to be furnished to me during the present year not to be less than one hundred dollars and not more than one hundred dollars by Thomas Devenport of said state and county, and which said amount of supplies shall be shown by a correct account thereof do hereby bargain, sell, and convey, unto him the said Thomas Devenport all the crop of cotton, corn and other products to be raised on W. B. Stewarts [sic] plantation in said county during the present year to gether [sic] with all the stock of cattle, horses, mules and agricultural implements therein, and it is further agreed by me that I will deliver to the said Devenport at his ware house in the town of Fayette in said county of all the crops so raised by me to be by him

42. Hammond, The Cotton Industry, 144; Woodman, King Cotton and His Retainers, 296–97; Shugg, Origins of Class Struggle, 110. Theodore Saloutos, "Southern Agriculture and the Problems of Readjustment, 1865–1877," Agricultural History, XXX (1956), 72, traces the lien back to colonial days.

the said Devenport shipped to market. It is also agreed by me that I will pay the usual charges and interest on said amount of supplies, but this deed is upon the expressed condition that when the said amount of supplies and merchandise shall have been fully paid for out of the proceeds of said crop or otherwise then this obligation shall cease and be of no effect.[43]

As did Devenport, most merchants sought to increase their protection by taking mortgages on any implements or livestock owned by their customers. To secure an advance for the year 1871 and for an outstanding indebtedness of $700, Jeff and Elijah Copelan, Claiborne County freedmen, had to grant their supplier not only a pledge of their crops but also a mortgage on one mare, two horses, a wagon and harness, and all their farm tools. Others with less property had fewer commitments but were also less able to acquire extensive credit.[44]

The lien gave storekeepers significant control over the crop. It bound producers to turn over their cotton as soon as it was ginned and baled, and left all marketing decisions to the discretion of the merchant. Few went so far as the Port Gibson firm that required customers to accept the following provision in their contracts: "The net proceeds, after paying expenses, to be applied by Louis Kiefer and Co. to payment of my indebtedness to them, and as they may think best for their security." But few had to. The authority of the supplier was presumed.[45]

The lien system provided a measure of security for merchants. It also prevented potentially debilitating rivalries. Conditions existed for a highly competitive situation. The rush to storekeeping after

43. Lien, January 25, 1873, in Jefferson County Deed Records, Vol. BB, p. 166. In the early years after the war, merchants often wrote interest charges into their agreements. These ranged from 8 to 10 percent. By the 1870s, however, interest payments were either taken for granted or included without reference to a specified rate.

44. Mortgage and lien, April 18, 1871, in Claiborne County Deed Records, Vol. II, p. 573, Mississippi Department of Archives and History, Jackson.

45. Lien, May 2, 1871, in Claiborne County Deed Records, Vol. II, p. 505. While suppliers apparently encouraged a concentration on cotton, there is virtually no evidence that they pressed for contractual provisions stipulating its growth. On those rare occasions when a lien referred to the nature of the crop to be raised, corn was included. Most often the agreement simply called for a lien on "all crops." For the role of the merchant in the perpetuation of the one-crop economy, see, in particular, Ransom and Sutch, *One Kind of Freedom*, Chap. 8.

Table 21.  NUMBER OF CUSTOMERS SUPPLIED BY
LOCAL MERCHANTS ON SELECTED PLANTATIONS IN CONCORDIA
PARISH, 1878

| | Merchant | | | | | |
|---|---|---|---|---|---|---|
| | Mrs. M. Farrell | Isaac Friedler | Isadore Lemle | Nathan Lorie | Morris Wexler | Peter Young |
| Plantation | | | | | | |
| Arnandlia | 0 | 12 | 3 | 24 | 1 | 1 |
| Lake Place | 0 | 17 | 8 | 0 | 10 | 1 |
| Potowamut | 12 | 9 | 2 | 12 | 9 | 0 |
| Scotland | 0 | 4 | 1 | 1 | 3 | 5 |
| Sycamore | 0 | 29 | 4 | 19 | 7 | 0 |
| Wecama | 0 | 5 | 0 | 9 | 8 | 1 |
| White Hall | 0 | 6 | 1 | 2 | 12 | 4 |
| Windermere | 3 | 16 | 0 | 2 | 13 | 0 |
| Total | 15 | 98 | 19 | 69 | 63 | 12 |

SOURCES: Various affidavits of open account, July 20–September 24, 1878, in Concordia Parish General
Mortgages, Vol. U, pp. 339, 373, 400, 407, 414, 424. Concordia Parish Courthouse, Vidalia.

the war brought together clusters of merchants in large and small
towns throughout the region. Contrary to a recent study by
Roger L. Ransom and Richard Sutch, there were likely to be
within any given community at least half a dozen suppliers with
easy access to the same plantations, hence the same customers.[46]
Many merchants dealt widely within a locality. In Concordia Parish, for example, Isadore Lemle furnished freedmen on nineteen
separate plantations, Nathan Lorie on thirty, Morris Wexler on
thirty-one, and Peter Young on twenty-seven. And there is every
evidence that many plantations were served by more than one supplier. Table 21 provides figures on eight plantations in Concordia
Parish in 1878.

As these figures demonstrate, while some merchants had a larger

46. Ransom and Sutch, *One Kind of Freedom*, Chap. 7. Compare Higgs, *Competition
and Coercion*, 57.

**Table 22.** TENANTS' ACCOUNTS WITH SUPPLIERS, THREE PLANTATIONS, 1878

| Plantation | Number of Tenants Supplied | Tenants with Accounts with More Than One Merchant |
|---|---|---|
| Potowamut | 45 | 1 |
| Scotland | 13 | 1 |
| Sycamore | 56 | 2 |
| Total | 114 | 4 |

SOURCES: Various affidavits of open account, July 20–September 24, 1878, in Concordia Parish General Mortgages, Vol. U, pp. 339, 373, 400, 407, 414, 424.

trade than others, tenants had access to several suppliers, with all the implications such a situation holds for marketplace competition. In fact, such competition was limited. Although merchants would willingly sell goods for cash at any time, they would not extend credit to someone who had already pledged his crops. Table 22 provides evidence from three plantations on the preceding list. Of a total of 114 tenants on Scotland, Sycamore, and Potowamut, only 4 had accounts with more than one storekeeper. Of these 4, 2 secured a second account as members of squads. Since their partners did not have additional debt obligations, the merchants involved accepted only slightly greater risks than normal. That leaves just 2 individuals with credit from more than one storekeeper. George Kennedy on Scotland owed $80.30 to Morris Wexler and $29.35 to Peter Young. Jack Black of Sycamore was indebted to Wexler for $96.40, to Isaac Friedler for $308.00, and, jointly with Curtis Black, to Nathan Lorie for $245.55. It appears that Black enjoyed an uncommon reputation for reliability, although the possibility exists that there were two men of the same name on the plantation.

The crop lien effectively put a damper on competition during the growing season. But in the winter, before the producer had pledged his forthcoming cotton, things were somewhat different. Charles Nordhoff found in 1875 that the freedmen "are quite able to transfer their traffic to new points and do so." P. Fennell of Concordia Parish provides a good example. In 1868, as a tenant on Morville, he procured supplies from Nathan Lorie. Four years later, he moved to Waterloo and dealt with Peter Young. In 1875, now on Cotton Grove, he was furnished by J. S. Gaynor. And the following year, renting a tract of Saint Genevieve plantation, he got his advances from Michael Pheland. There is no indication that any of these merchants found Fennell's business undesirable. His account of $250 in 1875 represented a substantial increase over the $75 he had received in 1868. Apparently by his own choice he moved his trade around from year to year.[47]

For those less successful than Fennell, opportunities were correspondingly less attractive. And individuals who came out in debt at the end of the harvest had dim prospects indeed. To be sure, the lien was not a self-perpetuating contract. A tenant whose crop production was insufficient to liquidate his financial obligations was not legally bound to renew his pledge for the forthcoming year. But merchants had little interest in competing for poor credit risks, as there was scant profit to be made from apparently unproductive laborers. Furthermore, as has already been noted, suppliers routinely protected their interests by demanding mortgages on their customers' tools and stock. Tenants who wished to avoid foreclosure had to bind themselves to their old agents for another year and generally on less favorable terms.

Most storekeepers did not have the capital to engage in perilous rivalries. And there were serious drawbacks to acquiring a very large clientele; overseeing freedmen demanded a lot of time and effort, and suppliers were wary of spreading their operations too thin. Consequently, the margin of difference between what one merchant and his competitor might offer was narrow. Nevertheless, that margin did exist, and to give the Fennells of the region their due, it must be emphasized that they were willing to play off one proposal against the next in the interest of securing the most generous arrangement available. They had to. Once the tenant had

47. Nordhoff, *The Cotton States*, 81; pledges of crops, April 29, 1868, March 1, 1872, July 5, 1875, in Concordia Parish General Mortgages, Vol. O, p. 311, Vol. P, p. 643, Vol. R, p. 545; lien on crops, May 4, 1876, in Concordia Parish General Mortgages, Vol. S, p. 532.

put his mark to a contract, he found himself trapped in a system that permitted no second thoughts.

The crop lien drew storekeepers into the cotton-marketing process. Many were quick to expand into outright purchasing of the staple for profitable resale. There were precedents for such activities. Before the war, a number of firms, principally in Natchez and Vicksburg, regularly bought cotton in anticipation of price increases. Furthermore, almost every merchant took part in the "speculative manias" that periodically swept the antebellum South. More important, some storekeepers purchased the bales of farmers and small planters who did not have access to the commission houses of New Orleans or Natchez. In Grand Gulph, for instance, the firms of Pearson & Hume and W. P. Holloway & Co. performed this service. However, the output of small producers was limited, and most antebellum merchants saw little to be gained from an investment in purchasing.[48]

Things proved radically different after the war. Storekeepers began to buy cotton, one or two bales at a time in the late 1860s, in large quantities during the following decade. Danjean & Co. of Port Gibson is a case in point. In 1866 it accepted a few bales from freedmen in payment of outstanding debts. This was followed within two years by a tentative move into purchasing, an experiment that evidently met with success, for the concern subsequently undertook full-scale development of this side of its business. By 1875, Danjean was one of the major buyers of cotton in Claiborne County. Other firms in the region followed a similar course, and, by the mid-1870s, merchants routinely included "purchasing" in descriptions of their services. "The best Market Price for COTTON," boasted the circulars of Meyer Eiseman of Fayette. The letterheads of both Johnson & McGilvary of Grand Gulph and its competitor Sandusky & Morehead promised "special attention" to the buying of the staple.[49]

The large companies in Natchez and Vicksburg now expanded

48. Atherton, *The Southern Country Store*, 48; Hammond, *The Cotton Industry*, 116; R. G. Dun & Co. Collection, Mississippi VI, 130, 136, 152, Mississippi II, 6.

49. Danjean Records, I, 76, II, *passim*; notice, January 4, 1872, in Darden Family Papers, Box 1, Folder 9; Sandusky & Morehead to Lewis Clarke, February 3, 1873, in Clarke Letters and Papers.

their purchasing activities. On a single day in March, 1881, for example, C. L. Holden of Natchez bought sixty-three bales from one customer and Benjamin Pendleton took in thirty-four from another. Nevertheless, it was not the dealers in the city who were the most conspicuous beneficiaries of the changing pattern of trade. That title belongs to the many merchants in the towns and at the crossroads who, picking up seasonal consignments, turned to purchasing on a modest scale.[50]

These developments were not unique to the Natchez district. Throughout the cotton South, storekeepers became buyers. In their efforts to explain this phenomenon, historians have concentrated on postwar advances in the areas of communication and transportation. The standard interpretation goes something like this. As the lien drew a portion of the crop into the hands of the local merchant, it gave him an increasingly prominent role in the marketing system of the South. Manufacturers took note of the situation and, aided by the growth of a comprehensive railway network that permitted direct shipments north, sent buyers to tap this new source of cotton. At the same time, the arrival of the telegraph in many inland towns and the laying of the transatlantic cable gave storekeepers access to current information about fluctuations and trends in the cotton market. Direct sales from merchants to manufacturers became practicable; local purchase for the purpose of profitable resale was no longer attended with great risk. The storekeeper became buyer and seller. In the words of Harold Woodman, "The intervening services of the cotton factor became superfluous."[51]

There can be little question of the importance of the railroad and the telegraph in opening up the interior regions of the South. They stimulated the growth of towns, linked communities directly to the North, and indeed provided a means for manufacturers to bypass coastal commission houses. But we should be wary of accounts that resolutely fix on technological progress to account for the development of the merchant as cotton buyer. The history of the Natchez district tells another story.

50. [Ayres] Ledger, 1880–81 (MS in possession of Ayres and Emily Haxton, Natchez), 131.
51. Hammond, *The Cotton Industry*, Chap. 10; Woodman, *King Cotton and His Retainers*, 96–97, 272–88.

As late as the 1880s, railroads were of little consequence in the counties and parishes of the region. Such lines as existed from before the war were mere adjuncts to the river trade; their purpose was to facilitate the shipment of cotton to depots along the Mississippi, from where it could be sent by steamboat to New Orleans. The few miles of track laid during Reconstruction served much the same end. In other words, improvements in transportation do not explain the rapid involvement of local merchants in the purchasing of cotton.[52]

It is suggestive that, during these years, only a few members of the gentry chose to dispose of their cotton in the district. Lewis Clarke of Claiborne County sold some of his bales to the Grand Gulph firm of Johnson & McGilvary, while in Wilkinson County Mrs. T. V. Noland regularly disposed of her crops to Joseph & Hart, a Woodville concern. But the vast majority of planters, as before the war, marketed their bales through New Orleans commission houses, and many continued to do so into the twentieth century. More often than not, the large landowner who sold locally was deeply in debt to the purchasing merchant.[53]

Planters had sound financial reasons for maintaining their antebellum marketing patterns. "You speak of selling in Natches [sic]," wrote Buckner & Co. to James Gillespie of Adams County in 1868. "We think this would not be to yr. interest, as businesses there purchase for sale in this market and generally make a profit."[54] What was true for Natchez in the late 1860s was true for the rest

52. "Historical and Other Notes on Port Gibson and Claiborne County" (MS in Maggie Williams Musgrave Papers, Z 1114, Mississippi Department of Archives and History, Jackson); "Address to the Jefferson County Agricultural, Mechanic, and Manufacturing Association, May 28, 1880" (MS in Joseph D. Shields Papers, Box 4, Folder 11, Department of Archives and Manuscripts, Louisiana State University, Baton Rouge), 26; "Transportation" (Typescript in W.P.A. Records, RG 60, for Warren County, Mississippi Department of Archives and History, Jackson), 66; Taylor, *Louisiana Reconstructed*, 398; Leland H. Jenks, "Railroads as an Economic Force in American Development," *Journal of Economic History*, IV (1944), 12–13.

53. Receipt, January 28, 1869, in Clarke Letters and Papers; Julia Tigner Noland and Blanche Connelly Saucier, *Confederate Greenbacks: Mississippi Plantation Life in the 70's and 80's* (San Antonio: Naylor Co., 1940), 166.

54. Buckner & Co. to James A. Gillespie, October 31, 1868, in Gillespie Papers. Storekeepers occasionally ventured into speculative purchasing in anticipation of a hoped-for upswing in the New Orleans market. When this happened, some planters chose to sell locally for as long as the uncharacteristically high prices continued. See, for example, C. D. Ven-

of the region through Reconstruction and into the 1880s. Local merchants sold their cotton through those same factors who serviced the former slaveholders. Johnson & McGilvary, for instance, sent their bales to J. W. Champlin, while Danjean & Co. of Port Gibson dealt with John Burnet & Co. The ledgers of the New Orleans commission house of Nalle & Cammack for 1880–1881 record large consignments from Natchez area merchants. From September 1, 1880, to March 25 of the following year, the firm received 317 bales from A. Beekman, 627 from George Payne, 238 from M. Lemle, 459 from A. Perrault & Co., 139 from S. & A. Jacobs, and 196 from A. & M. Moses. To encourage continued patronage, factors secured rebates and reduced shipment charges for their clients. Such efforts met with notable success. Of the many Vicksburg firms engaged in the purchase of cotton in 1875, only two sold directly to manufacturers. The situation could hardly have been different in the smaller communities of the region.[55]

The local merchant evolved as a buyer not because of changes in the marketing pattern of the region but, on the contrary, because he suddenly had an increased opportunity to take advantage of traditional trade arrangements. The spread of tenancy meant that a large proportion of the cotton crop was now in the hands of small producers, principally freedmen, who, handicapped by their illiteracy and bound tightly by the lien system, were scarcely in a position to avail themselves of the benefits of the more distant markets. Thanks to low shipment costs, merchants were able to make a profit by purchasing at slightly below the New Orleans price. Joe Gray Taylor discovered records of a Madison Parish storekeeper who, in 1879, shipped 15 bales of cotton to his factor at a cost of $18.75 for freight and $12.59 for insurance, or about $.005 per pound. The standard 2.5 percent commission charge would have increased this figure hardly at all. In October, 1873, the Port Gibson concern of S. Bernheimer & Sons bought cotton

tress to Chas. Gallagher, October 11, 1872, receipt, January 18, 1879, both in Trask-Ventress Family Papers, Folders 208, 314.

55. R. G. Dun & Co. Collection, Mississippi, VI, 144S; Danjean Records, II, 222, 274, 466, 475; [Ayres] Ledger, 1880–81; "Professional and Civic Leaders, II" (Typescript in W.P.A. Records for Warren County); King, *The Great South*, 53.

at $.16 per pound with the knowledge that a factor would resell the bales in New Orleans at $.175 or $.18.[56]

The tenant was a captive client. As Thomas Clark has noted, the small producer "was practically forced by the general understanding among merchants to sell his cotton where he bought his supplies and fertilizer, in order to guarantee the creditor an opportunity to collect his bills. Persons having remnants of bales found it difficult . . . to sell them, except to merchants who had control of supplies."[57]

We are left with the revealing paradox of tenants selling their share of the crop in one market while the landlord disposed of his in another. For example, James A. Gillespie of Hollywood regularly shipped his cotton to New Orleans in 1868, but his freedmen had to content themselves with buyers in nearby Natchez. Similarly, although James Surget marketed bales from his Concordia Parish plantation through the commission house of S. B. Newman & Co. in 1878, his tenants sold their cotton to Morris Wexler and Isaac Friedler, the local merchants who supplied them. Occasionally a conscientious former slaveowner agreed to let his freedmen include their surplus cotton in his consignments to New Orleans. But the number of planters who provided this service was comparatively small, and the situation was not without its ironies. "We note your report of the unwillingness of your Freedmen to sell their cotton at present prices," wrote Jurey & Harris to Nancy Pinson, "and in reply beg to say that in view of the general war in Europe, and the certainty of a large crop made in this country, we see no prospect of an advance that would justify them in holding; the most experienced and sagacious Planters and factors are free sellers at current quotations, and are generally apprehensive of low prices later in the season."[58]

---

56. Taylor, *Louisiana Reconstructed*, 397; S. Bernheimer & Sons to Lewis Clarke, October 3, 1876, in Clarke Letters and Papers.

57. Thomas D. Clark, "The Furnishing and Supply System in Southern Agriculture Since 1865," *Journal of Southern History*, XII (1946), 38.

58. Notices of sale, November 28, 1867, March 9, 1868, both in Gillespie Papers; J. F. Moriarty to Jas. Surget, October 4, 1878, accounts notice, March 10, 1879, both in possession of Mrs. Douglas MacNeil, Natchez; Jurey & Harris to Mrs. N. and S. A. Pinson, November 18, 1870, in Pinson Papers.

Storekeepers had always been an influential force in the lives of the white farmers and small planters of the district. But they now gradually began to extend their authority over the former slaves, branching more and more into matters that used to be solely the concern of the gentry. By the early 1870s, local merchants performed all manner of services for their freedmen customers, from paying taxes, lodge bills, and church dues, to arranging for medical care and funerals. They regularly took trips or sent agents into the countryside to inquire after their clients. And some were known to ride through the fields on inspection trips.[59] In brief, their power was growing. And, as interested observers, the former slaveowners took note.

### III

Naturally the gentry did not view this challenge to their authority dispassionately. Many who had willingly abdicated the role of supplier were made uneasy by the resulting sequence of events. At one time, they had been petty lords directing scores of chattels. Now they found their influence sorely circumscribed and their power shared with others. Much more was involved here than damaged pride. At stake was control of the labor force, and of cotton.

At the heart of the conflict lay the lien system. Merchants were not the only ones to recognize the value of the lien. Landlords routinely wrote crop pledges into their leases to protect themselves against defaulting renters. Invariably disputes arose over which party was to have first call on the crop. Tenants complicated matters by withholding from potential suppliers information about previously negotiated obligations. The result was a contractual tangle that bred confusion and, quite often, rancor.

In January, 1870, Henry Ambrose and Elijah Bowman rented a portion of a plantation in Adams County from James Surget and Katherine Minor. The two freedmen consented not to remove any cotton from the place "until the balance of rent is paid." As se-

59. E. J. Larkin Diary (MS in Department of Archives and Manuscripts, Louisiana State University, Baton Rouge), March 5, 1878; Darden Diary, II, October 13, 1873; Woodman, *King Cotton and His Retainers*, 302, 308, 329; Clark, *Pills, Petticoats and Plows*, 75.

curity they granted Surget and Minor a mortgage on their crops. Two months later, Ambrose and Bowman contracted with the firm of Lafayette Thomas & Co. for supplies of meat, molasses, and meal. Again they pledged their cotton, and now bound themselves to ship it "as soon as gathered and baled, and in condition to be sent to market to be sold by said parties of the second part [Thomas & Co.], and the proceeds to be applied by them in payment of the sums due." It is not clear how the conflicting claims of landlords and merchant were resolved in this particular instance, but it could hardly have been in a manner satisfactory to both parties. The content of later contracts written by Surget and Minor suggests that the two former slaveowners had recurring difficulties with local suppliers. After 1872 they were careful to add the following specific provision to all their leases: "And to give Jas. Surget and K. S. Minor full protection against any Liens of persons who may Supply Provisions or Supplies of any Kind to the said ——— —— during the year 187– or of any hands who may be employed by said ——— in Cultivating said Land the said ——— doeth by these presents bargain Sell transfer and alien to Jas. Surget and K. S. Minor all the Crops of Cotton and Corn that may be raised on said Lands during the year 187– by way of Mortgage."[60] Such contractual jockeying was all part and parcel of the elaborate maneuvering by which planters and merchants struggled to establish the superiority of their respective claims.

The lien laws of Mississippi and Louisiana attempted to address this chaotic situation. The Mississippi statute of 1867 conferred a "prior lien" on those who furnished materials "necessary for the cultivation of a farm or plantation." A lessor was not entitled to the benefits of the law unless he also provided essential supplies. "The statute implies," ruled the Mississippi Supreme Court in 1873, "that the debtor already has the land ready to be cultivated, and offers this lien 'prior' over all others, to him who will supply the agriculturalist the means wherewith to make the crops." Con-

60. Agreements, January 1, March 21, 1870, in Adams County Deed Records, Vol. PP, p. 774, Vol. QQ, p. 13; leases, February 1, 1873, in Adams County Deed Records, Vol. RR, p. 241, Vol. SS, pp. 214, 242.

versely, the Louisiana law of 1874 recognized the claim of the landlord over that of the supplier.[61]

The unambiguous language of the legislation did not, however, prevent conflict. For one thing, under most leases landlords supplied their tenants with implements and perhaps livestock. As a result, Mississippi planters and merchants were occasionally drawn into dispute over who was actually furnishing the "necessary" materials. Furthermore, former slaveowners who did not choose to provide any goods to their freedmen attempted periodically to skirt the Mississippi law through legal technicalities. As we have seen, Katherine Minor and James Surget argued that a landlord's "mortgage" was somehow superior to a supplier's lien. The Mississippi Supreme Court rejected this and similar stratagems in the mid-1870s, testimony itself to the fact that imaginative planters were continuing to seek loopholes.[62]

The principal reason that the laws did not resolve the situation, however, was simply that planters and merchants regularly ignored them in practice. Many Mississippi landowners claimed prior lien rights as lessors, apparently confident that they could use their personal standing to overcome any legal objections. G. Malin Davis of Adams County included a proviso in his contracts obligating his freedmen "not to encumber, sell, dispose of or remove any part [of the crop], nor permit the same to be disposed of or removed until said rent is fully paid and satisfied." Benjamin Humphreys of Claiborne County, nephew of the former governor of the same name and someone who could hardly have been ignorant of the legal situation, required his tenant Calvin Brazan to set aside his first two bales for rent. Brazan's Port Gibson merchant

61. *Laws of the State of Mississippi Passed at a Called Session of the Mississippi Legislature Held in the City of Jackson, October, 1867* (Jackson, 1867), 569; *Wm. B. Stewart, use, etc.* v. *Virgil Hollins et al.,* in State Supreme Court of Mississippi, *Mississippi Reports,* XLVII (Chicago: Callahan, 1873), 708–712; *Acts Passed by the General Assembly of the State of Louisiana at the Second Session of the Third Legislature Begun and Held in New Orleans, January 5, 1874* (New Orleans, 1874), 114. See also Harold D. Woodman, "Post–Civil War Southern Agriculture and the Law," *Agricultural History,* LIII (1979), 328–29.

62. Lease and mortgage, January 25, 1871, in Claiborne County Deed Records, Vol. II, p. 133; Harris, *Presidential Reconstruction,* 173; lease, February 1, 1873, in Adams County Deed Records, Vol. RR, p. 241; *Stewart, use, etc.* v. *Hollins et al.,* 710.

agreed to this arrangement, persuasive evidence that influential planters could indeed use their standing to bend the law.[63]

Similarly, across the river, Louisiana merchants continued to secure their advances with crop pledges, despite the preferential treatment accorded landlords in the 1874 statute. Nathan Lorie of Concordia Parish won the following concession from the prominent planter Alfred Vidal Davis in 1876: "Of the first cotton picked out by each squad, said Davis and said Lorie shall take alternative bales until Davis gets the number of bales due him for lease and Lorie gets a quantity equal in value to the Supplies furnished by him."[64]

The preceding instances are revealing. Control of the cotton crop often came down to negotiations between parties in which economic influence and social position had much to do with advantages won. Individual planters and storekeepers feuded, bargained, reached compromises, confronted new difficulties, and sought new compromises. Not all disagreements were resolved, and there is evidence of continuing friction into the twentieth century. But it is clear that at some point the relationship between planter and merchant came to be characterized more by stability than by ongoing adjustment.

No doubt some sort of partnership was assured from the moment the landowner came to understand the central role that the store was destined to play in the life of the postbellum plantation. Nevertheless, the evidence suggests that a durable *modus vivendi* did not appear until the long and deep depression that settled on the nation following the Panic of 1873. The tightened conditions of credit that accompanied the depression forced many merchants to curtail advancing to tenants and drew the former slaveowners back into the process of furnishing the freedmen. "A large number of our Bayou Sara & Woodville merchants are flat broke & shut up," wrote Samuel Postlethwaite in February, 1874, from Westmoreland. "Those that aint quite broke have shut down advancing

63. Lease, February 10, 1881, in Adams County Deed Records, Vol. XX, p. 45; mortgage and lien, April 17, 1871, in Claiborne County Deed Records, Vol. II, p. 484.

64. Contract of lease and supplies, March 1, 1875, in Concordia Parish General Mortgages, Vol. R, p. 408.

to negroes who are unable to get any supplies except from planters who are fortunate enough to be able to draw on the merchant."[65]

Brought together to sustain the new supply system, landlords and merchants sought ways to resolve their existing differences. In the process, they moved toward an accommodation that would preserve for each of them a voice in the plantation regime. The accommodation finally reached took a variety of forms, most of which called for some sharing of authority and responsibility. The most common formula had the merchant continuing to furnish the labor force, with the planter serving as middleman. Every time a tenant wished to make a purchase, he had to obtain an order from his landlord. He would present the order to the relevant storekeeper, who would charge the goods in question to the landlord's account. At the end of the year, the planter would pay the merchant, the tenant would pay the planter.

Agreements of this nature can be found several years prior to the depression; thereafter they became commonplace. Although George W. Montgomery operated a commissary on his Madison Parish plantation in 1876, he regularly wrote orders for his freedmen so that they could procure items that he did not stock. The Ventress brothers of Wilkinson County had accounts for their tenants with at least four separate Woodville firms in the late 1870s and early 1880s.[66]

Such arrangements had advantages for both merchant and planter. The former gained a measure of security; recalcitrant tenants were no longer his immediate concern and crop failures were less certain to result in unpaid bills. The landowner, freed of the threat of a competing lien, assured himself final authority over the growing crop. At the same time, he evaded the practical burdens involved in running a furnishing operation, in particular the necessity of finding credit at the beginning of the year to stock supplies. Together landlord and merchant exercised rigid control over the

65. Sam Postlethwaite to Uncle [James] Gillespie, February 22, 1874, in Gillespie Papers. See also R. A. Sessions to A. K. Farrar, November 17, 1874, in Farrar Papers.

66. Danjean Records, I, 25, 26, 103, 193, 210; Montgomery Account Books, V, 28, 52; receipts, March 5, 1879, May 24, 1887, receipt, January 11, 1879, receipt, March 1, 1884, all in Trask-Ventress Family Papers, Folders 282, 287, 279.

purchasing activities of the producer. It became impossible for a tenant to make even the smallest credit acquisition without falling under the narrow scrutiny of both parties. "Georg [*sic*] Barr, F. M. of C. wanted fifty cents of tobacco," wrote a Woodville merchant to Nancy Pinson in September, 1867. "I have charged it to your accounts, if not satisfactory I will *erased* [*sic*] from the book the first time you will come to town. It is not my habit in giving negroes goods without an order, but this being tobacco, I labored under the impression you would not refused [*sic*]."[67]

From the point of view of the tenant, there was another serious drawback to the order system. As middleman, the planter had the opportunity to increase still further the inflated credit prices of the merchant. Interest of about 10 percent per year seems to have been standard, not to mention the straight markup that most landlords presumably added. The records of the Prospect Hill plantation of B. H. Wade demonstrate the uneven way in which one man took advantage of the situation. Table 23 compares what Wade paid a storekeeper for supplies bought by a freedman on March 15, 1890, with what he charged the freedman for the same goods.

The evidence is scanty—accounts are available for few plantations—but it seems likely that the majority of landholders were no more consistent than Wade. The average proprietor evaluated each item separately and decided what to charge only after considering the nature of the article, the circumstances of the tenant involved, and his own financial needs. No doubt some landlords were more guided by constraints of conscience than were others. One thing seems certain. The already crushing financial obligations of the tenant were increased even more by the evolution of the planter as middleman for the storekeeper.[68]

Some landowners allowed merchants to run stores on their plantations. In 1874, Volney Stamps leased two acres of Bowling Green in Claiborne County to Solomon Marx for this purpose. The fol-

67. K. Mandell to Mrs. N. S. Pinson, September 18, 1867, in Pinson Papers.

68. Thomas D. Clark and Albert D. Kirwan, *The South Since Appomattox: A Century of Regional Change* (New York: Oxford University Press, 1967), 89. See also leases, April 22, 1870, January 1, 1875, in Adams County Deed Records, Vol. QQ, p. 111, Vol. UU, p. 415.

**Table 23.   PRICE MARKUPS BY B. H. WADE**

| Item | Price Paid by Wade | Price Charged by Wade | Markup |
|---|---|---|---|
| 30½ yds. stripes | $2.30 | $3.05 | 33% |
| 20 yds. domestic | $1.80 | $2.20 | 22% |
| 9 balls thread & 2 spools | .25 | .40 | 60% |
| 10 yds. bleached domestic | .90 | $1.25 | 39% |
| 1 pair pants | $1.75 | $2.25 | 29% |
| flour | .50 | .50 | 0% |
| sugar | .10 | .10 | 0% |
| 1 shirt & collar | .90 | $1.25 | 39% |
| 2 pairs socks | .20 | .40 | 100% |
| 10 yds. dress goods | $1.75 | $2.40 | 37% |
| 2 pairs hose | .20 | .40 | 100% |
| buttons | .25 | .35 | 40% |
| 2 handkerchiefs | .20 | .40 | 100% |
| general merchandise | .45 | .45 | 0% |

SOURCES: Account notice, March 15, 1890, "Book of Invoices of B. H. Wade, 1889–92," Prospect Hill Plantation Ledger, 1890–93, p. 10, all in Battaille Harrison Wade and Family Papers, Mississippi Department of Archives and History, Jackson.

lowing year, Antonio Yznaga del Valle permitted H. C. Miller to operate a store on his Concordia Parish property. Arrangements of this kind provided the merchant with a base for widespread business in the surrounding countryside. Charles Hester ran a store on the estate Brushey Bayou in Concordia Parish in 1875. From there, he was able to secure customers on over half a dozen nearby plantations. Although merchants normally took sole responsibility for these enterprises, at times planters provided financial backing much as before the war.[69]

The logical culmination of these developments was the planta-

69. Lease, March 1, 1874, in Claiborne County Deed Records, Vol. PP, p. 531; affidavit for supplies, September 21, 1875, in Concordia Parish General Mortgages, Vol. S, p. 62; R. G. Dun & Co. Collection, Louisiana XXII, 19, Louisiana IV, 240.3.

tion store owned and managed by the landowner himself. The plantation store of the 1870s and beyond was fundamentally different from those undertakings that appeared at the end of the war. Then the planter had stocked up on large quantities of perfume and liquor, colorful clothing and flashy trinkets, hoping to turn the financial inexperience of the freedman into a quick fortune. Now he concentrated on everyday needs. Profit was not an incidental goal of the later ventures but it was decidedly secondary to the establishment of control over the labor force.

The size of the later stores reflects the limited financial commitments and objectives of their proprietors. Most were very small, indeed little more than commissaries. Henry Magruder, son of a wealthy Claiborne County slaveholder, ran an enterprise in the 1870s whose sole purpose was to provide goods to the hands on his three estates. William H. Noble and Eugene Osgood of Wilkinson County kept a store just to service their own Longside and Riverside places. Some planters, more ambitious no doubt, sought a wider clientele. Lane Brandon of Wilkinson County furnished J. J. Winn's tenants as well as his own. C. R. Byrnes of Belvedere in Claiborne County had customers on several neighboring plantations.[70]

Most planters directed no more than $3,000 a year into their operations, and many were content to spend half that sum. Henry Magruder kept only about $500 in stock on hand, Osgood and Noble only about $2,000. Profits were correspondingly low. Records of the store run by the Bisland family at Mount Repose, their plantation in Adams County, are particularly revealing in this regard. During the hectic period from December 15 to December 31, 1884, total sales amounted to $409.00. On Christmas Eve, the most active day of the year, the Bislands grossed $81.00. By contrast, business from July 15 to July 31, 1882, brought in only $117.75, ranging from a one-day low of $3.00 to a high of $20.00. In general, things were a little better than during July, noticeably worse than during December—in other words, hardly the stuff

70. R. G. Dun & Co. Collection, Mississippi VI, 144V, Mississippi XXII, 183; Brandon Account Books, I, 139; C. R. Byrnes to Nellie [Metcalfe], August 1, 1880, in possession of Mr. and Mrs. Bazile Lanneau, Natchez.

from which fortunes are made. The Mount Repose store showed a balance of only $73.00 at the end of 1882, $261.30 at the end of 1883, $238.92 at the end of 1884.[71]

In a recent study of Alabama, Jonathan Wiener has suggested that landowners conceived the plantation store as a means of undermining the growing authority of the local merchant. He contends that planters established direct links with wholesalers, and thereby seriously weakened the economic base of the storekeeper. The situation in the Natchez region casts serious doubt on the general applicability of such an interpretation. Local landowners bought much of their stock in the district. Under the circumstances, the plantation store did little more than simplify the role of the landlord as middleman for the storekeeper. Consider, for example, the Mount Repose operation. The Bislands procured their stock from I. Lowenburg, Rumble & Wensel, Marx & Scharff, H. Frank, P. Neihysel, F. A. Dicks, and H. M. Gastrell, all merchants in nearby Natchez. Lewis Clarke of Claiborne County supplied his plantation store through Johnson & McGilvary, the leading firm in Grand Gulph. It is true that, to the disadvantage of some shopkeepers, landlords made a few purchases outside the region. But, for these, they turned to their old agents the factors, not to wholesalers.[72]

During the years when many planters were first putting up stores on their estates, a small element of local merchants began to acquire a significant financial interest in land and plantations. To some extent this was accomplished through leasing. The Natchez concern of I. Lowenburg & Co. contracted with Charlotte Surget for her Cheripa and Concordia places from 1870 to 1875 at $2,000 a year. The firm also took a part interest in Morvin, a neighboring plantation belonging to Eustace Surget, for the same period of

71. R. G. Dun & Co. Collection, Mississippi VI, 144V, Mississippi XXII, 183; Mount Repose store ledger, 1882–84 (MS in possession of Dr. and Mrs. William Godfrey, Natchez). See also R. G. Dun & Co. Collection, Louisiana IV, 233, 237, Mississippi XI, 356.

72. Jonathan M. Wiener, *Social Origins of the New South: Alabama, 1860–1885* (Baton Rouge: Louisiana State University Press, 1978), 78; Mount Repose store ledger, 1882–84; Johnson & McGilvary to Lewis Clark[e], April 19, 1872, account notices, April 17, February 21, 1871, invoice, January 9, 1872, all in Clarke Papers; Elgin Journal, January 1, 1883–July 31, 1884 (MS in possession of Mr. and Mrs. Hyde D. Jenkins, Natchez), November 2, 7, 12, 19, 1883.

**Table 24.**   ACREAGE OWNED BY MERCHANTS

|  | 1861 | 1870 | 1879 |
| --- | --- | --- | --- |
| Adams County | 80 | 6,242 | 19,928 |
|  | 1860 | 1868 | 1879 |
| Claiborne County | 0 | 2,361 | 16,054 |
|  | 1860 | 1871 | 1880 |
| Concordia Parish | 4,758 | 3,393 | 11,316 |

SOURCES: U.S. Bureau of the Census, MS Population Schedules for Adams County, Claiborne County, Concordia Parish, 1860, 1870, 1880; U.S. Bureau of the Census, MS Agricultural Schedules for Claiborne County, Concordia Parish, 1860; Adams County Land Rolls, 1861, 1870, 1879; "Report of State Tax, 1868," in Records of the Auditor of Public Accounts, Box 85; Claiborne County Land Rolls, 1879; Concordia Parish Assessment Rolls, 1871, 1880.

time.[73] But, for most storekeepers, leasing represented a temporary expedient. The real goal was landownership.

Some merchants were able to buy small tracts here and there from struggling farmers. Those who amassed extensive holdings, however, generally did so at the expense of large slaveowners unable to adjust to the demands of the postwar economy. For instance, when Catherine S. Daniell went bankrupt in 1868, Moses Kaufman of Port Gibson bought her China Grove plantation at public auction for only $250. That same year, Louis Kiefer of Claiborne County purchased 813 acres from the insolvent estate of Harriet Mitchell.[74]

The interest of the storekeeper in acquiring property was hardly a new phenomenon. Ambitious antebellum merchants had commonly turned their profits into land and slaves. But whereas before the war the individual who acquired a stake in the countryside was likely to sell his store, now he held on to it. As a result, during Reconstruction and beyond, there was—as Table 24 demon-

73. Leases, November 4, 1870, January 1, 1871, in Concordia Parish General Mortgages, Vol. P, pp. 89, 91.

74. Deeds, June 9, 13, 1868, in Claiborne County Deed Records, Vol. GG, pp. 231, 306; deed, May 6, 1872, in Claiborne County Deed Records, Vol. JJ, p. 48; deed, May 30, 1881, in Claiborne County Deed Records, Vol. VV, p. 632.

strates—a striking increase in the acreage owned by the merchant class (see Appendix I).

The increasing tendency for merchants to hold on to their stores as they acquired land had major implications for the economic structure of the merchant class (see Table 25). It meant that there now existed a segment of that class at the highest levels of the planting hierarchy. This development was of some consequence even in Natchez. Merchants had been by no means unimportant in

Table 25.   MERCANTILE ENTERPRISES, BY ACREAGE, 1860–1880

|  | 0 | town lots* | 1–199 | 200–499 | 501–999 | 1,000+ |
|---|---|---|---|---|---|---|
| *Adams* | | | | | | |
| 1861 | 30 | 62 | 1 | 0 | 0 | 0 |
| 1870 | 80 | 27 | 0 | 0 | 6 | 1 |
| 1879 | 77 | 45 | 4 | 2 | 1 | 6 |
| *Claiborne* | | | | | | |
| 1860 | 24 | 21 | 0 | 0 | 0 | 0 |
| 1868 | 29 | 11 | 3 | 2 | 2 | 0 |
| 1879 | 41 | 6 | 3 | 2 | 4 | 6 |
| *Concordia* | | | | | | |
| 1860 | 2 | 3 | 1 | 1 | 1 | 0 |
| 1871 | 4 | 5 | 0 | 0 | 1 | 0 |
| 1880 | 17 | 5 | 1 | 1 | 0 | 1 |
| *Natchez Merchants with Land in Concordia Parish* | | | | | | |
| 1860 | — | 0 | 0 | 0 | 0 | 2 |
| 1871 | — | 0 | 0 | 0 | 1 | 2 |
| 1880 | — | 4 | 0 | 0 | 1 | 3 |

SOURCES: U.S. Bureau of the Census, MS Population Schedules for Adams County, Claiborne County, Concordia Parish, 1860, 1870, 1880; U.S. Bureau of the Census, MS Agricultural Schedules for Claiborne County, Concordia Parish, 1860; Adams County Land Rolls, 1861, 1870, 1879; "Report of State Tax, 1868," in Records of the Auditor of Public Accounts, Box 85; Claiborne County Land Rolls, 1879; Concordia Parish Assessment Rolls, 1871, 1880.

* Those who owned both town property and land in the countryside are not included in this category. They are listed according to the number of acres they held.

the city before the war; but as the figures demonstrate, they had a more prominent stake in its Adams County and Concordia Parish environs afterward. Still, it was in the predominantly rural areas that the most profound change took place. Here the storekeeper had acted out a decidedly secondary role during the antebellum years. Now, as the figures for Claiborne County reveal, a select group of merchants climbed to the top of the planting economy. By 1879, Louis Kiefer had accumulated 2,404 acres, his competitor Englesing & Frankenbusch, 2,381 acres. The Barrot brothers had done almost as well, as had D. A. Jones. Things were much the same elsewhere throughout the district. Each community produced a handful of storekeepers who successfully joined thriving mercantile operations and full-scale planting.[75]

The merchant who acquired a plantation was not the mirror image of the landowner who opened a store on his property. The former usually had clients on a large number of plantations and depended heavily on merchandising for his profits. But if the merchant-turned-planter was not exactly the same as the planter-turned-merchant, the two still had much in common. They represented the highest form of accommodation reached by landowner and supplier: formal merger. In each was vested undivided authority over labor and the cotton crop.

This formal merger has captured the attention of historians precisely because it bluntly reveals the new relations that evolved during the postwar years. But we should be wary of according it more importance than it deserves. At no time did most storekeepers acquire extensive real estate. Indeed, emancipation created the conditions for the proliferation of a propertyless element doing a limited business. Furthermore, at least before 1880 the average planter did not have a store on his estate.

But these qualifications did not mean that the accommodation between planter and merchant was of no effect or somehow incomplete. As we have seen, individual landlords and suppliers fashioned partnerships of their own, principally through the order

75. Claiborne County Land Rolls, 1879. See also R. G. Dun & Co. Collection, Mississippi VI, 144Z, Mississippi II, 9, Mississippi XXI, 91G, 145, Louisiana XXII, 37, Louisiana IV, 229.

system or some variation thereof. Together they exercised authority over the freedman, together they controlled the cotton crop. In the Natchez district of the New South, planters and merchants lived in close accord.

## IV

The results of the alliance between planters and merchants were as might be expected for the freedman. After a number of years in which he had enjoyed continual improvement in his working conditions and heightened expectations, he found himself once again trapped in a state of dependence. Some blacks, deeply in debt and with mortgages on their personal property, had little choice but to remain with the same landlord year after year. Most continued to move around from time to time—the limited evidence available for the Natchez district suggests that debt peonage was rare during Reconstruction[76] (see Appendix II)—but were unable to make significant strides toward landownership and genuine economic independence. The gentry and merchants used the differential between cash and credit prices to reduce the profits of the freedmen. And they used the lien system to protect themselves against the vagaries of the cotton market. In any season of short crops or low prices it was the tenants who would suffer first and most severely. Not infrequently a former slave who had slowly and painstakingly accumulated some capital over an extended period of time lost it all in one bad harvest. Thirty-five years after the war, the number of freedmen and their descendants who owned land in the district was still insignificant (see Table 26). Blacks remained the mudsills of society, forced to contract themselves out each year as renters and hired hands.

With the alliance of planters and merchants, the transformation of the Natchez district plantation can justifiably be said to have come

76. The pervasiveness of debt peonage is a matter of some debate. See, for example, Ransom and Sutch, *One Kind of Freedom*, 162–70; Higgs, *Competition and Coercion*, 72–74. Regarding freedman mobility, see William Cohen, "Negro Involuntary Servitude in the

Table 26.   BLACK LANDOWNERSHIP, 1900

| | Number of Farms | | |
|---|---|---|---|
| County | Operated by Blacks | Owned by Blacks | Percentage Owned |
| Adams | 2,386 | 147 | 6% |
| Claiborne | 2,299 | 170 | 7% |
| Jefferson | 2,898 | 214 | 7% |
| Warren | 3,481 | 181 | 5% |
| Wilkinson | 2,072 | 194 | 9% |
| *Parish* | | | |
| Concordia | 1,396 | 18 | 1% |
| Madison | 2,357 | 27 | 1% |
| Tensas | 2,235 | 48 | 2% |
| Total | 19,124 | 999 | 5% |

SOURCE: U.S. Bureau of the Census, *Twelfth Census of the United States* (10 vols.; Washington, D.C.: Government Printing Office, 1902), Vol. V, Pt. 1, pp. 88–89, 96–97.

to a close. Relations between landowners and black laborers, paternalistic prior to the war, had now been defined along radically different lines. The former slaveowners, after struggling for a time to resist substantive change, had accepted the consequences of Emancipation and—along with the mercantile elite—established their dominance over the new order. The freedmen, after enjoying a period of relative influence and securing a number of substantial concessions, had fallen back into a position of subservience. The New South plantation had emerged, and in a form that would last for decades.

South, 1865–1940: A Preliminary Analysis," *Journal of Southern History*, XLII (1976), 33. Cohen suggests that planters took steps to restrict black mobility only when there was a labor shortage. The evidence for the Natchez district through the 1870s suggests, to the contrary, that it was precisely when labor was in short supply that planters were most likely to fall into competition for the services of freedmen.

# Concluding Remarks

Historians disagree rather starkly over whether the society that came into existence in the South after the war differed fundamentally from the society that had gone before. At issue is the very nature of southern distinctiveness itself. The most influential spokesman on this question remains C. Vann Woodward. The history of the South, he writes, unlike the history of the rest of the nation, seems to be "characterized more by *dis*continuity." Southerners "repeatedly felt the solid ground of continuity give way under their feet." This was particularly true, he believes, during the era of the Civil War and Reconstruction. "A great slave society"—a society that he elsewhere has described as "a paternalistic order, perhaps the most paternalistic of the slave societies of the New World"— "had grown up and miraculously flourished in the heart of a thoroughly bourgeois and puritanical republic. It had renounced its bourgeois origins and elaborated and painfully rationalized its institutional, legal, metaphysical, and religious defenses. It had produced leaders of skill, ingenuity, and strength who, unlike those of other slave societies, invested their honor and their lives, and not merely part of their capital, in that society. When the crisis came, they, unlike the others, chose to fight. It proved to be the death struggle of a society, which went down in ruins." Into this shattered world, he contends, came new leaders with a new way of life. The old planting aristocracy gave way to an elite dominated by merchants, financiers, and industrialists, aggressive, materialistic in the extreme, cloaking their behavior in "a cult of archaism, a nostalgic vision of the past,"[1] but otherwise conspicuously bour-

---

1. C. Vann Woodward, *American Counterpoint: Slavery and Racism in the North-South Dialogue* (Boston: Little, Brown, 1971), 13–46, 275, 276, 249, 281; C. Vann Woodward, *Origins of the New South, 1877–1913* (Baton Rouge: Louisiana State University Press,

geois. The South they created was in the image of the North, if imperfectly so.

Until recently the most noteworthy alternative to this interpretation came from a journalist, Wilbur Cash, in his evocative *The Mind of the South*.

> The extent of the change and of the break between the Old South that was and the South of our time has been vastly exaggerated. The South, one might say, is a tree with many age rings, with its limbs and trunk bent and twisted by all the winds of the years, but with its tap root in the Old South. Or, better still, it is like one of those churches one sees in England. The facade and towers, the windows and clerestory, all the exterior and superstructure are late Gothic of one sort or another, but look into the nave, its aisles, and its choir and you find the old mighty Norman arches of the twelfth century. And if you look into its crypt, you might even find stones cut by Saxon, brick made by Roman hands.[2]

Cash was principally concerned with developments beyond the plantation. But his interpretation of the ruling class bears directly on the subject at hand. He agrees with Woodward in one basic respect: the typical member of the southern elite in the decades following Reconstruction was a merchant or factory owner, a "hard, energetic, horse-trading type of man," a man who was prepared "to give himself to business with a single-minded devotion." But, unlike Woodward, he argues that the ruling class before the war was made up of similar—and in many cases the same—men. The large slaveholders, he maintains, were ambitious, self-reliant, acquisitive, often unscrupulous individuals. Cash suggests that they had some "paternalistic" inclinations, but the message that comes across is quite different. As Woodward has observed, "He seems to be saying that they were all bourgeois, and therefore the Old South was bourgeois too, and therefore essentially indistinguishable from the New South."[3] As Cash himself has stated, "So far from having reconstructed the Southern mind in the large and in

---

1971), 154. See also C. Vann Woodward, *The Burden of Southern History* (Rev. ed.; Baton Rouge: Louisiana State University Press, 1968), 134–49.

2. W. J. Cash, *The Mind of the South* (New York: Vintage Books, 1941), x. It might be noted that Cash wrote his interpretation a decade before publication of *Origins of the New South*, Woodward's principal work.

3. Cash, *The Mind of the South*, 153, 154; Woodward, *American Counterpoint*, 277–78.

its essential character," the war and its aftermath "strengthened it almost beyond reckoning, and . . . made it one of the most solidly established, one of the least *reconstructible* ever developed."[4]

In the past decade, there has been an outpouring of works on the social and economic origins of the New South. In terms of the debate over continuity and change, two different groups of studies deserve particular attention.[5] Certain neoclassical economists have turned to highly developed theoretical models and advanced econometric techniques to explore the character of the labor system that came into existence after the war. They have not all arrived at the same conclusions, but the general methodological approach they use draws attention to a central theme of the story of Reconstruction that has often been overlooked: sharecropping, squad labor, tenancy, and other features of the postbellum regime can be properly understood only if it is recognized that they originated in a market environment.[6]

All the same, the scholars concerned have tended to present their conclusions in a manner that obscures the complexity of the historical experience in the South. Implicit in their work is the assumption that the gentry and the former slaves acted rationally (in the sense understood by economists). Although the authors themselves make few assertions about human motivation, the impression is created that individuals entered the marketplace as informed participants, ready to adjust their expectations to the forces of

---

4. Cash, *The Mind of the South*, 109.

5. This discussion deals only with works that explicitly or implicitly take sides in the debate over continuity and change. Of necessity, a number of significant studies on Reconstruction are neglected because they either do not contribute to this particular debate or contribute in an ambiguous manner. In the latter category would fall the two most sensitive investigations of developments on the plantation, James L. Roark, *Masters Without Slaves: Southern Planters in the Civil War and Reconstruction* (New York: Norton, 1977), and Leon F. Litwack, *Been in the Storm So Long: The Aftermath of Slavery* (New York: Knopf, 1979).

6. See, for example, Joseph D. Reid, Jr., "Sharecropping as an Understandable Market Response: The Post-Bellum South," *Journal of Economic History*, XXXIII (1973), 106–130; Stephen J. DeCanio, *Agriculture in the Postbellum South: The Economics of Production and Supply* (Cambridge: Massachusetts Institute of Technology Press, 1974); Robert Higgs, *Competition and Coercion: Blacks in the American Economy, 1865–1914* (New York: Cambridge University Press, 1977); Ralph Shlomowitz, "The Transition from Slave to Freedman: Labor Arrangements in Southern Agriculture, 1865–1870" (Ph.D. dissertation, University of Chicago, 1978).

supply and demand and sensible to the costs and benefits of alternative labor arrangements. The resulting allocation of risks and potential profits, we are told, was optimal—given the existing material circumstances of planters and freedmen.[7]

While developments in an established labor market may or may not unfold in so logical a fashion, the history of the Natchez district suggests that an entirely different process takes place in a market that is emerging where none has previously existed. In the immediate aftermath of the war, neither the gentry nor the former slaves evidenced much of what might be termed a market consciousness. The perceptions of social interaction held by the freedmen had largely been formed under slavery. As for the planters, although they understood the nature of market activities, they believed that the inherently childlike personality of the Negro would eventually require a paternalistic labor settlement outside the marketplace. Even when they were drawn into competition for the services of the former slaves, their conduct was for a time constrained by the mistaken conviction that blacks were not responsive to marketplace incentives and would, in any case, soon be replaced by European and Chinese laborers. It is a moot point whether the labor system that had its origins in this atmosphere of uncertainty and misapprehension represented the best possible solution to the problems of the planters, the former slaves, or the region. But it seems scarcely credible that the New South plantation would have taken the form it did if the gentry—or freedmen, for that matter—had known in 1865 what they knew a decade later.[8]

Much of the writing of the neoclassical economic historians seems to imply that the structure of the new regime was not only distinctly bourgeois but little influenced by the ideological legacy

7. As neoclassical economists, Roger L. Ransom and Richard Sutch (*One Kind of Freedom: The Economic Consequences of Emancipation* [New York: Cambridge University Press, 1977]) trace the origins of the New South plantation to developments in the marketplace. However, unlike Higgs, DeCanio, Shlomowitz, and Reid, Ransom and Sutch take into account the ideological legacy of the antebellum period and, indeed, argue that it hindered the market in producing a settlement advantageous to either the freedmen or the region.

8. For a more extensive discussion of the works of the neoclassical economic historians, see Harold D. Woodman, "Sequel to Slavery: The New History Views the Postbellum South," *Journal of Southern History*, XLIII (1977), 525–41.

of the antebellum period. An entirely different interpretation has lately been offered by a group of Marxist scholars.[9] The character of the New South, they contend, was in essence the same as that of the Old South, and the Old South was altogether antibourgeois. That the war and Reconstruction produced no radical change in the orientation of the region they attribute primarily to two factors. First—and this is an argument presented by Jay R. Mandle—the paternalistic nature of the antebellum plantation derived from the structure of the "plantation economy" and not from slavery. Since the ownership of land in the region was not significantly widened as a result of the war, the plantation was able to survive, and with it, paternalism. Second—and here we are dealing with the work of Jonathan M. Wiener and Dwight B. Billings—the ruling class of the New South was dominated by families who had roots in the antebellum elite, retained the values of the large slaveholders, and were determined to allow no substantive modifications in the shape of the society. What the Marxists offer, in effect, is Cash's theme of continuity, but turned inside out. The continuity they describe is marked by antibourgeois, rather than bourgeois, tendencies.

The works of the Marxists have helped correct earlier misconceptions regarding the fate of the antebellum elite after the war. As the present study confirms, the old gentry held on to their place at the top of the local economic hierarchy and continued to have a significant—though not the only significant—voice in the regime. No doubt, too, as Billings and Wiener have contended, planters in certain areas of the South took steps to restrict or control the development of manufacturing, much as they had in the past.[10] But

9. Jonathan M. Wiener, *Social Origins of the New South: Alabama, 1860–1885* (Baton Rouge: Louisiana State University Press, 1978); Dwight B. Billings, Jr., *Planters and the Making of a "New South": Class, Politics, and Development in North Carolina, 1865–1900* (Chapel Hill: University of North Carolina Press, 1979); Jay R. Mandle, *The Roots of Black Poverty: The Southern Plantation Economy After the Civil War* (Durham, N.C.: Duke University Press, 1978).

10. Billings, *Planters and the Making of a "New South,"* Chaps. 4–6; Wiener, *Social Origins*, Chaps. 5–7. For a challenge to their position, see David Carlton, "'Builders of a New State'—The Town Classes and Early Industrialization of South Carolina, 1880–1907," in Walter J. Fraser, Jr., and Winfred B. Moore, Jr. (eds.), *From the Old South to the New: Essays on the Transitional South* (Westport, Conn.: Greenwood Press, 1981), 43–62.

to demonstrate that the New South was antibourgeois in nature, it is necessary to do more than show that the old elite remained powerful and antagonistic to particular kinds of industrial development. It is necessary to establish that the social basis that supported the new regime and created the outlook of the ruling class was itself antibourgeois.

This Jay Mandle attempts to do in *The Roots of Black Poverty*. In a plantation economy, he asserts, landowners use nonmarket mechanisms to ensure themselves a large supply of disciplined laborers. With no real likelihood of escaping their subservient condition, workers have little choice but to accept a paternalistic arrangement in which they are guaranteed certain rights in return for deference and obedience. Where, prior to Emancipation, slavery had been used to keep blacks in a state of dependence, subsequently the same thing was accomplished—though with somewhat less effect—through sharecropping, violence, and the denial of alternative job possibilities.[11]

One can clearly imagine a free society in which the opportunities of laborers have been so limited that a paternalistic order evolves. Such a society, indeed, is what the planters of the Natchez district had in mind at the end of the war, when they bound their former slaves to contracts instituting antebellum plantation law and then, a few months later, tentatively supported the implementation of the Black Codes. But paternalism in the South had derived from slavery, not from the plantation, and the gentry proved unable to sustain by calculation what was no longer dictated by social force. When the freedmen took to the road and introduced the marketplace into the labor settlement, the old relations did not merely weaken; they crumbled. Interaction on the plantation now began to take on a new form. As Mandle acknowledges, although without grasping the significance of his observation, relations between planters and freedmen "may have experienced a sharp change in which economic calculation assumed increasing importance."[12] In

11. Mandle, *Roots of Black Poverty*, Chaps. 1–3.

12. Mandle differs with the most important Marxist scholar of the antebellum period, Eugene D. Genovese, who argues, as the present study does, that paternalism was rooted in slavery. See, especially, Eugene D. Genovese, *The World the Slaveholders Made: Two Essays*

fact, those relations were now explicitly tied to the monetary value of goods and services provided. Here is the explanation for the substantial evidence of growing bourgeois sensibilities among Natchez area planters during the years following the war.

True, the former slaveowners learned to use the new conditions to reduce the freedmen to a state of dependence. But manipulation of the cash nexus—the principal means of exerting control over the freedmen—merely confirmed the collapse of the old order.[13] That is, the authority of the gentry was now predicated on behavior that directly contradicted the notion that capital and black labor had enduring and reciprocal rights and obligations. Of course, in so restrictive an environment it was inevitable that some planters and former slaves would reach individual accommodations of a paternalistic type. Certain black families remained on the same estate year after year, developing close personal bonds with their landlords or employers and securing guaranteed care and protection in return for loyalty and deference. But, unlike slavery, free labor is founded on the principle of equality—equality of opportunity in the marketplace. And there is little indication that the majority of former slaves in the Natchez district were willing to abandon even this theoretical equality for the benefits of an arrangement that conferred legitimacy on their subservience. In general, freedmen disavowed any duties beyond those for which they specifically received compensation, and planters refused to acknowledge a responsibility to any but a few favored hands.

The history of the Natchez district, then, points to a profound break between the plantation regime of the old order and the plantation regime of the new. This break reflected not the demise of the antebellum ruling class, as some have allowed, but its transformation. In the words of Harold Woodman: "New conditions forced new ways and the result was not simply a return to prebourgeois ways but a major alteration in the planters' relationship to their

---

in Interpretation (New York: Pantheon Books, 1969); Eugene D. Genovese, Roll, Jordan, Roll: The World the Slaves Made (New York: Pantheon Books, 1974). Mandle, Roots of Black Poverty, 30–31.

13. Eugene D. Genovese, The Political Economy of Slavery: Studies in the Economy and Society of the Slave South (New York: Vintage Books, 1967), 30.

workers and to the outside world—in short, a major alteration in the planter class."[14] How close the gentry of the New South era came to resemble the manufacturers of the Northeast or the great farmers of the Midwest in terms of, say, investment practices or patterns of consumption remain subjects for further investigation. But in terms of their interaction with labor and their resulting perspective on the nature of human relations, they were, like other members of the American ruling elite, fundamentally bourgeois.

One final point, although it really lies beyond the scope of this investigation. That the plantation had been organized in a paternalistic fashion before the war should not obscure the fact that southern society had itself been dualistic. Landowners had dealt with black laborers in one way, with white laborers in another. Perhaps the most far-reaching consequence of the transformation of the plantation—and the most significant break with the past— was the elimination of this duality. The mechanisms used by the planters and merchants of the New South to control the freedmen were to a significant extent the same mechanisms they used to control white tenants and hired hands—high credit prices, crop liens, mortgages, manipulation of the supply system. This is not to deny that, because of their color, many freedmen suffered threats and physical abuse in their daily lives. But the principal means of restricting the opportunities and controlling the behavior of black laborers were class-determined and also used against whites.[15] In other words, with the transformation of the plantation, the previously existing class basis for racial differentiation in the region had broken down. As historians of the agrarian revolt and of race relations have made clear, the results of this development left their own distinctive marks on the origins of the New South.

14. Woodman, "Sequel to Slavery," 547.
15. Perhaps the major constraint facing blacks and blacks alone was northern racial prejudice. Blacks simply did not have many employment opportunities outside the South. Mandle, *Roots of Black Poverty*, Chap. 2.

# Research Methods

## Landholding

For the various tables on landholding (acreage and wealth) in
Chapters One, Four, and Six, circumstance, not choice, has dictated which years have been examined. The Louisiana tax records
are fragmentary before the war; only a few Mississippi land rolls
remain from the period under consideration. Fortunately, those
records that are available for Concordia Parish, Claiborne County,
and Adams County are sufficient to give a reasonably good idea of
the economic structure of the Natchez district before and after the
war. Note, however, that, as no complete tax records are available
for antebellum Concordia Parish, it has been necessary to use the
agricultural schedules from the manuscript census of 1860. The
discrepancy between sources undoubtedly introduces some bias
into the Concordia figures. It is likely that the census taker overlooked some landowners, principally smallholders. As a result,
some of the increase in acreage evident after the war, and in the
number of landowners (Table 8), is probably a function of the
sources used. The reasons for not relying on census data after
the war are familiar enough. Suffice it to say that the figures taken
on wealth in 1870 were considered so suspect that they were never
published. And in 1880 no attempt was even made to take such
information. Too, census takers counted tenants as landholders in
1880, making it impossible to separate renters from owners.[1]

## Persistence

*Persistence* is defined as the percentage of those with 1,000 or
more acres who had belonged to the slaveholding elite before the

---

1. See Roger W. Shugg, *Origins of Class Struggle in Louisiana: A Social History of
White Farmers and Laborers During Slavery and After, 1840–1875* (Baton Rouge: Louisiana State University Press, 1972), 235–36.

war; this, of course, includes not only those who had been large slaveowners themselves but also their spouses and children (as identified in the population schedules of the manuscript census of 1860). Here, the slaveholding elite is comprised of those who owned fifty or more slaves in 1860 (according to the slave schedules of the manuscript census of that year) plus, for Adams and Claiborne counties, those who held 1,000 or more acres on the tax lists of 1861 and 1857, respectively, but were not listed in the census slave schedules. The reason for this second step is that the census enumerator apparently overlooked several large slaveholders. The danger is that one or two of the individuals added may actually *have* owned no slaves and held their land only for speculative purposes. If there were such individuals in the district, their numbers would have been so small as to introduce no more than a slight bias into the figures. No such additional step has been possible for Concordia Parish, there being no land rolls available for the antebellum period. The census taker probably overlooked a few large slaveholders in the parish who subsequently appear on the tax records after the war, and therefore the persistence rate is presumably slightly understated (Tables 13, 14). Finally, the Concordia Parish Assessment Rolls for 1873 and 1880 list absentees in a separate category. Evidently by *absentee* is meant, not an individual who simply resides outside the parish, but someone who neither works nor rents his or her land—a speculator, in other words. Absentees have not been included in the large planter class, on the grounds that their land was worth very little and they played no significant social or economic role in the parish. It is worth noting, however, that most such speculators did not belong to the antebellum elite.

### Merchants

I identified the merchants through the population schedules of the manuscript census for 1860, 1870, and 1880. I then traced the same men in the land rolls to determine who owned real estate and how much. There are two problems. First, there is always some margin of error involved in tracing individuals across different records. As a result, I undoubtedly missed one or two instances of merchant landholding. However, the error would be minor and of no more consequence for the postbellum years than for the period before the war. Second, for reasons already discussed, it has not always been possible to find a tax list for the same year as the census. Consequently, it is almost certainly true that some of the men who were listed as merchants in the census were no longer at that profession (or had not yet entered it) when I found them (or failed to find them) in the land rolls. Unfortunately this problem is unavoidable. All the same, it is far from clear that the time lag between census and tax rolls creates a systematic bias. The weight of the evidence is strong (Tables 20, 24, 25), and if the specific figures are themselves open to doubt, the general trends to which they point almost certainly are not. To minimize the problem as much as possible, I have used the acreage figures in the agricultural schedules of the 1860 manuscript census for Concordia Parish and Claiborne County. Tax records in these communities were not available for a period within two years either before or after the 1860 census. Similarly, no land rolls exist for Claiborne County between 1867 and 1878. However, in Box 85 of the Records of the Auditor of Public Accounts (Mississippi Department of Archives and History, Jackson), there is a complete list of taxes paid on acreage owned in the county in 1868. I have used the numbers in that list. Insofar as a merchant had not paid his taxes, he will be mistakenly listed as landless. As a result, I have probably slightly overstated the propertyless element in 1868. On the other hand, the list was complete through April, 1869, the number who failed to pay their taxes was apparently small, and, in any case, such individuals were liable to forfeit their property for nonpayment and thus stood on the precipice of the landless class.

# Labor Turnover on Four Plantations, 1871–1874

Attempts by historians to determine the extent of debt peonage in the Black Belt have been severely constrained by lack of information regarding labor turnover on individual plantations. In the Adams County Deed Records (Adams County Courthouse, Natchez) can be found a set of contracts between tenants and landlords on four Adams County estates—two owned by Katherine Minor, one by James Surget, and one by them jointly. If complete, these records suggest that, in any given year during the 1870s, a significant minority of blacks took to the road in search of new opportunities (see Table 27). Although there was a solid core of permanent tenants on the four plantations, over one-quarter of the freedmen who rented each year were newcomers. Furthermore, only 45 percent of those who contracted in 1871 were still around

**Table 27.** TURNOVER OF FREEDMEN ON FOUR ADAMS COUNTY PLANTATIONS, 1871–1874

|  | Total Tenant Force | Tenants Remaining from 1871 | | | Percentage of Total Tenant Force Which Was New Each Year |
|---|---|---|---|---|---|
|  |  | Number | Percentage of Total Tenant Force | Percentage of Original (1871) Tenant Force |  |
| 1871 | 42 | — | — | — | — |
| 1872 | 38 | 23 | 61% | 55% | 39% |
| 1873 | 64 | 20 | 31% | 48% | 56% |
| 1874 | 62 | 19 | 31% | 45% | 27% |

SOURCES: Various leases, 1871–74, in Adams County Deed Records, Vols. PP, QQ, RR, SS, TT, Mississippi Department of Archives and History, Jackson.

three years later. It is difficult to know how representative was the collective experience of these particular estates. It does seem fair to say, however, that as members of very respected and successful families in the Natchez district, Katherine Minor and James Surget probably treated their tenants no worse and perhaps better than did most of their neighbors. If so, the pattern of recurring annual turnover apparent on their plantations was widely repeated throughout the community.

# Selected Bibliography

PRIMARY SOURCES
**Manuscripts**

Baker Library, Harvard Graduate School of Business Administration, Boston
    R. G. Dun & Co. Collection.
Department of Archives and Manuscripts, Louisiana State University, Baton Rouge
    Bower, Garner and Harrison Papers.
    Brandon Account Books.
    Britton, Audley Clark, and Family. Papers.
    Conner, Lemuel Parker, and Family. Papers.
    Douglas, Emily Caroline. Papers.
    Duncan, Stephen. Correspondence.
    Duncan, Stephen, and Stephen, Jr. Papers.
    Farrar, Alexander K. Papers.
    Foster, James, and Family. Correspondence.
    Foster, James, and Family. Papers.
    Gillespie, James A., and Family. Papers.
    Good Hope Plantation Papers.
    Hunter Brothers Business Records.
    Inman, Benajah R., and Family. Papers.
    Jenkins, John C., and Family. Papers.
    Johnson, William T., and Family. Memorial Collection.
    Larkin, E. J. Diary.
    McGehee, J. Burruss. Papers.
    McGehee, James Stewart. Papers.
    Mercer, William Newton. Papers.
    Minor, William J., and Family. Papers.
    Montgomery, George W. Account Books.
    Montgomery, Joseph A., and Family. Papers.
    Pinson, Mrs. Nancy. Papers.
    Shields, Joseph D. Papers.
    Stratton, Joseph B. Papers.

Manuscript Department, William R. Perkins Library, Duke University, Durham, N.C.
  Clarke, Lewis. Letters and Papers.
  Foster, Kate D. Diary.
  James, Joshua. Papers.
  Nutt, Haller. Papers.
  Pedrick, John C. Papers.
  Routh, John. Papers.
  Shoemaker, Isaac. Diary.
  Tompkins, Charles Brown. Papers.
  Wailes, Benjamin Leonard Covington. Letters and Papers.
Louisiana State Library, Baton Rouge
  W.P.A. Source Material.
Mississippi Department of Archives and History, Jackson
  Allen, James S. Plantation Book, Z 14.
  Allen, James S., and Family. Papers, Z 1239.
  Archer Family Papers, Z 27.
  Archer-Finlay-Moore Papers.
  Aventine Plantation Diary, Z 175.
  Baker, T. Otis. Papers, Z 72.
  Danjean, J. H., and Co., Ltd. Records, Z 917.
  Darden Family Papers, Z 82.
  Davis, Joseph E., and Family. Papers, Z 1028.
  Drake, Benjamin M., and Family. Papers, Z 995.
  Drake-Satterfield Papers, Z 96.
  Ellett-Jefferies Family Papers, Z 410.
  Fonsylvania Plantation Diary, Z 442.
  Forbes, Alden Spooner. Diary, Z 752.
  Freeland, Thomas. Papers, Z 774.
  Hamilton, Charles D., and Family. Papers, Z 98.
  Hughes, William, and Family. Papers, Z 68.
  Humphreys, George Wilson, and Family. Papers, Z 29.
  Humphreys Family Papers, Z 1099.
  Jefferson College Papers, Z 59.
  Jones, Archibald K., and Family. Papers, Z 1235.
  Jones-Smith Plantation Journal, Z 890.
  Maury, James H. Papers, Z 733.
  Minute Book of Port Gibson Female Academy, Z 1331.
  Musgrave, Maggie Williams. Papers, Z 1114.
  Paxton, A. J., Sr. "Reminiscences," Z 555.

Sessions, J. F. Papers, Z 608.
Snodgrass, John, and Family. Papers, Z 624.
Stockwell, Eunice J. Papers, Z 629.
Swain, Samuel Glyde. Papers.
Timberlake, Alcinda. Papers, Z 648.
Trask-Ventress Family Papers, Z 607.
Trinity Episcopal Church Records, Z 517.
Wade, Battaille Harrison, and Family. Papers, Z 270.
Wade, Walter. Plantation Diaries, Z 270.
Whitehurst, William N. Papers, Z 15.
Woodville Methodist Church Records, Z 993.
W.P.A. Records, RG 60.
Young, Thomas. Papers, Z 1203.
Southern Historical Collection, University of North Carolina, Chapel Hill
Allen, James, and Charles B. Papers.
Coulson, George Hiram. Papers.
Douglas Papers.
Fowler, Joseph S. Papers.
Hamilton, W. S. Papers.
Hughes Family Papers.
Ker, Mary Susan. Papers.
King, Thomas Butler. Papers.
Lovell, William S. Plantation Records.
Minor Family Papers.
Pattison, William J. Papers.
Perkins, John. Papers.
Polk, Leonidas. Papers.
Quitman Family Papers.
Richardson-Farrar Papers.
Stamps, Mary. Papers.
Tweed, Robert. Papers.
Whitmore, Charles. Diary.
Withrow, Adoniram Judson. Papers.
Tulane University Library, New Orleans
Cummings-Black Family Papers.
Stamps-Farrar Family Papers.

## Private Collections, Natchez

In possession of Ayres and Emily Haxton
  Ayres Family Papers.
In possession of Dr. and Mrs. William Godfrey
  Mount Repose Store Ledger.
In possession of Mr. and Mrs. Bazile Lanneau
  Metcalfe Family Papers.
In possession of Mr. and Mrs. Boyd Sojourner
  Jackson, Dempsey P. Memoranda.
  Sojourner, A. H. Contract.
In possession of Mr. and Mrs. Hyde D. Jenkins
  Jenkins Family Papers.
In possession of Mrs. Waldo Lambdin
  Pine Ridge Grange Records.
In possession of Mrs. Douglas MacNeil
  Surget-Minor Family Papers.

## Government Records

### Federal Census

MS Agricultural Schedules for Claiborne County, Concordia Parish,
  1860.
MS Population Schedules for Adams County, Claiborne County, Jeffer-
  son County, Warren County, Wilkinson County, Concordia Parish,
  Madison Parish, and Tensas Parish, 1850, 1860, 1870, 1880.
MS Slave Schedules for Adams County, Claiborne County, Jefferson
  County, Warren County, Wilkinson County, Concordia Parish, Madi-
  son Parish, and Tensas Parish, 1850, 1860.

### County and Parish Records

Adams County Courthouse, Natchez
  Adams County Chancery Court Records.
  Adams County Deed Records.
  Adams County Land Rolls, 1879.
  Adams County Probate Records.
  Adams County Record of Lands Sold for Taxes.
Concordia Parish Courthouse, Vidalia
  Concordia Parish Conveyance Records.
  Concordia Parish General Mortgages.
Louisiana State Capitol, Baton Rouge
  Concordia Parish Assessment Rolls.

Mississippi Department of Archives and History, Jackson
    Adams County Land Rolls.
    Claiborne County Chancery Court Records.
    Claiborne County Deed Records.
    Claiborne County Land Rolls.
    Jefferson County Deed Records.
    Wilkinson County Chancery Court Records.

**Official Papers**

Mississippi Department of Archives and History, Jackson
    Governors' Correspondence.
    Records of the Auditor of Public Accounts.

**Published Documents**

U.S. Bureau of the Census. *Eighth Census of the United States*. Washington, D.C.: Government Printing Office, 1864–1866.
———. *Ninth Census of the United States*. Washington, D.C.: Government Printing Office, 1872.
———. *Tenth Census of the United States*. Washington, D.C.: Government Printing Office, 1883–1888.
U.S. Department of Agriculture. *Report of the Commissioner of Agriculture, 1867*. Washington, D.C.: Government Printing Office, 1868.
———. *Report of the Commissioner of Agriculture for the Year 1874*. Washington, D.C.: Government Printing Office, 1875.

**Published Reminiscences and Contemporary Sources**

Anderson, John Q., ed. *Brokenburn: The Journal of Kate Stone, 1861–1868*. Baton Rouge: Louisiana State University Press, 1972.
Butler, Pierce. *The Unhurried Years: Memoirs of the Old Natchez Region*. Baton Rouge: Louisiana State University Press, 1948.
Davis, Robert M. *The Southern Planter, the Factor and the Banker*. New Orleans: n.p., 1871.
Dennett, John Richard. *The South as It Is: 1865–1866*. Edited by Henry M. Christman. New York: Viking Press, 1965.
Eaton, John. *Grant, Lincoln and the Freedmen: Reminiscences of the Civil War with Special Reference to the Work for the Contrabands and Freedmen of the Mississippi Valley*. New York: Longmans, Green, 1907.
Fulkerson, H. S. *Random Recollections of Early Days in Mississippi*. Vicksburg: Vicksburg Printing and Publishing Co., 1885.

Gresham, Matilda. *Life of Walter Quintin Gresham, 1832–1895*. Vol. I. Chicago: Rand, McNally, 1919.

Hogan, William R., and Edwin A. Davis, eds. *William Johnson's Natchez: The Ante-Bellum Diary of a Free Negro*. Baton Rouge: Louisiana State University Press, 1951.

[Ingraham, Joseph Holt]. *The South-West: By a Yankee*. Vol. II. New York: Harper, 1835.

King, Edward. *The Great South*. New York: Arno Press, 1969.

Kingsford, William. *Impressions of the West and South During a Six Weeks' Holiday*. Toronto: A. H. Armour, 1858.

Knox, Thomas W. *Camp-Fire and Cotton-Field: Southern Adventure in Time of War*. New York: Blelock, 1865.

Murray, Elizabeth Dunbar. *My Mother Used to Say: A Natchez Belle of the Sixties*. Boston: Christopher Publishing House, 1959.

Noland, Julia Tigner, and Blanche Connelly Saucier. *Confederate Greenbacks: Mississippi Plantation Life in the 70's and 80's*. San Antonio: Naylor Co., 1940.

Nordhoff, Charles. *The Cotton States in the Spring and Summer of 1875*. New York: D. Appleton, 1876.

Olmsted, Frederick Law. *The Cotton Kingdom*. Edited by Arthur M. Schlesinger. New York: Knopf, 1953.

Powers, Stephen. *Afoot and Alone: A Walk from Sea to Sea by the Southern Route*. Hartford: Columbian Book Co., 1872.

Rawick, George P., Jan Hillegas, and Ken Lawrence, eds. *The American Slave: A Composite Autobiography*. Supplement, Series 1. Vols. VI–X. Westport, Conn.: Greenwood Press, 1977.

Reid, Whitelaw. *After the War: A Southern Tour*. Cincinnati: Moore, Wilstach & Baldwin, 1866.

Russell, Robert. *North America, Its Agriculture and Climate: Containing Observations on the Agriculture and Climate of Canada, the United States, and the Island of Cuba*. Edinburgh: A. and C. Black, 1857.

Stratton, Jos. B., D.D. *Address Delivered July 23rd, 1875, Before the Trustees, Professors and Students of Jefferson College, Washington, Adams County, Miss*. Natchez: Democrat Book and Job Print, 1875.

Strode, Hudson, ed. *Jefferson Davis: Private Letters, 1823–1889*. New York: Harcourt, Brace & World, 1966.

Trowbridge, J. T. *The South: A Tour of Its Battlefields and Ruined Cities*. New York: Arno Press, 1969.

Wailes, B. L. C. *Report on the Agriculture and Geology of Mississippi*. Jackson: E. Barksdale, 1854.

Yeatman, James E. *Report to the Western Sanitary Commission, in Regard to Leasing Abandoned Plantations, with Rules and Regulations Governing the Same.* St. Louis: Western Sanitary Commission Rooms, 1864.

## SECONDARY SOURCES

Atherton, Lewis A. *The Southern Country Store, 1800–1860.* Baton Rouge: Louisiana State University Press, 1949.

Bettersworth, John K. *Confederate Mississippi: The People and Policies of a Cotton State in Wartime.* Baton Rouge: Louisiana State University Press, 1943.

Billings, Dwight B., Jr. *Planters and the Making of a "New South": Class, Politics, and Development in North Carolina, 1865–1900.* Chapel Hill: University of North Carolina Press, 1979.

Blassingame, John. *The Slave Community: Plantation Life in the Antebellum South.* Rev. and enl. ed. New York: Oxford University Press, 1979.

Boyle, James E. *Cotton and the New Orleans Cotton Exchange: A Century of Commercial Evolution.* New York: Country Life Press, 1934.

Brandfon, Robert L. *Cotton Kingdom of the New South: A History of the Yazoo Mississippi Delta from Reconstruction to the Twentieth Century.* Cambridge: Harvard University Press, 1967.

Cash, W. J. *The Mind of the South.* New York: Vintage Books, 1941.

Clark, Thomas D. *Pills, Petticoats and Plows: The Southern Country Store.* Norman: University of Oklahoma Press, 1964.

Clark, Thomas D., and Albert D. Kirwan. *The South Since Appomattox: A Century of Regional Change.* New York: Oxford University Press, 1967.

DeCanio, Stephen J. *Agriculture in the Postbellum South: The Economics of Production and Supply.* Cambridge: Massachusetts Institute of Technology Press, 1974.

Eaton, Clement. *The Waning of the Old South Civilization, 1860–1880's.* Athens: University of Georgia Press, 1968.

Fogel, Robert William, and Stanley L. Engerman. *Time on the Cross: The Economics of American Negro Slavery.* Boston: Little, Brown, 1974.

Fredrickson, George M. *The Black Image in the White Mind: The Debate on Afro-American Character and Destiny, 1817–1914.* New York: Harper & Row, 1971.

Garner, James Wilford. *Reconstruction in Mississippi*. New York: Macmillan, 1901.

Genovese, Eugene D. *The Political Economy of Slavery: Studies in the Economy and Society of the Slave South*. New York: Vintage Books, 1967.

———. *Roll, Jordan, Roll: The World the Slaves Made*. New York: Pantheon Books, 1974.

———. *The World the Slaveholders Made: Two Essays in Interpretation*. New York: Pantheon Books, 1969.

Gerteis, Louis S. *From Contraband to Freedman: Federal Policy Toward Southern Blacks, 1861–1865*. Westport, Conn.: Greenwood Press, 1973.

*Goodspeed's Biographical and Historical Memoirs of Mississippi, Embracing an Authentic and Comprehensive Account of the Chief Events in the History of the State and a Record of the Lives of Many of the Most Worthy and Illustrious Families and Individuals*. 2 vols. Chicago: Goodspeed Publishing Co., 1891.

Gutman, Herbert G. *The Black Family in Slavery and Freedom, 1790–1925*. New York: Pantheon Books, 1976.

Hammond, M. B. *The Cotton Industry: An Essay in American Economic History*. New York: Johnson Reprint Corp., 1966.

Harris, William C. *Presidential Reconstruction in Mississippi*. Baton Rouge: Louisiana State University Press, 1967.

Higgs, Robert. *Competition and Coercion: Blacks in the American Economy, 1865–1914*. New York: Cambridge University Press, 1977.

James, D. Clayton. *Antebellum Natchez*. Baton Rouge: Louisiana State University Press, 1968.

Kane, Harnett T. *Natchez on the Mississippi*. New York: Morrow, 1947.

Litwack, Leon F. *Been in the Storm So Long: The Aftermath of Slavery*. New York: Knopf, 1979.

Magdol, Edward. *A Right to the Land: Essays on the Freedmen's Community*. Westport, Conn.: Greenwood Press, 1977.

Mandle, Jay R. *The Roots of Black Poverty: The Southern Plantation Economy After the Civil War*. Durham, N.C.: Duke University Press, 1978.

Menn, Joseph Karl. *The Large Slaveholders of Louisiana, 1860*. New Orleans: Pelican Publishing Co., 1964.

Novak, Daniel A. *The Wheel of Servitude: Black Forced Labor After Slavery*. Lexington: University of Kentucky Press, 1978.

Otken, Charles H. *The Ills of the South: Or, Related Causes Hostile to the General Prosperity of the Southern People*. New York: G. P. Putnam's Sons, 1894.

Oubre, Claude F. *Forty Acres and a Mule: The Freedmen's Bureau and Black Land Ownership*. Baton Rouge: Louisiana State University Press, 1978.

Painter, Nell Irvin. *Exodusters: Black Migration to Kansas After Reconstruction*. New York: Knopf, 1977.

Phillips, Ulrich Bonnell. *American Negro Slavery: A Survey of the Supply, Employment and Control of Negro Labor as Determined by the Plantation Regime*. Baton Rouge: Louisiana State University Press, 1966.

Powell, Lawrence N. *New Masters: Northern Planters During the Civil War and Reconstruction*. New Haven: Yale University Press, 1980.

Ransom, Roger L., and Richard Sutch. *One Kind of Freedom: The Economic Consequences of Emancipation*. New York: Cambridge University Press, 1977.

Roark, James L. *Masters Without Slaves: Southern Planters in the Civil War and Reconstruction*. New York: Norton, 1977.

Rowland, J. Dunbar. *History of Mississippi, the Heart of the South*. Vol. I. Chicago: S. J. Clarke, 1929.

Shannon, Fred A. *The Farmer's Last Frontier: Agriculture, 1860–1897*. New York: Farrar & Rinehart, 1945.

Shugg, Roger W. *Origins of Class Struggle in Louisiana: A Social History of White Farmers and Laborers During Slavery and After, 1840–1875*. Baton Rouge: Louisiana State University Press, 1972.

Stampp, Kenneth M. *The Peculiar Institution: Slavery in the Ante-Bellum South*. New York: Vintage Books, 1956.

Sydnor, Charles S. *A Gentleman of the Old Natchez Region: Benjamin L. C. Wailes*. Westport, Conn.: Negro Universities Press, 1970.

———. *Slavery in Mississippi*. New York: D. Appleton-Century, 1933.

Taylor, Joe Gray. *Louisiana Reconstructed, 1863–1877*. Baton Rouge: Louisiana State University Press, 1974.

van den Berghe, Pierre L. *Race and Racism: A Comparative Perspective*. New York: Wiley, 1967.

Watkins, James L. *King Cotton: A Historical and Statistical Review, 1790–1908*. New York: Negro Universities Press, 1969.

Wharton, Vernon Lane. *The Negro in Mississippi, 1865–1890*. New York: Harper & Row, 1965.

Wiener, Jonathan M. *Social Origins of the New South: Alabama, 1860–1885*. Baton Rouge: Louisiana State University Press, 1978.

Wiley, Bell Irvin. *Southern Negroes, 1861–1865.* New Haven: Yale University Press, 1965.

Wilson, Theodore Brantner. *The Black Codes of the South.* University, Ala.: University of Alabama Press, 1965.

Woodman, Harold D. *King Cotton and His Retainers: Financing and Marketing the Cotton Crop of the South, 1800–1925.* Lexington: University of Kentucky Press, 1968.

Woodward, C. Vann. *American Counterpoint: Slavery and Racism in the North-South Dialogue.* Boston: Little, Brown, 1971.

———. *Origins of the New South, 1877–1913.* Baton Rouge: Louisiana State University Press, 1971.

Wright, Gavin. *The Political Economy of the Cotton South: Households, Markets, and Wealth in the Nineteenth Century.* New York: Norton, 1978.

### Articles

Bull, Jacqueline P. "The General Merchant in the Economic History of the New South." *Journal of Southern History,* XVIII (1952), 37–59.

Calhoun, Robert Dabney. "A History of Concordia Parish, Louisiana." *Louisiana Historical Quarterly,* XV (1932), 44–67.

Clark, Thomas D. "The Furnishing and Supply System in Southern Agriculture Since 1865." *Journal of Southern History,* XII (1946), 24–44.

Cohen, William. "Negro Involuntary Servitude in the South, 1865–1940: A Preliminary Analysis." *Journal of Southern History,* XLII (1976), 31–60.

Davis, Ronald L. F. "The U.S. Army and the Origins of Sharecropping in the Natchez District—A Case Study." *Journal of Negro History,* LXII (1977), 60–80.

Greenberg, Kenneth S. "The Civil War and the Redistribution of Land: Adams County, Mississippi, 1860–1870." *Agricultural History,* LII (1978), 292–307.

Griffin, Richard W. "Problems of the Southern Cotton Planters After the Civil War." *Georgia Historical Quarterly,* XXXIX (1955), 103–117.

Holmes, George K. "The Peons of the South." *Annals of the American Academy of Political Science,* IV (1893–1894), 265–74.

Ransom, Roger L., and Richard Sutch. "Debt Peonage in the Cotton South After the Civil War." *Journal of Economic History,* XXXII (1972), 641–69.

Reid, Joseph D., Jr. "Sharecropping as an Understandable Market

Response: The Post-Bellum South." *Journal of Economic History*, XXXIII (1973), 106–130.

Rister, Carl Coke. "Carlota: A Confederate Colony in Mexico." *Journal of Southern History*, XI (1945), 33–50.

Saloutos, Theodore. "Southern Agriculture and the Problems of Readjustment, 1865–1877." *Agricultural History*, XXX (1956), 58–76.

Sellers, James L. "The Economic Incidence of the Civil War in the South." *Mississippi Valley Historical Review*, XIV (1927–1928), 179–91.

Thompson, Edgar T. "The Natural History of Agricultural Labor in the South." In *American Studies in Honor of W. K. Boyd*. Durham, N.C.: Duke University Press, 1940.

——. "The Plantation: The Physical Basis of Traditional Race Relations." In *Race Relations and the Race Problem*, edited by Edgar T. Thompson. Durham, N.C.: Duke University Press, 1939.

Wiener, Jonathan M. "Class Structure and Economic Development in the American South, 1865–1955." *American Historical Review*, LXXXIV (1979), 970–1006.

Wiley, B. I. "Vicissitudes of Early Reconstruction Farming in the Lower Mississippi Valley." *Journal of Southern History*, III (1937), 441–52.

Woodman, Harold D. "Post–Civil War Southern Agriculture and the Law." *Agricultural History*, LIII (1979), 319–37.

——. "Sequel to Slavery: The New History Views the Postbellum South." *Journal of Southern History*, XLIII (1977), 523–54.

Zeichner, Oscar. "The Transition from Slave to Free Agricultural Labor in the Southern States." *Agricultural History*, XIII (1939), 22–32.

## Theses and Dissertations

Coussons, John Stanford. "The Federal Occupation of Natchez, Mississippi, 1863–1865." M.A. thesis, Louisiana State University, 1958.

Ganus, Clifton. "The Freedmen's Bureau in Mississippi." Ph.D. dissertation, Tulane University, 1953.

Moore, Ross H. "Social and Economic Conditions in Mississippi During Reconstruction." Ph.D. dissertation, Duke University, 1937.

Shlomowitz, Ralph. "The Transition from Slave to Freedman: Labor Arrangements in Southern Agriculture, 1865–1870." Ph.D. dissertation, University of Chicago, 1978.

Thompson, Edgar T. "The Plantation." Ph.D. dissertation, University of Chicago, 1932.

# Index